Auschwitz

Auschwitz

Nazi Extermination Camp

Second Enlarged Edition

Interpress Publishers
Warsaw 1985

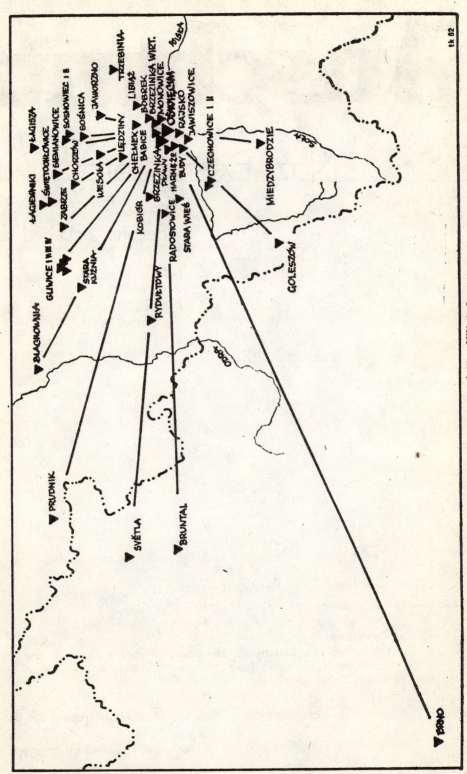

The Auschwitz camp and its affiliated camps

CONTENTS

Józef Buszko: Foreword 7

Danuta Czech: Konzentrationslager Auschwitz — A Historical Outline 13
    1. Genesis of the Camp. 2. The Building, Expansion and Development of the Camp and its Subsidiaries. 3. The Splitting up of the Auschwitz Camp. 4. The Gradual Winding up of the Camp. 5. The Camp Chain of Command

Tadeusz Iwaszko: The Prisoners 45
    1. Arrest and Detention in the Camp. 2. Transport. 3. The Reception and Registration of Transports. 4. The Marking of Prisoners. 5. Breakdown of the Prisoners by Age and Nationality. 6. Quarantine. 7. Living and Sanitary Conditions. 8. Clothing. 9. Food. 10. The Prisoner's Day. 11. Contact with the Outside World. 12. The Camp Hospital

Franciszek Piper: Extermination 87
    I. The Political and Racist Premises for Extermination . . 89
    II. Methods of Indirect Extermination 93
        1. Hunger and Disease. 2. Work. 3. Punishments and Executions
    III. Methods of Mass Extermination 110
        1. Lethal Injections. 2. The Gas Chambers and Crematoria
    IV. At the Sources of New Concepts in Extermination . . . 127
        Sterilization Experiments. 2. Other Pseudomedical Experiments

Barbara Jarosz: The Resistance Movement in and around the Camp 133
    1. The Conditions in which the Camp Resistance Movement Worked. 2. The Emergence of a Clandestine Movement Inside the Camp. 3. The Resistance Movement in the Camp Vicinity. 4. Forms of Activity of the Camp Resistance Movement

Andrzej Strzelecki: The Liberation of the Camp and Aid to the Freed Prisoners 157
    1. The Liberation of the Camp. 2. Aid to the Liberated Prisoners

Kazimierz Smoleń: The Prosecution of the Auschwitz Criminals . 171

    1. Legal Foundations of the Prosecution and Punishment of War Criminals. 2. The International Military Tribunal. 3. The Nuremberg Trials of 1947—49. 4. The Legal Bases of the Punishment of War Criminals in Poland. 5. The Auschwitz Criminals Before the Supreme National Tribunal. 6. The Auschwitz Criminals Before the Courts of Other Countries

SS Ranks and their Wehrmacht Equivalents 201
Bibliography 203

Foreword

The International Military Tribunal at Nuremberg described the Nazi concentration camps as one of most shameful means of terror used against the population of the occupied countries, and defined the crimes committed in them as crimes against humanity.

In the government apparatus of the Third Reich the concentration camps were the main instrument of implementing the Nazi policy of terrorizing, exploiting the labour resources of and physically exterminating conquered peoples, mainly Slav, above all the Polish nation and the peoples of the USSR, as well as Jews and persons considered to be such under the Nuremberg Laws of 1935.

In the Nazi plans for a future "order" in Europe after a victorious conclusion of the war, the Polish nation was the first to be removed from the territories intended for Germanization and incorporation into the "Greater Reich". The crimes committed against the Polish people in the years 1939-45 were a prelude to the implementation of the programme of exterminating the nations of eastern Europe contained in the Generalplan Ost prepared by the Reich Main Security Office (RSHA).

Revealing the truth about Konzentrationslager Auschwitz, the largest of all the concentration and extermination camps created on a gigantic scale by the system of Nazi rule, must be accounted a particularly weighty undertaking whose significance extends far beyond the realm of scholarship, concerning as it does the whole of mankind. To present even in the most general outline all the factors which made possible the existence for nearly five years of this centre of extermination where some four million people met their deaths is to perform an elementary duty towards the writing of history and is at the same time a moral directive which constitutes a warning against every criminal ideology.

Founded in May 1940 on the outskirts of the town of Oświęcim, which *following its incorporation into the Third Reich received the name of Auschwitz, the concentration camp was initially intended as an instrument of terror against the conquered Polish nation, as a place where hundreds of thousands of Polish patriots could be first isolated and then exterminated. Gradually, however, as the camp's expansion proceeded, it assumed the character of an enormous international "death combine" in which people from all the countries occupied by Nazi Germany were murdered en masse. From March 1942 to the end of the camp's existence those imprisoned in the camp included, besides Poles, Americans, Austrians, Belgians, Britons, Bulgarians, Croats, Czechs, Dutchmen, Frenchmen, Germans, Greeks, Gypsies, Hungarians, Italians, Jews, Letts, Lithuanians, Norwegians, Romanians, Russians, Serbs, Slovaks, Slovenes, Swiss and Turks.*

Among the prisoners of various nationalities the largest group was always constituted by Poles and Polish citizens of Jewish origin, followed by citizens of the USSR, Yugoslavia and France. Particularly numerous — besides Polish Jews — were Hungarian, Czech, Slovak, German, Greek and Dutch Jews.

The camp contained men and women, adults, children, young people and old, people of various political affinities, professions and religious denominations. Most of them were people who had never had anything to do with any kind of political activity. They had been transported to the camp solely on account of their national or racial origin.

In March 1942, about three kilometres from the main camp (Stammlager), known as KL (for Konzentrationslager) Auschwitz I, there arose a huge camp at Brzezinka which was called KL Auschwitz II — Birkenau, after which another extension camp — or Aussenlager — Auschwitz III was built, to which belonged KL Monowitz and about 40 subsidiary camps situated mainly on the territory of Upper Silesia. A particular role in this gigantic complex of camps was played by Birkenau where, alongside the concentration camp where men and women were intended to undergo gradual extermination, from spring 1942 onwards a camp of immediate extermination was located. Here people were gassed in specially constructed chambers, the corpses being buried in pits and, in a later period, burned in crematoria or on pyres. Some idea of the scale of this extermination may be gained from the fact that the number of those murdered and subsequently cremated in the summer of 1944, i.e. when the incoming transports were most numerous, came to about 20,000 every twenty-four hours. The total number of victims gassed at KL Birkenau comes to 3.5 million.

Besides those prisoners who were never entered in the camp records and were driven straight from the railway siding to the gas chambers, there passed through the concentration camp at Oświęcim over 400,000 persons who were registered and given numbers. Of this number, about

340,000 perished of disease, hunger, inhuman treatment, exhausting physical labour or as a result of summary individual or mass executions.

The camp complex was constantly and systematically expanded so that it might in future be able to contain about a quarter of a million prisoners who were to provide the work force for various enterprises run by the SS and German industrial concerns. To Auschwitz, as to all the extermination camps, there was a constant influx of enormous transports of prisoners directed thither by the Gestapo, which carried out mass round-ups on the streets, conducted home arrests, and evacuated the populations of specific urban districts or entire regions of the country.

The fundamental and ultimate purpose of all the Nazi concentration camps was to cause the death of the prisoners they contained after previously extracting the maximum of labour from them. Extraordinarily harsh conditions of existence, hunger, disease, inhuman treatment and labour exceeding human endurance led to extreme physical and mental exhaustion, the result of which was inevitably death.

Even if prisoners had not been tortured in Auschwitz, even if there had been no executions, or mass murders, even if the inmates had not been forced to perform exhausting physical labour, the very living conditions and diet would have been enough to cause an enormous mortality rate, which rate was considerably higher in KL Auschwitz than in the other Nazi concentration camps. Even the former commandant of the camp, Rudolf Höss, stated as much in his memoirs.

The camp diet was such that the majority of prisoners could expect to live — according to the kind of work they performed — from three to six months.

The Auschwitz camp provided thousands of workers as slave labour. When the prisoners returned from work in the evening, exhausted, battered, often bleeding, they carried on their backs or dragged along in carts their comrades who had dropped from exhaustion or been shot down on the spot by the SS. It was a procession of shadows and corpses, for which the camp orchestra, composed of prisoners, had to provide music. The corpses of those who had been murdered were laid out on the Appellplatz (parade ground), as the camp authorities were chiefly concerned that the number of prisoners immediately after return to the camp should agree with the roll. The orders issued by the camp command clearly encouraged and rewarded the murder of prisoners.

The working conditions for prisoners employed in German firms outside the camp, for which the managements of these firms were responsible, were as a rule just as hard as those in the camp. Prisoners who were weak, undernourished, or unifit for work were selected for the gas chambers and their place was taken by new contingents. In this way the number of workers laid down in the contract between the SS and a given firm was constantly supplemented.

Hunger, extremely exhausting labour and insanitary conditions caused incessant epidemics of infectious diseases: typhus, typhoid fever, tuberculosis, numerous skin diseases, etc. Peculiar methods of treatment were applied in the camp hospital. During the first phase of the camp's existence, treatment there was a fiction; later, in connection with the growing demand for labour in the armaments industry, patients were treated, but only those who seemed capable of a quick return to work. The rest were killed with phenol injections or sent to the gas chambers.

It must moreover be stressed that the SS doctors, despite the basic principles of the ethics of their profession, not only did not treat the sick, but conducted criminal experiments on them which, if they did not cause the victim's death, resulted in incurable illness or permanent disablement. One of the main aims of such experiments was to find ways of mass sterilization intended to serve the biological destruction of entire nations.

The SS doctors also took part in the killing of prisoners. They carried out inspections of the sick in the hospital and in the blocks, after which they would decide whether a person was to live or die, without any medical examination, purely on the basis of external appearance. A prisoner who at first glance appeared to be emacited or sickly was marked down by the Nazi doctor for extermination.

The selection of people for the gas chambers was a fixed, systematically repeated procedure in the camp. In this way were disposed of those slaves who were no longer capable of work and whose place was constantly being taken by new arrivals. This fate befell not only the old and the sick, but also perfectly healthy children who were too young for the work required of them. Pregnant women were dealt with similarly.

Particularly bestial treatment was meted out in the Auschwitz camp to Soviet prisoners of war. They died very quickly from general exhaustion or diseases against which they had no resistance left, or they were murdered by the SS.

From the spring of 1942 the Auschwitz camp became a place of extermination of Jews transported there from nearly all over Europe. The enormous transports were directed straight from the railway sidings to the gas chambers. Only those who were young, strong and healthy were placed in the camp for a while until their labour potential was exhausted, after which they shared the fate of their fellows.

The documentary materials gathered immediately after the war reveal that the entire complex of gas chambers and crematoria was built with a view to systematically exterminating human beings on a scale unprecedented in the history of mankind. Indeed from the first tests of the gassing method of killing people to the end of the camp's existence constant, feverish efforts to improve its efficiency by the use of all technical means were in evidence.

The extermination operation was kept a close secret. In order to destroy all trace of the crimes committed, the camp authorities blew up the gass chambers and crematoria, but the ruins and the plans and other documents which have survived give an idea of the size of these murder installations and make it possible to reconstruct the way in which they were used.

Today the campsite is recognized as a Monument to the Martyrdom of the Polish and Other Nations, and there is also a State Museum.

The purpose of this book is to present as briefly as possible the basic information concerning all that went to make up the functioning mechanism of Konzentrationslager Auschwitz, which, without any exaggeration, deserves the name of "the hell of Oświęcim". The book consists of five closely inter-related sections by different authors, the first of which deals with the genesis of the camp, the history of its construction and further expansion; the second describes living conditions in the camp; the third concerns the various methods of extermination used; the fourth discusses the organizational structure and manifestations of the resistance movement inside and outside the camp; while the fifth is devoted to the prosecution and sentencing of war criminals associated with Oświęcim.

It should be noted that the first attempt at a concise history of the camp at Oświęcim was the book by Jan Sehn, the third edition of which appeared over twenty years ago. Since that time research on the Nazi occupation of Poland has made considerable progress. Given this state of affairs, the need arose for a new publication on the subject of Oświęcim which would take account of the research of the past twenty years, which has made it possible to define a number of facts more accurately and to present them in a fuller light.

This book is also addressed to a wide range of readers who are not Polish and hence not adequately informed about the war and Nazi occupation in Poland. The authors and publishers are also concerned to make these facts available to the younger generation whose knowledge of the events of the last war is derived above all from the accounts of their elders.

To reveal the mechanism of the Nazis' criminal activity is also — as we have already mentioned — to give warning against every criminal ideology whose purpose is to glorify nationalism, sow hatred among peoples and incite war which in present conditions carries the threat of total annihilation. In this context it should be remembered that the symbolic slogan "never again" has come to mean much more than might have appeared immediately after the collapse of Hitler's Germany. Today it is well understood that this slogan places on all people of good wil the obligation of striving to ensure peaceful coexistence between nations.

Recalling the crimes committed in the Nazi concentration camps not only does not hinder the cause of normalizing international relations. On the contrary, a properly understood normalization of these relations is impossible without a change of consciousness, without drawing conclusions from the past, without a full realization and assessment of the consequences of the criminal ideology of Hitlerism. Nor does this attitude clash with the necessity of prosecuting and punishing those Nazi criminals who have so far escaped justice.

It is a moral duty towards all those who perished brutally murdered, a duty arising from the sense of justice deeply rooted in every honest person, to know the tragic fate of the countless victims of Hitlerism and to keep alive the memory of them.

JÓZEF BUSZKO

Danuta Czech

Konzentrationslager Auschwitz
— A Historical Outline

1. GENESIS OF THE CAMP

The project of founding a concentration camp at Oświęcim arose in Wrocław in the office of the Higher SS and Police Leader for the South East *(Höhere SS- und Polizeiführer Südost), SS-Gruppenführer* Erich von dem Bach-Zelewski. His subordinate, the inspector of the Security Police and Security Service *(Inspekteur der Sicherheitspolizei und des Sicherheitsdienstes — Sipo u. SD), SS-Oberführer* Arpad Wigand submitted such a project at the end of 1939, prompted by reports of the overcrowding of the prisons of Upper Silesia and the Dąbrowa Basin, which impeded the security police in its task of carrying out terrorist and repressive measures against the Polish population. Justifying this proposal, *SS-Oberführer* Wigand stressed that the resistance movement in Silesia and the General Government was intensifying, which meant that mass arrests were necessary, and the existing concentration camps were inadequate for holding all those arrested.

Wigand pointed to Oświęcim as a suitable place for a concentration camp. He considered that the existing barracks there could be used for holding prisoners straight away. The situation of the barracks outside the town in the fork of the Vistula and Soła rivers, in the region called Zasole, would make possible a future expansion of the camp and also its isolation from the outside world. A further argument was provided by Oświęcim's convenient railway connections with Silesia, the General Government, Czechoslovakia and Austria.

In the first days of January 1940, the Inspector of concentration camps, *SS-Oberführer* Richard Glücks, sent to Oświęcim a commission headed by the then camp commander *Schutzhaftlagerführer)* of Sachsenhausen, *SS-Sturmbannführer* Walter Eisfeld. After its inspection of the site the commission declared that the Oświęcim barracks were unsuitable for conversion into a camp.[1]

---

[1] Statement of the accused Rudolf Höss. Archive of the Oświęcim State Museum (APMO). Trial of the former commandant of the concentration camp at Oświęcim before the Supreme National Tribunal in Warsaw (hereafter *Höss Trial*), t. 21, k. 26.

This opinion was not shared by the HSSPF Office in Wrocław as on 25 January the chief of the *SS-Hauptamt* (Head Office) informed *Reichsführer SS* Heinrich Himmler, that according to a report by *SS-Gruppenführer* von dem Bach-Zelewski "a camp will soon be set up near Oświęcim, which is conceived as a kind of state concentration camp".[2]

On 1 February 1940, with a view to taking a final decision concerning the site of the planned camp, *Reichsführer SS* Himmler ordered that inspections be made of the police prison at Welzheim and the transit camp at Kislau (both in the district of the *HSSPF Südwest*), the camp at Frauenberg near Admondt (in the district of the *HSSPF Alpenland*), the camp at Sosnowiec and the camp at Oświęcim (both in the district of the *HSSPF Südost*).[3] On 21 February 1940 *SS-Oberführer* Glücks informed Himmler that the former Polish artillery barracks at Oświęcim, after the installation of certain sanitary amenities and the making of certain structural alterations, would be suitable for a quarantine camp (*als Quarantänelager geeignet*) and if the negotiations ordered by the chief of the security police concerning the handing over the barracks by the Wehrmacht were concluded, a quarantine camp would be immediately set up.[4]

As a result of these negotiations, on 8 April Air Force General Halm gave his consent to the renting out of the barracks and the drawing up of a contract concerning their transfer to the SS authorities.[5]

In connection with the finalization of the negotiations between the Wehrmacht and the SS, on 18-19 April 1940 another commission came to Oświęcim headed by *SS-Hauptsturmführer* Rudolf Höss[6] who had succeeded Eisfeld at the Sachsenhausen concentration camp. The commission stopped over in Wrocław to meet with Wigand and acquaint itself with the details of his project which envisaged the organization at Oświęcim of a transitional quarantine camp for Polish prisoners before their transfer

---

[2] APMO. Photocopies of *Allgemeine Erlasse des Reichssicherheitshauptamtes* (hereafter *Allgemeine Erlasse RSHA*), sygn. D-RF-3/RSHA 117a, k. 59.
[3] *Ibid.* k. 55.
[4] *Ibid.* k. 55—57.
[5] Voivodship State Archive in Katowice. Rejencja Katowice (hereafter *WAP Katowice, Zesp. RK*) 2905, fol. 119.
[6] Rudolf Höss had served in the concentration camps since 1 December 1934. In the space of four years he rose from the rank of *SS-Unterscharführer* to that of *SS-Hauptsturmführer*. On 4 May 1940 he was appointed commandant of *KL Auschwitz*. In this post he was promoted on 30 January 1941 to *SS-Sturmbannführer* and on 18 July 1942 to *SS-Obersturmbannführer*. In November 1943 Höss was recalled from the post of commandant of *KL Auschwitz*. From 10 November 1943 he performed the duties of head of *Amt DI* in *Amtsgruppe D* of the SS-WVHA (Economic Administration Head Office), being formally appointed to this post on 1 May 1944. On 2 April 1947 he was sentenced to death by the Supreme National Tribunal in Warsaw.

to concentration camps in the heart of the Reich. According to Wigand's plan the camp was to accommodate 10,000 prisoners. [7]

After Höss had submitted to Glücks a report of his inspection, Himmler on 27 April 1940 gave the order for the founding of a concentration camp at Oświęcim, the existing buildings to be added to by prisoner labour.

Höss, having been sent to Oświęcim again by Glücks, arrived there on 30 April accompanied by five SS men to carry out the preliminary work. On 4 May 1940 he was officially appointed commandant of *Konzentrationslager Auschwitz*. [8]

Höss began his preparations by informing the civil authorities in the Bielsko district, to which Oświęcim belonged, of the necessity of moving the 1,200 odd persons living in the barracks in the immediate vicinity of the camp, as the site was to become part of the camp area. [9] In order to get the site of the future camp ready, he acquired from the mayor of Oświęcim 300 local Jews who worked there throughout the whole of May and up to the middle of June. In the course of the alterations a dozen or so Polish workers resident in the neighbourhood were employed.

On 20 May 1940 *Rapportführer* Gerhard Palitzsch [10] brought to Oświęcim 30 prisoners, convicted criminals of German nationality selected at Höss's request from among the prisoners in the concentration camp at Sachsenhausen. These prisoners were given serial numbers 1 to 30 and placed in Block 1 of the camp. They were intended to act as trusties, constituting an extension of the SS apparatus and exercising immediate and cruel supervision over the prisoners in the camp and the work gangs. At the same time 15 SS men from an SS cavalry detachment in Cracow were sent to Oświęcim as members of the future garrison.

---

[7] APMO. *Höss Trial*, t. 21, k. 27; photocopies. Zesp. *Allgemeine Erlasse RSHA*, sygn. D-RF-3/RSHA/117a, k. 55—57.
[8] Jan Sehn in his introduction to the Polish edition of the Höss memoirs (*Wspomnienia Rudolfa Hössa komendanta obozu oświęcimskiego* — hereafter *Höss Memoirs*), Warsaw 1965, p. 16.
[9] *WAP Katowice*. Zesp. RK 2910, fol. 4.
[10] Gerhard Palitzsch had performed guard duties in *KL Lichtenburg*, *KL Buchenwald* and *KL Sachsenhausen*, where he was first a *Blockführer* and later a *Rapportführer*. In May 1940 he was transferred to *KL Auschwitz*. He was distinguished by peculiar sadism and personally shot prisoners with small calibre weapons against the Execution Wall in the courtyard of Block 11. After the creation of the family camp for Gypsies (BIIe) he took over the command of this camp. He appropriated for himself a large amount of money, valuables, clothing etc. originally belonging to people doomed to extermination. After being transferred to the subsidiary camp at Brno he was arrested and arraigned before an SS court. His fate thereafter is unknown.

On 29 May 1940 there was sent to Oświęcim from the Dachau concentration camp a group of prisoners known as an outside squad (*Aussenkommando*) in the charge of *Unterscharführer* Beck. The squad consisted of one German prisoner — the Kapo * — and 39 Polish prisoners — young men, mainly senior secondary school pupils from Łódz. The squad brought a waggonload of barbed wire and began to erect a fence around the future camp. The prisoners were accommodated in the cookhouse of the former barracks and employed in building the first provisional fence around the camp. Daily they were led across the barracks square (formerly used for horse riding) beyond the barracks from the direction of the road leading from Oświęcim to Rajsko. There they unwound the barbed wire onto wooden posts. The prisoners had no freedom of movement and were forbidden to make contact with the working Jews and civilian workers. The latter surreptitiously left food for them. The prisoners from Dachau came into contact with one of the criminals from Sachsenhausen from whom they learned of the planned transport to the camp of Polish prisoners from Tarnów. The prisoners were allowed to buy things in the SS men's canteen. For this reason they asked their *Kommandoführer, SS-Unterscharführer* Beck to try to have their money deposits transferred to Oświęcim and also for their own permanent transfer to Oświęcim. The money deposits arrived in the second half of June, but the prisoners were sent back to Dachau. As they were leaving they saw on the railway siding beside the camp a train with a transport of prisoners from Tarnów. The prisoners from Dachau were sorry to leave Oświęcim, where they could expect help from their fellow countrymen, in their own country. At that point SS-*Unterscharführer* Beck informed them that they were lucky that permission had not come from *KL Dachau* to let them stay in the Oświęcim concentration camp, for the latter was going to be hell on earth.[11]

On 14 June 1940 there arrived in Oświęcim from the prison at Tarnów the first transport of Polish political prisoners, numbering 728 men, sent by the *Sipo* and SD commander in Cracow. The prisoners were given the serial numbers 31 to 758 and placed in quarantine in the building of the former Polish Tobacco Monopoly, which was situated near the railway siding and divided by a barbed wire fence from the other buildings.

At the same time the staff was strengthened by the dispatch of a further 100 SS men plus officers and NCOs who took over posts in the command of the camp.

The post of adjutant was assumed by *SS-Obersturmführer* Josef Kramer[12] (seconded from *KL Mauthausen*). The post of *Lagerführer* (com-

---

[11] Account of former Dachau prisoner Edward Flakiewicz. Collections of Danuta Czech.

* Prisoner in charge of work squad.

[12] Josef Kramer held the post of adjutant until November 1940, and later became

pound chief) was held first by *SS-Obersturmführer* Karl Fritzsch (seconded from *KL Dachau*) and latter by *SS-Untersturmführer* Franz Xaver Maier (seconded from the *SS Totenkopf Division*). The post of chief of administration (*Leiter der Verwaltung*) went to *SS-Untersturmführer* Max Meyer (seconded from the Concentration Camp Inspectorate), that of head of the financial department (*Kassenleiter*) to *SS-Oberscharführer* Herbert Minkos (seconded from *KL Buchenwald*), the officer responsible for food supplies (*Sachbearbeiter für Verpflegung*) was *SS-Untersturmführer* Willi Rieck (seconded from *KL Dachau*), while billeting, uniforms for the SS and clothing for the prisoners (*Unterkunftsverwaltung*) were the domain of *SS-Hauptscharführer* Otto Reinicke (seconded from *KL Flossenbürg*). The camp doctors were *SS-Hauptsturmführer* Max Popiersch and *SS-Obersturmführer* Norbert Neumann. [13]

The head of the Political Department (*Politische Abteilung* or camp Gestapo) was *SS-Untersturmführer* Maximilian Grabner,[14] who had been assigned to this post by the Office of the Secret State Police (*Geheime Staatspolizeiamt*, i.e. Gestapo) in Katowice.

Five days after the arrival of the first Polish prisoners from Tarnów prison the population settled in the vicinity of the barracks began to be evacuated.

The first to be moved out were the inhabitants of the group of workers' huts situated near the railway siding of the Polish Tobacco Monopoly, since news of the intended arrests and liquidation of the settlement had leaked out to the persons concerned, some of whom abandoned their homes secretly by night. By 18 June 38 families had escaped, after having partially dismantled the wooden housing they had previously occupied. The evacuation operation was begun on 19 June 1940. The local labour office took part in it, supported by local police. 500 persons were arrested, of whom 250 were deported to forced labour in Germany. There remained temporarily in the settlement 30 persons unfit for work, children

---

Lagerführer of *KL Dachau*. In April 1941 he assumed the post of *Lagerführer* of *KL Natzweiler*, of which he became commandant in October 1942. From 8 May to 25 November 1944 he was commandant of *KL Auschwitz II*, and later of *KL Bergen-Belsen*. He was sentenced to death by a British military court on 17 November 1945 in the trial of members of the SS staff of *KL Bergen-Belsen* at Lüneburg. The sentence was carried out on 13 December 1945 at Hameln.
[13] APMO. Photocopies. Zesp. *Allgemeine Erlasse RSHA*, sygn. D-RF-3/RSHA/117/2, k. 166. The above-mentioned names were given in a register of posts in the headquarters of *KL Auschwitz* dating from 1 July 1940.
[14] Maximilian Grabner held the post of head of the Political Department until December 1943, when he was removed, arrested and, in 1944, sentenced by a special SS court to 12 years imprisonment. On 22 December 1947 the Supreme National Tribunal in Cracow sentenced him to death.

under 14, eight families whose members were employed by the camp SS, and 15 families whose members worked in the nearby coalmine at Brzeszcze. All these persons were marked down for resettlement outside the boundaries of the camp.[15] Some of those arrested were sent to the police camp at Sosnowiec, whence they were later transported to the camp at Oświęcim.

On 8 July 1940 some dozen families were evicted from the most attractive houses in Legionów, Krótka and Polna streets in the Zasole district. The operation was directed by the town council and camp SS. Those evicted were deported to forced labour in the Sudetenland, while their homes together with their entire contents were put at the disposal of the officers and NCOs of the camp staff and their families. Another eviction operation in the Zasole district was carried out in November 1940. Some of the houses thus made available were handed over to the families of the SS guards. The settlement that sprang up around the camp (*SS-Siedlung*) created a zone isolating the territory of the camp from the Polish population. In order to facilitate police operations in the event of escapes, 123 houses were demolished. For this purpose prisoners were employed from the so-called demolition squad (*Abbruchkommando*), and orders were given for the materials thus gained to be stored in the camp warehouses for future alterations to the camp.

Further evictions of the Polish population from the vicinity of the camp were closely associated with the plans of the following individuals:

(1) *Reichsführer SS* Himmler as regards the creation around the camp of an SS farming zone (*Gutsbezirk*) in which it was intended to develop experimental farming, stock and fishbreeding;

(2) *SS-Obergruppenführer* Reinhard Heydrich,[16] chief of the Reich Main Security Office (*Reichssicherheitshauptamt*, or RSHA) as regards the creation in Oświęcim of a second concentration camp for more serious cases;

(3) *Reichsmarschall* Hermann Göring, who was Hitler's plenipotentiary for the four-year plan, in connection with the project by IG Farben to build a synthetic fuel oil and rubber factory at Oświęcim.[17]

---

[15] *WAP Katowice, Zesp. RK* 2910, fol. 11 and 12.

[16] Reinhard Heydrich was at the same time *Reichsprotektor* of Bohemia and Moravia. After his assassination in Prague by the Czech resistance on 5 June 1942 he was succeeded in January 1943 by *SS-Obergruppenführer* Ernst Kaltenbrunner, who was condemned to death by the International Military Tribunal (hereafter IMT) in Nuremberg and hanged on 16 October 1946.

[17] As early as January 1941 Dr Otto Ambros, a member of the board of IG Farben, had acquainted himself in the Planning Office in Katowice with maps of the surrounding country and had decided on Oświęcim as the most favourable site for the building of new chemical works.

The decision to create an SS farming strip around the camp had been taken by Himmler, on the basis of the results of tests and reports submitted by Höss as early as November 1940.[18]

The chief of the RSHA, Heydrich, in an order of 2 January 1941, let it be known that *Reichsführer SS* Himmler had expressed his consent to the division of concentration camps into three categories, depending on the personality of the prisoner and the degree to which he constituted a threat to the state.

The Oświęcim camp was named by Heydrich *Konzentrationslager Auschwitz I* and included, together with Dachau and Sachsenhausen, in Category I, intended for prisoners who were "not serious offenders and absolutely capable of reform". Camps in Category II were designated by Heydrich for prisoners who were "more serious offenders, but still capable of being educated and reformed". In this category he included Buchenwald, Flossenbürg, Neuengamme and *Auschwitz II*, which not only did not exist at the time, but even Commandant Höss allegedly had no knowledge that such a camp was planned. In Category III, intended for prisoners who were "very serious offenders", especially those with a police record and asocials, Heydrich included the concentration camp at Mauthausen.[19]

From the above order it follows that the plan to create a second camp at Oświęcim — *Auschwitz II* — must have already arisen at the end of 1940.

On 10 February 1941 a special commission arrived at Oświęcim and under the direction of the camp commandant Höss worked out the main guidelines concerning the territorial scope and the number of persons to be evicted.

On 8 March 1941 the population of the village of Pławy was evicted in the space of 15 minutes. On 9 March the Jewish population was removed from Oświęcim to Chrzanów, and on 1 April the remaining residents of Legionów, Krótka, Polna and Kolejowa streets in Oświęcim were evicted, their vacated homes being put at the disposal of the families of SS men and of the German experts sent to work on the recently started building of the synthetic fuel oil and rubber factory, called the Buna-Werke, at Dwory, near Oświęcim. Between 7 and 12 April the Polish population of the villages of Babice, Broszkowice, Brzezinka, Budy, Harmęże and Rajsko was evicted.

As a result of these operations there were resettled in Brzeszcze and Jawiszowice the workers at the coalmine there and their families. 500

---

[18] APMO. *Höss Trial.* t. 21, k. 31, 32.
[19] APMO. Photocopies. Zespół *Erlass-Sammlung RKPA*, sygn. D-RF-3/RSHA/118/9, k. 607.

persons of Jewish origin were resettled in Chrzanów, and 1,600 Poles were deported to the General Government. All were deprived of the whole of their property.

The territory thus depopulated, about 40 square kilometres in area, was called the camp's zone of interest *(Interessengebiet)*. The zone constituted the land lying in the fork of the Vistula and Soła rivers, within boundaries running from Broszkowice along the Soła to the village of Bielany, thence through Łęki, Skidzin, Wilczkowice by Brzeszcze to the Vistula, and thereafter along the course of the river to the mouth of the Soła near Broszkowice. This area was constantly patrolled by the SS and the local Gestapo and police.

This huge extent of the camp's *Interessengebiet* was justified by economic and security considerations. In a letter to the inspector of concentration camps, Glücks, Höss wrote: "The local population is fanatically Polish, ready to undertake any action against the hated SS men, and every prisoner who succeeds in escaping will instantly receive help as soon as he reaches the first Polish farm." [20]

At the moment of its founding the concentration camp at Oświęcim contained twenty brick buildings, of which fourteen were single- and six were two-storied. Between 20 May 1940 and 1 March 1941, 10,900 persons, mainly Poles, were imprisoned in the camp.

Reichsführer SS Himmler came to Oświęcim for the first time on 1 March 1941. He was accompanied by the *Gauleiter und Oberpräsident* of Upper Silesia, *SS-Brigadeführer* Fritz Bracht, the Wrocław HSSPF *SS-Obergruppenführer* Ernst Schmauser, *SS-Oberführer* Glücks, *Regierungs-präsidenten*, and leading personalities of the IG Farben concern. After a thorough inspection of the camp and the surrounding terrain Himmler ordered the camp commandant, Höss, to

(1) extend the camp at Oświęcim until it was able to accommodate 30,000 prisoners;

(2) build near the village of Brzezinka a camp for 100,000 prisoners of war;

(3) supply IG Farben with 10,000 prisoners to build an industrial plant at Dwory near Oświęcim;

(4) prepare the entire area for farming purposes;

(5) build camp workshops for handicraft purposes.

He also indicated that large armament plants *(Rüstungsindustrie)* should be built near the camp, so that the SS should occupy a leading place in the equipping of the German army.

In an instruction issued after the inspection on 5 March 1941 Glücks passed on to the concentration camp commandants *Reichsführer SS*

---

[20] APMO. *Höss Trial*, t. 12, k. 10.

Himmler's order that they should accept the transfer from the military formations of the SS of all officers and NCOs fit for service in the concentration camps even while the war was still on. At the same time Glücks informed the commandants of Himmler's intention to build a settlement for SS men at Oświęcim.[21]

2. THE BUILDING, EXPANSION AND DEVELOPMENT OF THE CAMP AND ITS SUBSIDIARIES

The first sketch of a general plan for the expansion of the main camp (*Stammlager*) at Oświęcim was ready in broad outline by June 1941. The final detailed plan was confirmed by the SS Economic Administration Head Office (*Wirtschaftsverwaltungshauptamt* — WVHA) in December 1942 and passed on to the camp command for implementation.[22]

The area envisaged for expansion was bounded in the south by the Oświęcim-Rajsko road running along the river Soła and stretched northward as far as the railway tracks leading from Oświęcim to Jawiszowice. The general plan of expansion envisaged the creation of four sectors. In the first, western sector there was planned a housing estate for the SS with lawns, a sports pitch and a riding school. The second was to contain the camp headquarters and, as an extension of it, the economic-industrial area of the camp (warehouses, water works, workshops, etc.). The third, bordering on the headquarters and economic-industrial area, was to contain the concentration camp proper. The fourth, bordering the camp on the east, was to contain the barracks of the SS garrison.

For the camp itself an area 1,000 metres long and 400 metres wide was marked out. The buildings intended for the prisoners were to form two complexes divided by a square. The first complex was made up of the existing brick buildings — to which it was intended to add extensions — of the main camp. This complex was to contain 33 blocks for prisoners. After the demolition of warehouses and workshops between the two complexes it was planned to have a large *Appellplatz* in the space thus vacated. The two complexes combined were to have a total of 78 single-story buildings to accommodate prisoners.

Work on the extension of the camp was started in the summer of 1941. With the use of prisoner labour and the building materials derived

---

[21] APMO. Photocopies. Zesp. *Allgemeine Erlasse RSHA*, sygn. D-RF-3/RSHA/117/1. k. 91.
[22] APMO. Photocopies. *Konzentrationslager Auschwitz Generalbebauungsplan* (General Plan for the Extension of Auschwitz Concentration Camp), 12 November 1942, confirmed 5 December 1942, passed on to *KL Auschwitz* 18 January 143.

from the demolished houses in the Zasole district, the erection of eight single-story buildings was begun on the *Appellplatz* (on the site of the old riding school), the addition of another story to 14 of the existing single-story buildings was started, and a camp kitchen was built. Beyond the wire an administrative building for the SS was built.

By the autumn of 1944 a bridge had been built over the Soła with a road leading to the Oświęcim—Kęty—Bielsko highway and a new road to the Oświęcim railway station had been added, water pipes had been laid and a sewage system installed in the area where an extension of the camp was envisaged, and work had been begun on a pump station, a water works and a power station. Of the planned second complex 20 single-story buildings were completed on the so-called camp extension (*Schutzhäftlagererweiterung*). By the spring of 1944 five of the buildings were already in use as warehouses or tailoring workshops. Two buildings had been placed at the disposal of an SS doctor, Professor Carl Clauberg. In May the experimental station from Block 10 of the main camp was transferred thither together with some female prisoners on whom it was proposed to perform sterilization experiments. In October in other blocks 6,000 female prisoners transferred from the women's camp at Brzezinka were accommodated.

Furthermore a reception building (*Aufnahmegebäude*) for new arrivals was erected. In the summer of 1944 showers and disinfection chambers had been put in.

Both the plan for the camp's expansion and its partial realization permit the conclusion that the main camp at Oświęcim was built as a permanent establishment and was intended to serve in the future for many years to come for the imprisonment and annihilation of opponents of Hitler's Reich.

Together with the expansion of the camp, plans began to be made for the transformation of the town of Oświęcim, in order to give it as German a character as possible.

The siting of the IG Farben works at Dwory near Oświęcim was dictated by three considerations: first, the need to secure it against bombing raids; second, the existence of coalmines in the vicinity; and, third and most important, the proximity of the concentration camp at Oświęcim, with its possibilities of further expansion and its enormous labour force.

As a result of negotiations between representatives of IG Farben, WVHA and the camp command concerning the supply by the last mentioned of cheap labour to build the planned synthetic fuel oil and rubber factory, it was laid down that before the end of 1941 KL *Auschwitz* would supply about 1,000 prisoners consisting of skilled tradesmen and helpers, and in 1942 an additional 3,000 prisoners, which figure it would increase to 8,000 as the need arose, and that in the following years the number of prisoners employed would grow. It was agreed that the prisoners would be transported to work by train, and that the camp would build a railway bridge over the river Soła for this purpose. The length of the working day was fixed at 10-11 hours, and nine in winter. It was laid down that IG Farben would pay the command of *KL Auschwitz* 4 marks per work day in the case of a skilled worker and 3 marks in the case of a non-skilled worker.

Following these arrangements in April 1941 prisoners from Auschwitz began work on the construction of the Buna-Werke at Dwory near Oświęcim. To begin with the prisoners covered the first seven kilometres to work on foot and then travelled the remaining distance by train. They were very late in arriving at work as military transports had priority. In August 1942 the transport of prisoners to work was halted because of the outbreak of an epidemic of typhus in the camp.

The difficulties connected with transporting the prisoners to work and the consequent fall in productivity moved the IG Farben concern to build a separate camp for the prisoners near the Buna-Werke in the evacuated village of Monowice. At the end of October 1942 the prisoners were accommodated there. This camp until November 1943 bore the name *Lager Buna* and was treated as a branch camp of *KL Auschwitz*.

In the spring of 1941 a number of prisoner squads were set up in *KL Auschwitz* for work in the fields. Their task was to harvest the hay, cereals and root crops which had been sown and planted by the local peasants before their eviction from the camp's zone of influence. Next a start was made on the organization of large farms, including stockbreeding farms. In February 1942 *SS-Obersturmbannführer* Joachim Caesar arrived in Auschwitz, having been sent by the chief of WVHA to take up the post of director of farms at the camp.

In accordance with Himmler's order, in the years 1941—43 large farms for the raising of crops and stockbreeding were organized in the evacuated and razed villages and hamlets in the camp's zone of influence — in Babice, Budy, Harmęże, Pławy. In Rajsko an experimental plant station (*Pflanzenzuchtstation*), was set up, where research was devoted mainly to raising the kok-saghyz plant, the root of which contains a rubber-yielding substance. On the farms huts were either built or existing buildings adapted for the accommodation of prisoners of both sexes, thus giving rise to branch camps in Babice, Budy, Harmęże, Pławy and Rajsko.

Also expanded in the course of 1941 were the workshops already existing in the camp, as well as the SS enterprise *Deutsche Ausrüstungswerke* (*DAW*) which at a later period received orders to carry out repair work for the army.

The building of a camp at Brzezinka was begun in October 1941. By this time the camp at Oświęcim had attained a total complement of over

20,000 prisoners, as between 7 and 25 October about 10,000 Soviet prisoners of war had been brought from the POW camp at Lamsdorf (now Łambinowice) and had been interned in a separate section of the main camp.

The SS proceeded to demolish the farm buildings at Brzezinka and assemble the materials necessary for the future camp. For this work they used prisoners and POWs who had to be driven daily to Brzezinka, which was about three kilometres distant from the main camp. Because of the enormous overcrowding in the main camp, the Brzezinka camp — intended to hold 100,000 POWs — was built hastily, without the installation of a sewage and water supply system.

To direct the work of construction, *SS-Sturmbannführer* Karl Bischoff was seconded from *Amtsgruppe C* of WVHA in Berlin. Initially he was plenipotentiary of the Special Construction Board for the Building of a POW Camp of the Waffen SS in Oświęcim (*Sonderbauleitung für Einrichtung eines Kriegsgefangenenlagers der Waffen SS in Auschwitz*), but later became head of the Central Construction Board of the Waffen SS and Police in Oświęcim. In 1944 he was appointed head of the Construction Inspectorate of the Waffen SS and Police for Silesia and Bohemia.

The location plan of the POW camp at Brzezinka, dated 14 October 1941, was confirmed by Bischoff the following day and signed by the commandant of *KL Auschwitz*, Höss. According to this plan the area of the camp was to be divided by a main road into two parts. Beside the road a railway siding was planned. To the left of the main road and siding there was to be a quarantine camp, and to the right two camps (I and II). The whole area formed a compact rectangle surrounded by barbed wire fences and guarded by watchtowers. The sides of the rectangle were to measure 720 by 1,130 metres. According to the plan all three camps were to contain 174 brick-walled prison huts each.

Work began with the levelling and draining of the marshy terrain. Next the POWs and inmates were employed on the building of a road from the bridge over the railway track to the gateway of the future camp, the extraction of sand from the gravel pit, the unloading of materials and on the laying of foundations for the huts.

The cost of undertaking almost simultaneously the expansion of the main camp and its workshops, of farming the land in the zone of influence, of building the Buna-Werke and, finally, building the camp at Brzezinka, was very high.

In all this work of building and expansion between March 1941 and February 1942 many thousands of Polish inmates and Soviet POWs lost their lives.

The camp documents which have survived reveal that between 20 May 1940 and 31 January 1942, 26,288 inmates and 9,997 POWs — a total of 36,285 persons — were confined in *KL Auschwitz*. In this same period of time 2,435 inmates were transferred to other concentration camps, 76 were released, five escaped and 1,755 inmates and POWs were murdered — by shooting, phenol injections, or gassing with Cyclon B. Thus the number of inmates was reduced by a total of 4,271. The figures given concern only inmates and POWs mentioned in the camp records, i.e. those who received camp serial numbers.

According to the above data there should have been, on 31 January 1942, 32,041 inmates and POWs, whereas in fact the complement of inmates and POWs on that day numbered 11,449.[23] What happened then to the missing 20,565 inmates and Soviet POWs?

Schutzhaftlagerführer Fritzsch greeted newly arrived prisoners in the main camp with the words: "You have not come here to a rest home but to a German concentration camp, from which there is no way out except through the crematorium chimney."[24] These words hold the answer to the question posed above. About 2,500 inmates perished from starvation and harassment at the hands of the SS in the initial phase, that is between July 1940 and March 1941, and about 18,000 inmates and POWs died as a result of hunger, ill treatment and back-breaking labour, chiefly while engaged in the expansion of the main camp, the building of the Buna-Werke and of the camp at Brzezinka, during the period between 1 March 1941 and 31 January 1942.

On 1 March 1942 the camp for Soviet POWs on the site of the main camp was wound up, the 945 POWs[25] who remained and some of the prisoners being transferred to the Brzezinka camp then still under construction. In the course of March several thousand inmates were accommodated there. In the main camp, on the other hand, ten blocks were set aside and surrounded by a wall. This was the Women's Section (*Frauenabteilung*) which at first was subordinated to the women's concentration camp at Ravensbrück. In July 1942 it was made directly subordinate to the commandant of *KL Auschwitz*.

On 26 March 1942 the newly created Women's Section of *KL Auschwitz* received 999 German women prisoners from Ravensbrück and 999 Jewish women brought from Poprad in Slovakia. The women were given the serial numbers 1—1998. In the course of the month over 6,000 women were placed in the Women's Section.

The first Polish women political prisoners, 127 in number, arrived on 27 April from Montelupi prison in Cracow and Tarnów prison. They received the serial numbers 6784 to 6910.

On 17—18 July 1942 Himmler visited Oświęcim for the second time,

---

[23] APMO. Book of Daily Registers (*Stärkebuch*). Sygn. D-AuI-3/I, t. I, p. 25.
[24] APMO. *Materiały obozowego Ruchu Oporu* (Materials of the Camp Resistance Movement: hereafter Mat. oboz. Ruchu Oporu), t. VII, k. 464.
[25] APMO. *Stärkebuch*. Sygn. D-AuI-3/I, t. 1. p. 91.

accompanied by Bracht, Schmauser and the chief of *Amtsgruppe C* of WVHA, *SS-Gruppenführer* Heinz Kammler, who was in charge of construction for the concentration camps, the army, the SS and Police, as well as for the armaments industry. Visits were made to the farms, the experimental plant station at Rajsko, the laboratories, the land improvement works and the camp at Brzezinka, where two bunkers for killing people with Cyclon B gas were put into operation. These bunkers were made from two converted cottages which had belonged to the evicted peasants Harmata and Wichaj and were situated in the Buna-Werke, the hamlets of Brzezinka. Visits were also paid to the Buna-Werke, the main men's camp, the women's section, the workshops, the slaughterhouse, the bakery, the yard where building materials were stored, the warehouses containing property taken from the prisoners, known to the prisoners as "Canada", the SS warehouses and other items of interest.

Following his inspection, Himmler ordered Höss to speed up the expansion of the camp at Brzezinka, to liquidate the Jewish prisoners incapable of work and to build armaments factories.

By August 1942 there had been built at Brzezinka, on the site originally envisaged for a quarantine camp, two separate camps designated as Camp BIa (*Bauabschnit Ia* — Building Sector Ia) and Camp BIb. The latter camp was intended for men and had been functioning since March as a branch of *KL Auschwitz*. In the first half of August the Women's Section was transferred from the main camp to camp BIa where a Women's Concentration Camp (*Frauenkonzentrationslager*) was formed, which was also a branch of *KL Auschwitz*.

The plan of 14 October 1941 for the building of a camp at Brzezinka was realized only in part and had to undergo alteration as in the summer of 1941 Himmler has already marked out Oświęcim as the place for the mass extermination of the Jews, while Commandant Höss considered that Brzezinka was best fitted for this purpose.

The extermination of the Jews at Brzezinka was begun in January 1942. During his visit to Brzezinka, Himmler observed the entire process. He was present as the Jews were unloaded from the train, as the selection was made, at the gassing in the bunker and the removal of the corpses afterwards. The conclusions to be drawn from the experience thus gained were no doubt the subject of the final discussion before Himmler's departure. What was sought was a technical solution to the problem not only of mass murder but also of quickly destroying the bodies to remove all traces of the crime. The plan to exterminate millions of Jews assigned a special role to Brzezinka, and this must have exerted a fundamental influence on the change in the character of the camp and the original assumptions connected with its construction.

Thus the next plan, dated 15 August 1942 and also confirmed by Bischoff, envisaged the building at Brzezinka of a complex of camps for 200,000 POWs and extermination installations. Of the previous plan there remained only construction sector I with camps BIa and BIb. On the right of the main road and railway siding it was planned to have construction sector II (BII), and beside it construction sector III, later to be known to the prisoners as "Mexico". Construction sector IV (BIV) was to be located to the left of contruction sector I. Thus the order of sectors from left to right was: BIV, BI, BII, BIII. Sector IV was envisaged for 60,000 persons, sector I — i.e. camps BIa and BIb — for 20,000 persons, and sectors II and III for 60,000 each.

Each construction sector, with the exception of the already completed BI, was to be divided into six separate parts or camps separated from one another by barbed wire and with separate entrance gates. At each gate there was to be an SS guard room (*Blockführerstube*).

All that part of the camp where the prisoners were to have their living quarters was to be contained within a regular rectangle of 720 by 2.340 metres. In two rectangles jutting out from the western side of the camp, along the extension of the main road and the tracks of the railway siding, it was planned to build two crematoria. In the event four crematoria were built together with gas chambers, and it was planned to build one more, but time ran out before the plan could be realized.

In the blueprints, and also in the correspondence dealing with Brzezinka, the term *Kriegsgefangenenlager* (POW camp) or KGL is used. This designation was not abandoned until 31 March 1944.

Work on implementing the plan of 15 August 1942 had been begun much earlier. Already in July of that year the Construction Board, renamed the Central Construction Board of the Waffen SS and Police in Oświęcim, which was in charge of building the camps at Oświęcim and Brzezinka, had begun negotiations with various firms concerning the construction of not two but four large crematoria together with gas chambers. An offer accompanied by an estimate of 133,756.65 marks for the building of one crematorium (without crematorium installations) was lodged on 13 July by the firm of Hoch- und Tiefbau A.G. of Katowice. The building of the crematorium ovens and the installation of the necessary equipment in the gas chambers was undertaken by the firm of J.A. Topf und Söhne of Erfurt.

Both the Central Construction Board and the civil construction firms hired inmate labour from the camp command. In 1942 for example an average of 8,000 prisoners daily worked on the expansion of the camps. In the actual work of planning several hundred engineers and technicians from among the prisoners were employed, together with civilian staff and several hundred SS men.

The rate of construction was very rapid. Between March and June 1943 the building of four enormous crematoria together with gas chambers was completed at Brzezinka. After testing they were handed over to the command of *KL Auschwitz*.

In the course of 1943 construction sector II (BII) was completed. It contained six camps designated BIIa, BIIb, BIIc, BIId, BIIe and BIIf respectively, and also a camp where the plundered personal effects of Jews condemned to extermination were stored (*Effektenlager*). This last camp was designated BIIg.

Camps BIIb, BIIc, BIId and BIIe contained 32 prison huts each. In camp BIIa, there were 16 huts of the type known as *Pferdestallbaracken, OKH-Typ. 260/9*, originally intended as horse stables. There had been a time when each of these huts was intended to hold 52 horses; now they had 800—1,000 prisoners crammed into them.

The earliest of these camps to be put into commission was BIIe where a camp for Gypsies (*Familienzigeunerlager*) was created in February 1943. Between 26 February 1943 and 21 July 1944 a total of 20,967 men, women and children were placed in the Gypsy camp. About 1,700 persons were not entered in the camp records but were sent directly to the gas chambers as typhus suspects. On 2 August 1944 the camp authorities liquidated the Gypsy camp, gassing the 2,897 surviving men, women and children.

In July 1943 camps BIId and BIIf went into commission.

Camp BIId was intended for healthy prisoners employed in individual work teams. Prisoners whom the SS considered healthy and fit for work were transferred thither from the men's camp BIb. The average complement of the men's camp BIId (*Männerlager BIId*) in the years 1943-44 was about 13,000 prisoners.

In camp BIIf a men's prison hospital (*Häftlingskrankenbau, Lager BIIf*) was opened, to which sick prisoners were transferred from camp BIb on 23 July 1943. Ill-equipped and always overcrowded, for the prisoners it was "the antechamber to the crematorium". Initially it possessed about 2,000 and later 2,500 beds or bed places in collective bunks. The SS doctors removed the excess of sick patients by making selections for the gas chambers.

In August 1943 a quarantine camp *(Quarantänlager BIIa)* was set up in camp BIIa for newly arrived prisoners. The few weeks quarantine period constituted a test of physical endurance for prisoners. The average complement of the quarantine camp was between 4,000 and 6,000 prisoners.

In camp BIIb a family camp was set up for Jews from the ghetto camp at Theresienstadt (Terezin) in Bohemia. This camp was called *Familienlager Theresienstadt* or *Familienlager BIIb*. On 9 September 1943 it received 5,006, and on 16 and 20 December 4,964 men, women and children brought from the ghetto camp of Terezin. By March 1944,

1,100 persons from the September transport had died of hunger, disease and poor sanitary conditions, and on 9 March 1944, 3,791 men, women and children from the same transport were gassed. Only about 75 persons were spared — physicians and twins. On the latter camp doctor *SS-Hauptsturmführer* Josef Mengele conducted pseudomedical experiments.*

Next between 16 and 19 May 1944 there arrived at *Familienlager BIIb* 7,449 men, women and children from the ghetto camp at Terezin in three successive transports. This brought the camp complement up to about 11,000 prisoners. In the first days of July 1944, after a selection conducted by Mengele, 3,080 young and healthy men and women were transferred to other concentration camps. *Familienlager BIIb* was then liquidated with the gassing on 11-12 July of the same year of the 7,000 or so men, women and children who remained.

The huts in camp BIIc were initially used for storing the personal effects of Jews brought to *KL Auschwitz* for extermination.

In December 1943 on the extension of construction sector II (BIIg), between gas chamber and crematorium III and gas chamber and crematorium IV, a delousing station and bathhouse (called the Sauna) and a warehouse camp for personal effects (*Effektenlager*, known as "Canada II") were installed. The *Effektenlager* in sector BIIg was composed of 30 huts where all the belongings of those condemned to extermination were temporarily stored before being inspected, sorted, packed and dispatched to various Nazi establishments. Gold, objects of value, precious stones and currency were sent to WVHA and thence to the *Reichsbank*. The huts were permanently filled to overflowing, and heaps of unsorted baggage rose up between them. In this camp the SS employed over 2,000 prisoners of both sexes.

In the middle of May 1944 the Central Construction Board completed the railway siding and unloading ramp in the camp. The siding was situated by the main camp road between camps BIa and BIb on the one side and camps BIIa, BIIb, BIIc, BIIe and BIIf on the other. Inside the camp the siding possessed three tracks.

In June 1944, in camp BIIc and on the territory of the as yet uncompleted construction sector BIII, known to the prisoners as Mexico, a transit camp (*Durchgangslager*), also referred to as a depot camp (*Depotlager*) for Jewish women, chiefly from Hungary, was organized. Those who were young, healthy and fit for work, upon selection at the unloading ramp, were directed to camp BIIc. In camp BIII — "Mexico" — were kept Jewish women among whom there had not been time to make a selection. The Jewish women placed in camps BIIc and BIII were not registered and consequently received no camp numbers. They were merely "deposit-

---
* See p. 130.

ed" in Brzezinka and for weeks, in inhuman conditions of existence, they waited for the SS to decide their fate. As labour became necessary, some healthy Jewish women were shipped out to labour camps in the armaments factories of the Reich. Those who were sick, weak and emaciated waited until the gas chambers were able to receive them. Every week the SS doctors Josef Mengele and Heinz Thilo conducted selections among the inmates of camps BIIc and BIII. Smaller groups of selected women — of about 100 women each — were shot next to the ovens in crematoria II and III. The complement of camp BIIc, which was constantly supplemented by women from newly arrived transports, remained steady at a level of about 30,000 women, and in camp BIII it was even considerably higher.

At the end of September 1944 the SS proceeded to liquidate the inmates of camps BIIc and BIII. In the space of ten days over 40,000 Jewish women were gassed. On 3 October 17,202 Jewish women, who had been placed in camps BIIc and BIII as a "deposit", still remained alive. On 6 October camp BIII in "Mexico" was liquidated and 12,799 women and 961 girls, mainly Hungarian Jewesses, were transferred to camp BIIc.

Camp BIb, previously occupied by men, was — after the transfer of the male prisoners at the end of July 1943 to camps BIId and BIIf (the men's hospital) and the creation of camp BIIa (the quarantine camp) — designated as an extension of the women's concentration camp at Brzezinka. In camp BIb were kept chiefly women prisoners employed outside the camp.

Camps BIa and BIb, intended for 20,000 persons, in January 1944 held over 27,000 female prisoners. Despite high mortality caused by inhuman conditions of existence and constant selections, the complement of the women's camp on 12 July 1944 came to 31,406, and on 22 August to 39,234 prisoners. On 3 October — after the addition to its complement of the 17,202 Jewesses from the depot camp in "Mexico" — the women's camp *Auschwitz II* contained 43,462 prisoners.

The Nazi concentration camps, including the one at Oświęcim, constituted an enormous reserve of cheap labour. In implementing Hitler's order of September 1942 to stop building armaments factories beside concentration camps and instead to found concentration camps beside existing industrial plants, the command of *KL Auschwitz* in the years 1942-44 set up about forty branch camps, also known as subcamps. The following terms were used to describe them: *Arbeitslager, Nebenlager, Aussenlager, Zweiglager, Arbeitskommando* and *Aussenkommando*. These names were unconnected with any separate organizational structure. Subcamps directly served the economic needs of the SS (e.g. the farms in the camp's *Interessengebiet*), but most worked for the factories, mines and steelworks of such large German concerns as IG Farben, Berghütte, Ober-

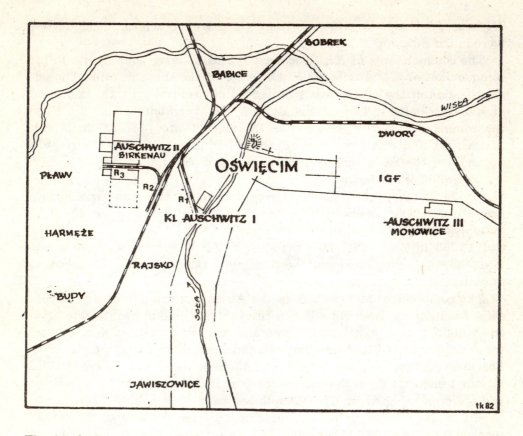

The Auschwitz camp complex

R_1 — railway siding at *KL Auschwitz I*
R_2 — railway siding at which Jewish transports were unloaded (the *Judenrampe*)
R_3 — railway siding inside the *Auschwitz II* camp (Birkenau)
IGF — site of the IG Farben works

KL Auschwitz I embraced the main camp. Its commandant was *SS-Obersturmbannführer* Liebehenschel.

KL Auschwitz II comprised all the camps at Brzezinka and the branch camps attached to farms. The commandant of *KL Auschwitz II* was *SS-Sturmbannführer* Fritz Hartjenstein. The office of *Schutzhaftlagerführer* (compound head) was performed by *SS-Untersturmführer* Johann Schwarzhuber in the men's camp and by *SS-Untersturmführer* Franz Hössler in the women's camp.

KL Auschwitz III comprised the ten branch camps at Monowice, Jaworzno, Jawiszowice, Świętochłowice, Łagisza, Wesoła near Mysłowice, Goleszów, Libiąż, Sosnowiec and Brno. The commandant of *KL Auschwitz*

III was *SS-Hauptsturmführer* Heinrich Schwarz whose headquarters were in the subcamp at Monowice.

The commandants of *KL Auschwitz II* and *III* were subordinate to the commandant of *KL Auschwitz I*, the senior of the three in rank. The administration of the camps was still carried out centrally by the command of *KL Auschwitz I*. The commandant of *KL Auschwitz I* still remained the commander of the SS garrison (*Standortältester des SS-Standortes Auschwitz*), and moreover was appointed industrial director (*Betriebsdirektor*)[28] of the SS enterprises within the camp's zone of influence with the exception of the farms.

On 20 January 1944 the total complement of the Auschwitz camps came to 80,839 prisoners of both sexes: 18,437 in *Auschwitz I*; 49,119 in *Auschwitz II* (22,061 in the men's camp, 27,053 in the women's camp); and 13,288 in *Auschwitz III* (including 6,571 at Monowice).[29] A month later the total complement of the Auschwitz camps was 73,669 prisoners of both sexes.[30]

The complement of prisoners in the Auschwitz camps underwent constant fluctuations. It would fall as a result of the high mortality rate caused by malnutrition, exhausting labour and consequent general debility, and would rise again with the arrival of another mass transport of prisoners. For example between 12 August and 17 September 1944 there arrived in four transports from the transit camp at Pruszków 13,000 men, women and children arrested in Warsaw following the outbreak of the uprising.

On 12 July 1944 the total complement of the Auschwitz camps had reached a figure of 92,208 prisoners of both sexes, and by 22 August it was 105,168. In addition, besides these prisoners entered in the camp register, there were at that time in the transit camps BIIc, BIIe and BIII at Brzezinka no less than 50,000 Jewish prisoners of both sexes.[31] Thus in August 1944 the number of prisoners in the Auschwitz camps exceeded 155,000.

4. THE GRADUAL WINDING UP OF THE CAMP

In view of the steady succession of German defeats on the Eastern front and the relentless onward march of the Red Army in the second half of 1944, the central authorities of the Third Reich ordered the com-

---

[28] Garrison order (*Standortbefehl*) No. 57/43 of 30 December 1943. APMO. *Zbiór rozkazów garnizonowych KL Auschwitz*, sygn. D-AuI-1/53.
[29] APMO. *Mat. oboz. Ruchu Oporu*, t. I, k. 60.
[30] *Ibid.* t. VII, k. 175.
[31] *Ibid.*, t. II, k. 94.

mandants of camps and prisons to prepare plans for evacuation and obliteration of all traces of the crimes that had been committed.

In August 1944 the SS authorities proceeded gradually to wind up the Auschwitz camps and to destroy the evidence of what had been done in them.

The winding up of the camps was carried out by the extermination of the "non-productive element" in the gas chambers and by transferring prisoners who were healthy and fit for work to concentration camps situated in the heart of the Reich.

Between 11 August and 4 October 10,000 Polish, Russian and Czech prisoners were transported to the concentration camps at Buchenwald, Sachsenhausen and Flossenbürg. In this same period (29 August—29 October) 3,824 prisoners from the men's quarantine camp BIIa at Brzezinka alone were gassed.

On 1 November 1944 the men's quarantine camp BIIa was liquidated. The healthy prisoners, staff and some of the doctors and nurses employed in the hospital there were transferred to the men's camp BIId, while the sick together with a dozen or so doctors and nurses were transferred to the men's hospital camp BIIf. On 24 November camps BIa and BIb were wound up, their surviving women prisoners being transferred to camps BIIb and BIIe. On 25 November by order of the chief of SS-WVHA, Pohl, the concentration camp *Auschwitz II-Birkenau* was joined to the main camp *Auschwitz I*, the resulting amalgam being again called *Konzentrationslager Auschwitz*, while the concentration camp *Auschwitz III* was renamed *Konzentrationslager Monowitz*.

This time the reorganization of the Auschwitz camp was connected with the considerable fall in the number of inmates caused by evacuation of prisoners to the Reich and the winding up of several camps at Brzezinka (BIa, BIb, BIIa and BIII).

Only *KL Monowitz* continued to expand. In the course of 1944 twenty branch camps were created, the last of them — *Hubertushütte* at Łagiewniki — being set up on 20 December, with 200 prisoners. They were employed in various parts of the ironworks on the most arduous and dirty tasks, in the cokery and gravel pit. The total complement of *KL Monowitz* in December 1944 was about 35,000 prisoners, including over 2,000 women.

In October 1944 the expansion of the main camp at Oświęcim was halted, as was work on the development of sector BIII at Brzezinka. No attempt was made to start work on construction sector BIV, but instead steps were taken to evacuate the warehouses containing building materials. Auschwitz had one of the largest stores of such materials attached to any concentration camp in the Third Reich.

The entry of Soviet troops into the Lublin region, the liberation of the concentration camp at Majdanek (24 July 1944) and the capture in the camp of several members of the SS staff forced the SS authorities to take action to obliterate all traces and destroy the evidence of the crimes committed in the Auschwitz camp where about four million people were murdered.

Already at the end of July 1944 the Political Department (camp Gestapo) had started to burn the registers containing the names of people who had been sent to their deaths in the Auschwitz gas chambers. Other departments of the camp administration also set about destroying files, registers and other camp documents.

In mid-October work was begun on the demolition of crematorium IV which had been destroyed by prisoners of the *Sonderkommando* during the revolt on 7 October 1944.* In November the gassings were halted, and *Reichsführer SS* Himmler ordered the destruction of the crematoria. Throughout November and December the technical installations of the gas chambers and in the ovens of crematoria II and III were dismantled for transportation to the Gross-Rosen concentration camp. Special squads of men and women prisoners were created to clean out, fill in and overlay with turf the pits where corpses had been burnt or where the ashes from the crematoria had been buried. The dismantling of the huts in camp BIII ("Mexico") was begun and the dismantled parts evacuated to Gross-Rosen. The warehouses containing the personal effects of Jews who had perished were hastily emptied, the most valuable objects being dispatched by train deep into the Reich and the remainder being destroyed.

The report of the head of the clothing warehouses in the main camp, *SS-Oberscharführer* Karl Reichenbach, reveals that in the period between 1 December 1944 and 15 January 1945 alone a total of 514,843 sets of men's, women's and children's clothing and linen were shipped out.

On 17 January 1945, 67,012 prisoners of both sexes presented themselves for the last roll call: 31,894 from *KL Auschwitz-Birkenau* and 35,118 from the subcamps constituting *KL Monowitz*.[32] On 18 January 1945 in the main camp the last camp serial number was issued: 202499. The recipient was a German criminal transferred on that day from *KL Mauthausen*.

In all over 400,000 persons figured in the camp registers.

Of the total number of prisoners entered in the registers and issued with camp serial numbers, there survived — among those transferred or evacuated or liberated in the Auschwitz camps — about 60,000 men and women.

---

* See p. 119.
[32] APMO. *Mat. oboz. Ruchu Oporu*, t. III, k. 208.

In relation to the some four million victims of the Auschwitz camps the figure of 60,000 survivors constitutes barely 1.5 per cent. Despite their terrible significance these figures can give no idea of the tragedy of the millions who perished, nor of the millions who mourn them to this day.

5. THE CAMP CHAIN OF COMMAND

The activity of the concentration camp at Oświęcim and of the other concentration camps was regulated within the state apparatus of the Third Reich by two offices belonging to Heinrich Himmler's central organization staff *(Reichsführung SS)*. These were the SS Economic Administration Head Office (WVHA), which decided on matters concerning the economic administration of the camps, and the Reich Main Security Office (RSHA), which through its branches supplied prisoners to the camp and decided on their fate thereafter (release, execution or extermination).

SS-WVHA was divided into five groups of offices *(Amtsgruppen)*: A, B, C, D and W. The most important of these for the concentration camps was *Amstgruppe D* which was composed of four offices: D — central office *(Zentralamt)*, DII — prisoner employment *(Arbeitseinsatz)*, DIII — hygiene *(Sanitätswesen und Lagerhygiene)* and DIV — concentration camp administration *(KL Verwaltung)*. The division of functions among offices DI—DIV was reflected in the organizational structure of the camp administration.

In prison after the war former commandant Höss reconstructed from memory the organizational scheme of *KL Auschwitz*.[33] On the basis of this scheme and surviving Nazi documents it is possible to reconstruct the organizational structure of the concentration camp at Oświęcim.

I. The Camp Command *(Kommandantur)*

At the head of the concentration camp stood the camp commandant who was responsible for all matters connected with the camp, above all for ensuring its total security. The camp commandant was at the same time the commander of the SS garrison of the camp and the director of the SS economic enterprises.

The first commandant of KL *Auschwitz* was *SS-Obersturmbannführer* Rudolf Höss (from 4 May 1940 to November 1943); the second was *SS-Obersturmbannführer* Arthur Liebehenschel (from 11 November

---

[33] *Höss Memoirs*, pp. 289—299.

1943 to 8 May 1944); and the third SS-*Sturmbannführer* Richard Baer [34] (from 11 May 1944 to the end of the camp's exitence).

Employed in the camp command were the adjutant to the commandant, a staff sergeant (*Stabsscharführer*) and a legal officer (*Gerichtsoffizier*). The mail censorship office (*Postzensurstelle*) was also located here.

After the division of the Auschwitz camp into three camps, the commandants of *KL Auschwitz II* (Birkenau) were *SS-Sturmbannführer* Fritz Hartjenstein (from 22 November 1943 to 8 May 1944), followed by *SS-Hauptsturmführer* Josef Kramer (from 8 May 1944 to 25 November 1944, i.e. to the next reorganization). The commandant of *KL Auschwitz III* (*KL Monowitz*) was *SS-Hauptsturmführer* Heinrich Schwarz (from 22 November 1943 to the liquidation of the camp in 1945).

II. The Political Department (*Politische Abteilung*)

This was the representative of RSHA in the camp and was independent of the commandant regarding its decisions as to the fate of prisoners, although it had to inform him of these decisions.

The Political Department was divided into the following sections: registration (*Registratur*), reception section (*Aufnahme Abteilung*), registrar's office (*Standesamt*), interrogation section (*Vernehmungsabteilung*), legal section (*Rechtsabteilung*) and records division (*Erkennungsdientes*). The Political Department had its cells in the individual camps of the Auschwitz complex.

The Political Department's sphere of activity embraced the following duties: keeping files on the prisoners, conducting correspondence with RSHA and with the Gestapo and Kripo (Criminal Police) stations which sent prisoners to the camp; the reception of prisoner transports; seeing to the security of the camp (combatting conspiratorial activities among the prisoners); conducting interrogations; keeping registrar's records; and running the crematoria.

---

[34] Richard Baer began his work in concentration camps in 1933 when he served as a guard in *KL Dachau*. In 1939 he was assigned to the Death's Head Division (*SS-Totenkopf*), from which he was transferred after suffering a contusion to *KL Neuengamme* as adjutant in 1942 and thence to Auschwitz the following year. After three days he was recalled to SS-WVHA as adjutant to Pohl, and in November 1943 he became chief of *Amt DI*. On 11 May 1944 he was appointed commandant of *KL Auschwitz I*. On 27 July he was made commander of the SS garrison at Oświęcim. After the evacuation of the Auschwitz camps he was named commandant of *KL Mittelbau*. Before the surrender he escaped to Styria (Austria). Until December 1960 he worked under an assumed name as a forestry worker in the vicinity of Hamburg. After his arrest in Frankfurt am Main he died suddenly in July 1963 while awaiting trial.

The Political Department was headed by an officer seconded from the Gestapo.

The first head of the Political Departmant was *SS-Untersturmführer* Maximilian Grabner. On 1 December 1943 the post was assumed by *SS-Untersturmführer* Hans Schurz.

III. Camp Supervision (*Schutzhaftlagerführung*), *Abteilung III*

This department was concerned with all matters relating to the direct management of the camp, such as accommodating, feeding and clothing the prisoners, their work and the maintenance of order in the camp. The compound head (*Schutzhaftlagerführer*) — as far as the prisoner was concerned the highest camp authority — performed the function of deputy to the commandant, was responsible for reports on the camp complement and for internal order in the camp, recommended to the commandant various types of punishment for the prisoners, took part in the infliction of punishment and was present at executions. To help him he had several camp marshals (*Rapportführer*) who reported to him, block leaders (*Blockführer*), and SS wardresses (*Aufseherinnen*) in the women's camp.

The chief *Lagerführer* of the main camp, and later of KL Auschwitz I, were, in order of appointment: *SS-Hauptsturmführer* Karl Fritzsch (to the end of 1941); *SS-Hauptsturmführer* Hans Aumeier (to 18 August 1943); *SS-Hauptsturmführer* Heinrich Schwarz (to 22 November 1943); *SS-Obersturmführer* Franz Johann Hofmann (to June 1944); and *SS-Hauptsturmführer* Franz Hössler (up to the liquidation and evacuation of the camp). The chief *Lagerführer* of the men's camp at KL Auschwitz II was *SS-Obersturmführer* Johann Schwarzhuber, and the women's camp from August 1943 to January 1944 Franz Hössler. Chief *Lagerführer* had their deputies who were known as deputy *Lagerführer*.

In the women's concentration camp (*Frauenkonzentrationslager*) at Brzezinka the function of chief supervisor (*Oberaufseherin*) was performed from 26 March to 8 October 1942 by Johanna Langefeld, from 8 October 1942 to November 1944 by Marie Mandel, and from 25 November 1944 to 18 January 1945 by Elisabeth Volkenrath. To help her the chief supervisor had supervisors (*Aufseherinnen*) who performed the functions of block leaders and heads of work gangs, corresponding to the functions of the *Blockführer* in the men's camp.

Commandant Höss who had a very poor opinion of the organizational skills of German wardresses, assigned SS officers and NCOs to help them by performing in the women's camp the functions of compound heads, *Rapportführer* and *Kommandoführer*.

IIIa. Department of Employment (*Arbeitseinsatz*), *Abteilung IIIa*

This department was concerned with the employment of prisoners, the organization of their work, the keeping of registers, the formation of work gangs (*Arbeitskommandos*), calculation of the wages due prisoners employed by various enterprises and firms. Watching over the prisoners during work was done by guards (*Postenführer* and *Kommandoführer*) who were members of the SS staff.

IV. Administration (*Verwaltung*), *Abteilung IV*

The tasks of this department included the management of the entire property of the camp, the supplying of the SS men and prisoners with food and clothing, heating, the maintenance of buildings (including the crematoria) and financial matters. It was in charge of all warehouses, including those containing the effects of the murdered, of the tailoring and repair shops, and also of the motor pool. Until June 1943 the Administration constituted Department IV of the Camp Command. On 1 July it was made an independent establishment bearing the name of Garrison Administration (*SS-Standortverwaltung*). In September 1944 it was renamed the Central Administration of the Waffen SS (*Zentralverwaltung der Waffen SS*). From July 1943 it was directly answerable to SS-WVHA. The successive heads of the administration were *SS-Hauptsturmführer* Rudolf Wagner (to the end of 1941); *SS-Sturmbannführer* Willi Burger (to June 1943) and *SS-Obersturmbannführer* Karl Möckel (from July 1943).

V. The Garrison Doctor (*SS-Standortarzt*), *Abteilung V*

The *SS-Standortarzt* was responsible for the SS men's state of health, for providing health care for the prisoners and for all sanitary installations, at first only in the main camp, but later also in its branches and — after the splitting up of the Auschwitz camp — also in *KL Auschwitz I, II* and *III*. The SS garrison doctor had under him the medical officers of the SS detachments (*SS-Truppenärzte*), who were responsible for treating the SS, the camp doctors (*Lagerärzte*), who were supposed to see to the health of the prisoners in the camp, SS dentists (*SS-Zahnärzte*) and the camp pharmacist (*SS-Lagerapotheker*). The SS camp doctors had assigned to them trained medical orderlies (*Sanitätsdienstgrade* — SDG). The successive garrison doctors were *SS-Hauptsturmführer* Dr. Max Popiersch (to September 1941); *SS-Hauptsturmführer* Dr. Siegfried Schwela (to May 1942); *SS-Obersturmführer* Oskar Dienstbach (to August 1942); *SS-Hauptsturmführer* Dr. Kurt Uhlenbrock (from 17 August 1942); and *SS-Obersturmbannführer* Dr. Eduard Wirths (from 6 September 1942 to 18 January 1945).

VI. The SS Troop Administration (*Truppenbetreung*), Abteilung VI

This department dealt with matters of training for the SS.

Other Organizational Units

The agricultural department (*Landwirtschaft*) occupied itself with the development of farming and stockbreeding, and also with research into the introduction of proper cultures. It was headed by *SS-Obersturmbannführer* Joachim Caesar, who was equipped with wide powers. The powers of the camp commandant in relation to this department were not defined by WVHA.

The Central Construction Board of the Waffen SS and Police at Oświęcim was directly subordinated to WVHA and was concerned with the planning, construction and extension of the Auschwitz camps and extermination installations. It was headed by *SS-Sturmbannführer* Karl Bischoff, and in 1944 by *SS-Obersturmführer* Werner Jothann. From July 1943 the administrative affairs of the Central Construction Board were conducted by the garrison administration.

In the fascist-police system of the Third Reich the Auschwitz camp performed two functions:

(1) that of a concentration camp in which the extermination of prisoners was carried out gradually;

(2) that of an extermination centre in which thousands of people were done to death immediately upon their arrival at the camp.

The authorities of *KL Auschwitz*, its administration and armed staff together constituted "a criminal organization created to implement the Hitlerite programme of the subjugation, physical and moral degradation and gradual biological debilitation of conquered peoples to the point of total extermination, through the application in the camp at Oświęcim established for these purposes of a system of terror, refined torments and the total exploitation of prisoners, through the extreme exploitation of their labour while they were alive, the mass plunder of their property and the utilization of their dead bodies for the aims of the war economy of the Third Reich".[35]

On 18 January 1945 the camp authorities proceeded to organize a hasty evacuation. All prisoners capable of walking were led out of the

---

[35] APMO. Verdict of the Supreme National Tribunal in Cracow of 22 December 1947 in the trial against members of the SS staff of the Oświęcim-Brzezinka concentration camp. Sygn. Dpr.-ZOp/1a, k. 13.

Auschwitz and Birkenau camps and force-marched as far as Wodzisław Śląski. Thence they were transported deep into the Reich. Some of the prisoners, especially those from *KL Monowitz* and the subcamps, were marched to other concentration camps nearer Oświęcim. The evacuation — involving over 58,000 prisoners of both sexes — was the last but at the same time one of the most tragic chapters in the history of Oświęcim. The route followed by the marching columns was strewn with the corpses of prisoners shot after falling by the wayside.

Left in the Auschwitz camps without food or medical care were over 8,000 sick and utterly exhausted prisoners of both sexes, including several hundred children. Following the launching of the Red Army's Vistula/Odra operation, eight days earlier than planned, Oświęcim found itself in the operational zone of the First Ukrainian Front.*

On 27 January 1945 — a memorable day for the inmates — soldiers of the 60th Army of the First Ukrainian Front entered Auschwitz, liberating about 1,200 male prisoners in the main camp, about 4,000 female prisoners and 1,800 male prisoners in Brzezinka, and 1,800 prisoners at Monowice.

In direct combat for the liberation of *KL Auschwitz* and the town of Oświęcim and district, troops of the 60th Army of the First Ukrainian Front lost 231 men, but they prevented the SS from carrying out their intention of liquidating the wounded and destroying the few remaining camp buildings.

---

* In Soviet usage the term "front" is used in the sense of army group (Tr. note).

Tadeusz Iwaszko

The Prisoners

1. ARREST AND DETENTION IN THE CAMP

The terror introduced by the Nazis in Germany upon their accession to power against their political opponents required the appearance of a legal sanction for the mass arrests and detention of those arrested in concentration camps. The means found of sanctioning lawlessness was the institution of "preventive custody" (*Schutzhaft*) which was given a theoretical basis by the decree of 28 February 1933 concerning "the protection of the nation and the state". The general principles governing the application of "preventive custody" were made specific in a circular of the Interior Ministry issued on 25 January 1938 in which it was stated that "temporary arrest is a means of coercion used by the Secret State Police as a defence against all hostile intentions aimed at the nation and the state" and applies to persons "who by their behaviour threaten the property and security of the nation and the state".[1] Persons to whom "preventive custody" was applied were to be put in concentration camps. It should be emphasized that in principle "preventive custody" was for an indefinite period (it is true that the order mentions release but that could take place "only when the means has achieved its end". This phrase, by not defining exactly the conditions of release, made it possible to detain those arrested indefinitely).

The years that followed saw the addition of an entire series of amendments to this circular which simplified the procedure for applying "preventive custody", especially in relation to Poles and citizens of other conquered countries. An example of these changes is the RSHA decree of 27 August 1941 (issued in connection with the attack on the Soviet Union) ordering all releases from concentration camps to be halted and, citing a Himmler order, "for all troublemaking persons, Czechs and Poles hostile to Germany, and also communists and similar riff-raff to be detained in camps for in principle a long period of time".[2] On the

---

[1] APMO. Photocopies. Zesp. *Erlass-Sammlung RKPA*, sygn. D-RF-3/RSHA/118/9, p. 626.
[2] APMO. Photocopies. Zesp. *Erlass-Sammlung RKPA*, sygn. D-RF-3/RSHA/118/9, p. 629.

other hand the order of 9 May 1944 simplified to a minimum the procedure to be followed with prisoners sent in mass transports from the eastern territories (*Ostvolksangehörige*), as the registration of these prisoners was to be carried out only in the concentration camps.[3]

The formal, but disregarded basis of applying "protective arrest" and subsequently putting a prisoner in *KL Auschwitz* was a written "order for protective custody" (*Schutzhaftbefehl*) issued by Office IV or V of RSHA. As of May 1943 the right to issue such an order in the case of Poles passed to the local Gestapo organs in occupied Poland.

The above mentioned Office IV issued decisions to apply "protective custody" to political prisoners, homosexuals, Jehovah's Witnesses and certain persons arrested for the purpose of corrective education (*Besserungshäftlinge*) and also prisoners who in view of their nationality might eventually be extradited or German political emigrés overtaken by the tide of Nazi conquest and caught in the occupied territory. The sphere of competence of Office V on the other hand included the placing under "preventive arrest" (*Vorbeugungshaft*) of common criminals, Gypsies, so-called asocials and those detained for security reasons (*Sicherungsverwahrte*). Prisoners subjected to preventive arrest were transferred to concentration camps from the prisons in which they had been previously serving sentences handed down by the courts.

The form on which an order for protective arrest was written out, besides the personal data of the person arrested, contained reasons (*Gründe*) for the arrest, which for example in the case of the Polish woman prisoner Stanisława Olewnik were formulated as follows: "The results of the State Police investigation establish that the prisoner by her behaviour threatened the existence and security of the State [a fixed formula — T.I.] as she offered shelter to numerous Jewish escapees and prevented their arrest by the police."[4]

Prisoners placed in concentration camps on the basis of a "preventive custody order" were described as *Schutzhäftlinge*. It should be pointed out that the regulations concerning the drawing up of a preventive arrest order and the showing of same to the person arrested were generally followed only in the case of people from the Reich or the territories annexed to it. In the case of other arrested persons either no warrant at all was issued, or it was sent on to the camp after a considerable lapse of time, often when the prisoner was no longer alive.

The mass extermination of Soviet POWs and their imprisonment in

---

[3] APMO. Collection of orders issued by SS-WVHA (hereafter: Zesp. *Sammlung von Erlassen*), sygn. D-RF-9/WVHA/8/2, p. 51.

[4] APMO. Photocopies of personal file on Stanisława Olewnik, who died in camp 21 April 1944, sygn. IZ-11 (Gestapo Ciechanów), p. 16.

KL Auschwitz was carried out on the basis of orders issued by the high command of the armed forces and a decree of RSHA. In an order of 27 August 1941, the chief of the Security Police and SD directed: "Executions should be carried out only in the nearest concentration camps. Appropriate directives to commandants will be issued. Efforts will have to be made to provide secure accommodation for those Soviet POWs who are to be exterminated and transport must be organized in such a way as to exclude the pos ibility of escape." [5]

On the basis of separate repressive orders issued in 1940 and 1941 and supplemented in the following years the institution of "educative labour camps" (*Arbeitserziehungslager*, or AEL) subordinate to the Gestapo arose. In an order in 12 December 1941 it was stated: "To educative labour camps should be sent only those who avoid work or break their contracts, and those who are unwilling to work and whose behaviour amounts to sabotage or violates general work morale and who for this reason ought to be detained by the police." [6] This order was directed against the "thousands of workers forced to perform slave labour for the needs of the German war economy". On the basis of these orders, by July 1941 local police stations had already begun to send "prisoners for education" (*Erziehungshäftlinge*, or EH) for a limited period (up to 56 days) of "education", after which they were released from the camp. Over 10 per cent of the men and women sent "for education" to *KL Auschwitz* died.

On the basis of Hitler's order of 7 December 1941, signed by Wilhelm Keitel, chief of OKW (*Oberkommando der Wehrmacht* — High Command of the Armed Forces), prisoners indicated by the cryptonym *Nacht und Nebel*, or NN (Night and Fog) began to be sent to the Auschwitz concentration camp from 1942 onwards. The text of this order states: "Since the beginning of the Russian campaign communist elements and other anti-German circles have intensified their activities against the Reich and the occupation forces in the occupied territories... Hence the need for the most severe pro ecution of these criminals. If the criminal is not a person of German nationality, there exist only one possible penalty — the death penalty." [7] Such a fate also befell the majority of the 1,170 prisoners of French nationality who were deported to *KL Auschwitz* under this decree on 8 July 1942.

The sending of Jewish prisoners to *KL Auschwitz* in the period preced-

---

[5] *Biuletyn Głównej Komisji Badania Zbrodni Niemieckich w Polsce* (Bulletin of the Main Commission for Investigation of Nazi Crimes in Poland), Poznań 1949, Vol. V, p. 133.
[6] APMO. Photocopies. Zespół "Akta różnych urzędów III Rzeszy" (Documents of various central offices of the Third Reich), sygn. D-RF-3/141a, p. 164.
[7] *Der Prozess gegen die Hauptkriegsverbrecher vor dem Internationalen Militärgerichtshof* (hereafter *Der Prozess...*), Nuremberg 1949, t. XXXVII, p. 572.

ing the implementation of the mass extermination programme took place in accordance with existing decrees and with the application of the formula of "protective custody". From 1942 onwards RSHA issued special decrees in this matter, on the basis of which successive operations were carried out under the cryptonym of Final Solution of the Jewish Question (*die Endlösung der Judenfrage*) and as a result of which mass transports of Jews were sent to Oświęcim from all the countries occupied by the Nazis.

The creation in *KL Auschwitz* of a separate section for Gypsies (*Zigeunerlager*) and the placing in it of over 20,000 Gypsies was done on the basis of an order of 29 January 1943 issued by Office V of Gestapo headquarters in Berlin.[8]

2. TRANSPORT

The first transport of 30 prisoners was sent to *KL Auschwitz* on 20 May 1940. These were professional criminals (*Berufsverbrecher*) of German nationality, transferred to Oświęcim from *KL Sachsenhausen*. It was intended that they should take over auxiliary functions, as had been the practice for years in the Nazi concentration camps. An idea of the real role envisaged for them may be gleaned from the fact that the SS told them that in *KL Auschwitz* they would be dealing with Polish "criminals". This was a premeditated and cynical provocation. All reminiscences and accounts by prisoners who were in the camp at this time are filled with descriptions of the cruelties and various forms of harassment to which the Polish prisoners were subjected by the SS staff and the "green" * trusties. A long time was to pass before — thanks to the camp resistance movement — the hegemony of the "greens" was finally broken and an increasing number of trusty posts began to be filled by political prisoners.

From 14 June 1940 (on which day 728 political prisoners of Polish nationality arrived) prisoners were brought to *KL Auschwitz* either individually (*Einzeltransport*) or in collective transports (*Sammeltransport*) of several score persons. Some prisoners (especially Poles) were handcuffed or bound during the journey, which made the already hard travelling conditions even worse. Only from the nearest localities were prisoners brought by lorry; the others were transported as a rule in closed cattle waggons.

The journey, often lasting several days, in crowded, unventilated waggons containing about 80 prisoners each, the foul air and tormenting

---

[8] Hans Joachim Döring, *Die Zigeuner im NS-Staat*. Verlag für kriminalistische Fachliteratur, Hamburg 1964, pp. 214—218.

* See p. 58.

thirst, were but a foretaste of what awaited the prisoners after their unloading on the camp ramp. The sufferings of the deportees were intensified when the journey lasted days on end. For example the transports of Jews from the Nazi-occupied countries of France, Belgium, Holland, Greece and Italy lasted up to six day.

All transports were accompanied by a strong escort in order to prevent escapes. But despite extraordinary security measures, a few brave spirits did succeed in escaping from the waggons.

The prisoners brought to *KL Auschwitz* had often been previously detained in other concentration camps, prisons, transit camps (*Durchgangslager*) or ghettoes, which obviously had an important effect on their physical condition and mental state, especially in the case of those who had been subjected to interrogation and torture in the cells of the Gestapo. This concerned especially persons suspected of belonging to the resistance movement and who had been arrested as a result of treachery or provocation, partisans, members of the resistance movement caught bearing arms or in possesion of objects constituting material proof of their anti-Nazi activity. Such prisoners were held for months at a time in crowded prison cells where, with almost complete lack of exercise and negligible rations, frequently tortured, they were reduced to a state of extreme exhaustion.

The appalling state in which prisoners brought to *KL Auschwitz* travelled from other concentration camps is revealed by surviving fragments of correspondence concerning, among others, the transport of 1,500 prisoners brought from *KL Majdanek* on 8 July 1943, whom it was intended to use as labour. Upon the arrival of this transport the camp doctor *(SS-Lagerarzt)* Dr. Bruno Kitt carried out an examination of the new arrivals and established that out of 750 men, only 424 would be able after four weeks' quarantine to be put to work, while the remaining 326 prisoners were described by him as unable to perform any kind of work at all. Of the 750 women prisoners brought with the same transport, five died immediately upon arrival at *KL Auschwitz,* and the state of the remainder was similar to that of the men (moreover the women were suffering from scabies).

A discussion of the prison transports should also include some account of the conditions in which the final evacuation of January 1945 took place when the prisoners from *KL Auschwitz* — men and women — were removed to concentration camps deep in the heart of the Reich. Most of them had to cover scores of kilometres to embarkation points where they were loaded onto coal waggons. The tragic results of these transports, carried out in winter in many degrees of frost, have been described by one prisoner as follows:

"The waggons were terribly crowded. None of the prisoners was able to move or to change his position once he had adopted it. ...It is difficult for me now to describe exactly what happened during the journey. Without protection against the frost, the prisoners felt their strength ebbing away. Dantesque scenes took place. Everyone fought for the place he had occupied. The weak and the emaciated slid dying to the floor of the waggon... The heart-rending groans of the dying mingled with the shrieks uttered by some prisoners who were losing their reason. Biting, kicking and scratching their immediate neighbours, they were beginning to be dangerous".[9]

3. THE RECEPTION AND REGISTRATION OF TRANSPORTS

The unloading of rail transports of prisoners took place on a ramp beside the camp in the vicinity of the prison huts of *KL Auschwitz I*. In 1942 a second unloading ramp (*Judenrampe*) came into use for transports of Jews brought to Auschwitz for extermination (although some of them, following selection, were taken into the camp and registered). From May 1944 rail transports were unloaded at a special ramp situated within the perimeter of *KL Birkenau* between sectors BI and BII.

Besides rail transports, prisoners were also, as already mentioned, delivered to Auschwitz by lorries, which usually halted at the camp entrance. There the prisoners were unloaded and handed over to the SS authorities. The transports arrived at various times of day, often at night, when the glare of headlights, the beatings with rifle butts, the shouts and curses of the SS men and the barking of the dogs set on the prisoners intensified the dreadful impression made by this first encounter with the realities of camp life.

Once arrived at the camp, new arrivals (*Zugang*) were taken to buildings containing bath facilities. In *Auschwitz I* it was Block 26, while at Birkenau in sectors BIa and BIb special brick buildings popularly known as "Saunas" (*Saune*) were built. If a transport arrived at night, the prisoners spent the remainder of the night in these buildings or in some substitute hut, reception and registration not taking place until the following morning.

The first thing new arrivals had to do was to surrender all their clothing, including underwear, and all valuables, proofs of identity and miscellaneous possessions. All they were allowed to keep was a handkerchief and in the case of men, a trouser belt, everything else being placed in paper bags and sent to the *Effektenkammer,* where they were to remain

---

[9] Account of former prisoner of *KL Auschwitz* Józef Tabaczyński. APMO, Zespół "Oświadczenia", t. 44, k. 62.

for the prisoner's stay in the camp. Naturally no receipt was given, even to prisoners compelled to surrender valuable objects made of gold, watches or considerable sums of money. Next the prisoner received a card with his camp number before being taken to the camp barber where all his body hair was removed, an operation made all the more unpleasant in view of the great haste with which it was carried out and the bluntness of the instruments employed. The shaved parts were then rubbed with disinfectant.

After being undressed and shaven, the prisoners were then driven on the trot to the showers. This was usually the first opportunity for a long time to slake their thirst. But even this hygenic measure, impatiently awaited by most of the prisoners after the hardships of the transports, was accompanied by various harassments, usually in the form of making the water too hot or icycold. Those who tried to escape the scalding or freezing jets of water were beaten back into place.

The constant hustling, beating and curses had a shocking effect on the prisoners. It was particularly hard for women and girls who had to undress in the presence of jeering and mocking SS men. One of the women prisoners has described it as follows:

"As a 'Zugang' we entered the gates of the 'Sauna'. The 'Sauna' was ruled by German female prisoners, professional prostitutes... All were old, obese, ugly, with tousled hair, like witches out of a fairy tale, whose very appearance aroused fear and revulsion. It was these 'black triangles'*, also known in the camp as 'Puff Mamas', who greeted us with vulgar oaths and jeers, urging us on to undress quickly. Round the 'Sauna' strolled a young and oafish-looking SS man — this was the *Unterscharführer* in charge of the 'Sauna' ...How could we undress completely while this 'Uscha' was walking about... and had no intention of leaving. I was not yet familiar with the camp customs. We stood, embarrassed, looking at one another, waiting to see who would begin to undress first... I also undressed, but I stooped and picked up a blanket lying near me on the ground and covered myself with it. A Kapo jumped at me, tore the blanket from my shoulders, struck me hard in the face and shouted 'Heilige Madonna', which was supposed to mean, 'Look what a holy madonna!' — the SS man began to laugh loudly — she then added something obscene and all the German women cackled with laughter... so much did the fact that she had called me a 'heilige madonna' amuse them... The German unexpectedly approached me and struck me with a stick on my bare buttock, laughing loudly and crassly at his heroic deed."[10]

---

* See p. 58.
[10] Recollections of former prisoner of *KL Auschwitz* Maria Oyrzyńska (registered in the camp under the name of Slisz). APMO. Zespół "Wspomnienia", t. 63, k. 28.

After the showers came the issue of camp clothing, which meant proceeding to further buildings. Because of the need for speed and the generally large number of new arrivals, the prisoners, while being driven at a trot from the bathhouse, were thrown successive items of camp equipment. Thus in the space of about an hour a group of prisoners had formed, dressed in ill-fitting striped prison clothing, which was usually dirty and lice-ridden. The wooden clogs issued instead of shoes hampered movement, especially in winter on the ice-bound camp streets.

Throughout these operations — which of course took place in unheated, draughty huts (in *KL Auschwitz I* the prisoners undressed and awaited their clothing issue in the open air) — there rained down on the prisoners, who were generally ignorant of the German language, a hail of orders, instructions, the foulest curses and blows, both from the SS men present and the trusties. Terrified by this brutal treatment, the prisoners barely recognized their relatives and friends with hair shaved off and dressed in ill-fitting clothing.

The registration of newly arrived prisoners took place immediately after the issue of clothing, and consisted in filling out a personal form (*Häftlings-Personalbogen*). Besides his personal data, the prisoner was required to give the address of his next of kin. The personal forms, kept in the camp Political Department, constituted the basis for the drawing up in some dozen copies of a list of new arrivals (*Zugangsliste*), copies of which were distributed to the various camp departments (*Abteilungen*) where they were used as a basic source of information about prisoners. They served as the basis for opening auxiliary files which made it easier to keep records of the prisoners and draw up daily and periodic reports. Thus registered, the prisoner received a camp serial number which would serve instead of his name for the entire period of his stay in the camp. The registration procedure was concluded with the tattooing of the prisoner's camp number on his left forearm.

The concentration camp at Oświęcim was the only camp in which tattooing was introduced to mark the prisoners. The reason for this was the very high mortality rate among the prisoners, which occasionally rose to several hundred a day. Such a large number of deaths created difficulties in the identification of corpses, as it was enough to remove the deceased's clothing on which his camp number was marked for that number to be impossible to establish. In the camp hospital (*Häftlingskrankenbau*, where many prisoners died, the practice of writing a patient's camp number on his chest with indelible ink was introduced. Difficulties in identifying bodies were intensified in autumn 1941 when the mass extermination of Soviet POWs in *KL Auschwitz* was begun. It was then that the camp authorities decided to introduce tattooing. It was first used on several thousand Soviet POWs. The tattooing was done with a metal stamp to which were attached interchangeable numbers formed from needles about a centimetre long. This device, when applied sharply to the upper left breast, made it possible to tattoo the whole number at once. Dye was then rubbed into the bleeding punctures. The tattooed prisoners were so weak that they had to be propped against the wall while the operation was being carried out, so as not to fall over at the moment of application. In March 1942 the same method of tattooing began to be used in KL Birkenau on other emaciated prisoners whose state indicated imminent decease (only a few of the Polish prisoners who had numbers tattooed on their breast survived).

Because the use of a metal stamp turned out to be impractical, single-needle tattooing was introduced, whereby each digit of the camp number was pricked out separately. The place for the number was also changed to the left forearm. In this way Jewish prisoners were tattooed at Brzezinka from 1942 onwards, and in spring 1943 the camp authorities ordered the tattooing of camp numbers on all prisoners (both those already registered and new arrivals). Numbers were not tattooed on Germans nor on prisoners sent for "education". Some categories of prisoners also had additional symbols tattooed before the number, for example Jews (though not all) had signs in the shape of a triangle, Gypsies had the letter "Z" (for the German word for Gypsy, *Zigeuner*), and, from May 1944, Jewish prisoners were marked with the letters "A" or "B", to indicate the separate series of numbers issued in this period. In 1943, for unknown reasons, the prisoners of some transports had their camp numbers tattooed on the inner side of their left forearms.

After the introduction of tattooing, prisoners were identified by their camp numbers, which were visible on their forearms. At Brzezinka the dead were so laid out in front of the blocks that the arm with the tattooed number was visible.

Besides the tattooing of numbers, another element of registration was the photographing of prisoners from three angles. On the first shot, taken in profile, the prisoner's camp number and letter symbol of his category and nationality were marked. Jewish prisoners, who from spring 1942 were brought in mass transports, were not photographed. From 1943, in view of the difficulties in obtaining photographic materials, the practice of photographing was limited, and following an order from higher authority photographs were only taken in the case of "particularly" dangerous prisoners, e.g. persons occupying leading functions in the resistance movement. The photographs taken in KL Auschwitz were kept separately in the form of negatives and positive contact copies, and filing them was the business of the SS camp records division (*Erkennungsdienst*), a branch of the camp Gestapo.

Even during the carrying out of these apparently simple activities new arrivals were exposed to various harassments. To be photographed a proisner had to sit on a special revolving chair controlled by a lever which when suddenly released after the taking of the third shot resulted in the prisoner's being thrown to the floor to the delight of the assembled technicians.

4. THE MARKING OF PRISONERS

Every prisoner registered in *KL Auschwitz* received a camp number which he had to wear on his striped prison uniform in a precisely defined place. The number, stamped on a small strip of canvas, was sewn onto the blouse at the level of the left breast and on the outer seam of the right trouser leg. Each of the numerical series introduced in *KL Auschwitz* began from the number one.

The first was the series of numbers issued to male prisoners from May 1940 and continued up to January 1945, reaching a total of 202,499 numbers. Up to mid-May 1944 this series also embraced Jewish prisoners.

In October 1941 a second numerical series was introduced (continued until 1944), which covered about 12,000 Soviet POWs (some of the POWs exterminated in *KL Auschwitz* were not registered and hence not issued with numbers).

From January 1942 a separate series of numbers was introduced for *Erziehungshäftlinge* (prisoners sent for "education"), who had previously received numbers in the general men's series. When this new series was introduced its numeration also included those prisoners of the new category who had previously died or been released, whereas their previous numbers were reissued to other prisoners. This is the only case in the history of the Auschwitz camp of numbers being issued twice. In all about 10,000 prisoners received numbers in the "education" series. Female prisoners of this category received numbers in a separate series beginning with the number 1. About 2,000 women were registered in this series.

On 26 March 1942 the first female prisoners brought to *KL Auschwitz* were issued with numbers in a new series which was continued to the end of the camp's existence. In this series about 90,000 women were registered, including (up to May 1944) Jewish women prisoners.

Gypsies sent to *KL Auschwitz* (from February 1943) were given numbers in two series continued up to August 1944: one for men which ran to 10,094 numbers, and one for women, which ran to 10,873 numbers.

From mid-May 1944 onwards for newly arrived and registered prisoners of Jewish origin there were separate series (to avoid the issuing of excessively high numbers in the general series), which were to begin with A1 and end at A20,000, the next to begin with B1, and so on through the alphabet. In the case of men this was done up to about 15,000 in the B series, whereas in the case of women, through an oversight, the A series did not stop at 20,000 and was continued up to about 30,000.

Because of the destruction of camp documents by the SS authorities it is not possible to establish exactly the final number of every series. In sum, in the series here mentioned over 405,000 numbers were issued. This figure also includes about 3,000 numbers issued to "police prisoners" (*Polizeihäftlinge*),* who were not mentioned separately in the daily reports on the camp complement (*Stärkemeldung*).

As already mentioned, the numbers issued served the SS authorities for file-keeping purposes, while the tattoos facilitated identification of the corpses of executed or deceased prisoners, and also the identification of escapees on recapture. For this reason from 1944 in reports sent from *KL Auschwitz* concerning escapes, the escaped prisoner's camp number was given under the heading of "identification marks".

On the basis of the number worn by a prisoner on his camp uniform it was possible to determine the length of time he had spent in the camp. With every passing year, the number of prisoners who remained with low numbers issued in 1940, 1941 or 1942 was few. A low number indicated that a prisoner had gone through a lot and had acquired the experience necessary (if he was lucky at the same time) to survive several years in the camp. Thus it was not surprising that the SS authorities tended to get rid of such prisoners by including them in transports departing for camps situated deep inside the Reich. There the prisoner once again became part of a *Zugang*.

In the Nazi concentration camps there were various categories of prisoners. The category a given prisoner belonged to could be identified by the colour of the triangle on his camp uniform. These triangles were originally sewn on separately, and later (in *KL Auschwitz*) they were painted beside the number on the same square piece of canvas.

A red triangle indicated a political prisoner to whom "preventive custody" (*Schutzhaft*) had been applied, hence the use in the camp documents of the term *Schutzhäftlinge*. Until 1944 this was the most numerous category of prisoners in *KL Auschwitz*, among whom there predominated Polish prisoners who had been arrested for genuine anti-Nazi activity (as members of the resistance movement), or in the course of various repressive operations. This latter category also included those who were arrested — for example in 1940 in the streets of Warsaw — without any anti-German activity being proved against them, nor any attempt being made to do so. A similar fate befell the Poles inhabiting the environs of Zamość, who were evicted and placed in *KL Auschwitz* at the end of 1942 and the

---

* See p. 61.

beginning of 1943. It should be stressed that the Polish peasants brought from the Zamość region included children who were killed in the camp by phenol injections through the heart. Included in this same category were several thousand men, women, and children brought from Warsaw in August 1944 after the outbreak of the rising, part of the mass evacuation of Warsaw's civil population to concentration camps.

In 1943 women and children from the occupied territories of the Soviet Union (the regions of Minsk and Vitebsk) were brought to *KL Auschwitz* and also registered as *Schutzhäftlinge*. In short, the number of prisoners in this category depended on the current situation in the various occupied countries. As a result of intensified repression applied against the civilian population, the Nazi authorities sent to *KL Auschwitz* numerous transports of prisoners who were included in the category of political prisoners and had to wear red triangles on their camp uniforms.

A green triangle was used to distinguish the next category of prisoners, that of "professional criminals" (*Berufsverbrecher* — BV). Although this was a comparatively small group, initially (1940) almost exclusively composed of Germans, it was from among their number that the camp authorities appointed trusties who were responsible to some extent for keeping order inside the camp and in the blocks, and also for overseeing the prisoners at work. The "green" trusties, demoralized by long years of experience in Nazi jails and concentration camps, quickly became the terror of their fellow prisoners. Thus it was not surprising that the term "trusty" came to be associated in the minds of most prisoners at *KL Auschwitz* with a ruthless individual with criminal tendencies, who exploited the post entrusted to him to "set himself up" comfortably in the camp, which in practice meant such things as stealing the prisoners' starvation rations and enforcing obedience with beatings and terror. A certain number of the German trusties maintained fairly intimate relations with members of the SS occupying responsible posts in the command structure of the camp (to which belonged such men as *SS-Rapportführer* Gerhard Palitzsch). This concerned especially the group, mentioned earlier, of thirty criminals of German nationality brought on 20 May 1940 from *KL Sachsenhausen*, and the subsequent 100-strong group brought from the same camp on 29 August the same year. These prisoners, who constituted almost a separate caste favoured by the camp authorities, eagerly fulfilled the tasks entrusted to them and became a criminal tool of the SS.

In the Nazi concentration camps a separate category of "asocial" (*Asoziale* — ASO) prisoners existed, who were distinguished by a black triangle. The concept of "asocial" was of course none too precise and fairly widely interpreted. In *KL Auschwitz* this category included both prostitutes (chiefly of German nationality), and over 20,000 Gypsies. It should be explained that among the Gypsies were many settled families who before their arrest had supported themselves by working and had led conventional lives. This same colour was used to indicate Gypsy men who before being arrested and sent to *KL Auschwitz* had served in the German army.

There was a small group of prisoners in *KL Auschwitz* made up of Jehovah's Witnesses (*Internationale Bibelforscher-Vereinigung* — IBV) and clergy. The Jehovah's Witnesses were given violet triangles. The Catholic clergy — distinguished by a purple triangle — consisted mainly of priests and monks of Polish nationality, who had been put in the camp by the Nazi authorities in the course of various repressive actions aimed against the Polish intelligentsia. A considerable proportion of them died in *KL Auschwitz*, and the remainder were transferred to *KL Dachau* (only a few individuals remained in the camp).

An equally small group was made up of prisoners who wore a pink triangle and had been arrested on a charge of homosexual practices. In practice there were considerably more homosexual prisoners in the camp, as homosexuality was a fairly frequent phenomenon among the long-term prisoners, especially the common criminals of German nationality (BV), who in discharging various functions used force or the promise of improved conditions to make the prisoners in their charge comply with their wishes.

Prisoners who had been placed under preventive custody after serving sentences passed by a court and put in concentration camps (*Sicherungsverwahrte* — SV, PSV) wore a green triangle standing on its base.

From July 1941 there appeared a new category in *KL Auschwitz*: *Erziehungshäftlinge*, or prisoners sent for education. They did not wear triangles, merely having the letter E precede their camp numbers. In accordance with the relevant decrees *Erziehungshäftlinge* were supposed to be sent to "camps of education through labour" (*Arbeitserziehungslager* — AEL). Of course this was not observed in relation to those prisoners of this category placed in *KL Auschwitz*, where they were merely allotted part of one of the blocks. Initially *Erziehungshäftlinge* were disfigured on registration by having a strip of hair left on the crown of their shaven heads, which gave rise to the name "cockerels" by which they were generally known. Residing in the camp, supervised by SS guards, sent to perform the most arduous tasks and subject to all the rigours of life in Nazi concentration camps, they differed in no way from the other prisoners. Particularly tragic was the fate of the *Erziehungshäftlinge* sent to *KL Auschwitz* in 1941 and 1942. As a result of the primitive conditions in which they were kept, the hunger rations they received and a spreading typhus epidemic, a large number of these prisoners died of exhaustion or disease before the lapse of the 56 days they were allegedly to serve before being released from the camp. From January

1943 four huts of the camp at Monowice (later *KL Auschwitz III Monowitz*) were evacuated for male *Erziehungshäftlinge*, while women of this category, who had begun to be placed in the camp from 1943, were sent to the women's section of *KL Auschwitz II Birkenau*.

A separate category was created for Soviet prisoners of war (*Russische Kriegsgefangene* — RKG), the first transports of whom had been registered in the camp files in October 1941. For these prisoners nine blocks in the main camp were set aside and the words *Russisches Kriegsgefangenen Arbeitslager* (Labour Camp for Soviet Prisoners of War) were set up over the entrance gate to the section thus detached. Of course this inscription was a mere camouflage, as in fact the Soviet POWs were dealt with by the same camp authorities of *KL Auschwitz* and the regulations regarding the treatment of prisoners of war were not observed in relation to them. It is true they were allowed to retain their uniforms on which stripes and the letters SU (for *Sowjet Union*) were marked in oil paint. but in practice this had no meaning at all, and the way in which they were treated indicated that they had been brought to *KL Auschwitz* for the purpose of rapid extermination. In March 1942 the surviving Soviet POWs were transferred to *KL Birkenau*, causing the winding of the fictitious "POW camp". But in camp files and daily roll calls (*Lagerstärke*) "Soviet prisoners of war" continued to figure as a separate category.

For the Jews, who were entered in the camp statistics as a separate category of prisoners and who from 1943 constituted the most numerous group in *KL Auschwitz*, a badge was introduced in the shape of a six-pointed star composed of two overlapping triangles of different colours: one yellow to indicate a Jew in general, the other the colour indicating whichever of the above mentioned categories he happened to belong to. From mid-1944 the Jews wore triangle badges identical to those of all the other prisoners, only with an oblong yellow stripe over the triangles.

In 1944 yet another category was introduced in the Nazi concentration camps — that of civilian worker (*Zivilarbeiter* — ZA). On 14 February an order was issued to include in this category Russians and Poles unsuitable for Germanization (*Russen und nichteindeutschungsfähige Polen*). [11] In the few surviving documents of the former *KL Auschwitz*, especially in the general lists, it has not been established that such a category was in practice introduced, but there is no doubt that it existed in other Nazi concentration camps, such as Mauthausen and Flossenbürg. The above-mentioned order was probably meant to serve as a basis for the later practice of changing the category of prisoners transferred from *KL Auschwitz* to other concentration camps. Thus for example a Pole registered in *KL Auschwitz* as a political prisoner upon being transferred

---

[11] APMO. Zesp. *Sammlung von Erlassen*, sygn. D-RF-9/WVHA/8/1, pp. 38—39.

to *KL Mauthausen* was included in the category of "civilian workers" without being at all aware of this, as he continued to wear on his camp uniform the same badge: a red triangle with the letter P. In this way not only was a prisoner's category changed, but also his nationality. Prisoners from territories annexed to the Reich, such as Silesia or Poznań, were registered against their will as "Germans". Many of them were detained in *KL Auschwitz* for several years and, despite pressure, refused to sign the German nationality list (DVL). For this reason the statistical data of these camps, for example those of *KL Mauthausen,* regarding particular categories of prisoners and their nationality should be treated as falsified and not corresponding to reality.

From 12 February 1943 there were detained in *KL Auschwitz* so-called police prisoners (*Polizeihäftlinge* — PH), who were kept there because of the overcrowding of the remand prison at Mysłowice. Initially accommodated on the upper floor of Block 2 and later on the ground floor of Block 11, the "police prisoners" were not allowed to leave the quarters assigned to them. In relation to these prisoners the concentration camp played the role of a substitute for the remand prison. "Police prisoners" were allowed to retain their civilian clothes and did not have camp numbers tattooed on their forearms. They were issued numbers which did not, however, have to be worn on their clothing, but were printed on cards which they carried in their pockets. Upon the completion of the investigation and a "trial" (lasting merely a few minutes) before the Summary Police Court (*Polizei-Standgericht*), death sentences were carried out on the spot. Only a few prisoners of this category were registered in the camp files, and they were all persons who had been sentenced by the Summary Police Court to a term in a concentration camp. They then had to go through the whole procedure connected with this: surrendering their civilian clothing, being issued with camp uniforms, etc.

In *KL Auschwitz* there also existed a small category of so-called privileged prisoners (*Bevorzugte Häftlinge*). In theory any prisoner who had spent a long time in camp and whose conduct had been irreproachable and in accordance with the regulations could become privileged. In practice the SS authorities only softened the regime in relation to a small group of trusties, chiefly of German nationality, who were allowed to wear their hair longer, to possess a watch, and even to take Sunday walks in civilian clothing outside the camp perimeter (under the supervision of an SS guard). One such privileged prisoner in *KL Auschwitz* was Bruno Brodniewicz, a common criminal of German nationality who for several years held the function of "camp senior" (*Lagerältester*). [12]

---

[12] Account of former prisoner of *KL Auschwitz* Erwin Olszówka. APMO. Zespół "Oświadczenia", t. 72, k. 135.

Sometime in the winter of 1943/44 in *KL Auschwitz* from the several dozen prisoners of German nationality a "camp watch" (*Lageraufsicht*) was created. Its members received separate accommodation and special yellow armbands with the inscription *Lageraufsicht*. It was their task to supervise the work commandos. In practice they did not perform the role assigned to them, as their armbands made them identifiable from a distance, and whenever they approached the prisoner naturally feigned "productive" work.

In the Nazi concentration camps additional markings had to be worn by the members of the "penal company" (*Strafkompanie* — SK), who had a small piece of black cloth in the shape of a circle on their blouses. Prisoners considered to be dangerous or liable to attempt escape had a red circle with the letters IL (for *"Im Lager"* — in camp), which meant they were not to be allowed outside the camp fence and were to be specially watched. The consequences for prisoners in *KL Auschwitz* who had to wear such a badge were occasionally tragic, especially in the first years of the camp's existence. In 1942 a large number of Polish political prisoners were marked in this way before being transferred to Brzezinka and simply attached to the penal company. After a rebellion by the penal company on 10 June 1942 over 300 Polish prisoners wearing red circles went to the gas chamber. [13]

Painted or stamped in indelible ink on the triangle indicating a prisoner's category was the first letter of the name of his nationality in German (e.g. P for Pole). Prisoners of German nationality did not have letters.

The daily reports drawn up in the camp also took account of the division of the prisoners into different categories. Thanks to the activity of the camp resistance three such reports have survived: one for the prisoners of *KL Auschwitz I* for January 1944 and two for all parts of *KL Auschwitz* for 22 August and 2 September 1944 respectively. [14]

These reports reveal that in August 1944 the largest category of prisoners in *KL Auschwitz* was that of Jews, followed by that of political prisoners. In previous periods the situation had varied. Before the start of the mass extermination of the Jewish population the most numerous category had been that of political prisoners (above all Poles), while the number of prisoners in other categories varied largely in accordance with Nazi policy in a given period. Unfortunately the destruction by the SS authorities in January 1945 of nearly all the personal files has made it impossible to establish precisely the relative sizes of the various categories throughout the entire period of the camp's existence.

---

[13] Account of former prisoner of *KL Auschwitz* Józef Kret. APMO. Zespół "Oświadczenia", t. 4. k. 591—595.
[14] APMO. *Mat. oboz. Ruchu Oporu*, t. II, k. 60, 116, 133.

5. BREAKDOWN OF THE PRISONERS BY AGE AND NATIONALITY

In *KL Auschwitz* there were prisoners of various nationalities, creeds and professions. They included Americans, Austrians, Belgians, Britons, Bulgarians, Chinese, Croats, Czechs, Dutchmen, Egyptians, Frenchmen, Germans, Greeks, Gypsies, Hungarians, Italians, Jews, Letts, Lithuanians, Norwegians, Persians, Poles, Romanians, Russians (and other citizens of the Soviet Union), Slovaks, Spaniards, Swiss, Turks and Yugoslavs.

The number of prisoners of any given nationality underwent constant changes and depended on the transports sent to the camp. An analysis of the sources reveals that in the first years of the camp's existence (especially in 1940 and 1941) the majority of the prisoners were Poles, who in later years too, together with Polish citizens of Jewish origin, constituted the most numerous national group. Periodic falls in the number of Polish prisoners were caused by such things as their removal in mass transports (amounting even to several thousand at a time) to concentration camps situated deep in the Reich, such as Buchenwald, Gross-Rosen, Mauthausen, Neuengamme and Sachsenhausen. For example, from August 1944 — in view of the outbreak of the Warsaw Rising — most of the Polish and Russian prisoners were hastily sent away from *KL Auschwitz*, as the SS authorities wished to guard against the possibility of a rebellion being organized in the camp.

The breakdown of the prisoners by nationality was alternately influenced by such factors as high mortality and the selections, as a result of which tens of thousands of prisoners perished in a very short space of time. The mortality rate was particularly high in the first years of the camp's existence (over 80 per cent of prisoners brought to the camp died a few months after arrival), but the situation in this respect did not change in later years either. This is illustrated by the fact that of 12,757 Jewish prisoners — men and women — deported from Greece between 20 March 1943 and 16 August 1944 and registered in the camp, 1,838 remained alive on 21 August 1944. [15]

For all the reasons mentioned above the national composition of the prisoners of *KL Auschwitz* changed almost from day to day. Unfortunately lack of materials prevents a more thorough analysis of the changes occurring in the proportionate national representation of the prisoners, the few existing data enabling us merely to present by way of example the situation as it appeared on a few random dates.

The transports sent to *KL Auschwitz* and registered there contained

---

[15] APMO. Mat. oboz. Ruchu Oporu, t. IV, k. 262—271.

prisoners of all ages: children, youth, adults and old people. Following an order from higher authority the administrative offices of the concentration camps (*Abteilung II — Schutzhaftlagerführung*) prepared monthly reports in which the prisoners were divided into age groups (*Unterteilung in Alterstufen*) as follows: under 20, 20-30, 30-40, 40-50, 50-60, 60-70, 70-80 and over 80. These reports were drawn up on the last day of every month for prisoners currently in the camp, while separate reports were drawn up on identical forms for those who died in a given month.

Confirmation of the fact that, besides adults, juveniles and old people were brought to *KL Auschwitz* may be found in the partially preserved registers of new arrivals (*Zugangsliste*). For example among 525 Polish prisoners from Lublin registered in the camp on 9 January 1941 and issued with the numbers 8608-9132, apart from 17-year-olds there were also old people. The prisoner Szczepan Cyrulski who arrived with this transport and received the number 8806 was 83 years old.

Particularly tragic was the fate of both the youngest and the oldest prisoners. Apart from Polish children, Russian children (many of them from the environs of Minsk and Vitebsk), the children of Gypsies and Jewish children were sent to *KL Auschwitz*. Most of them were killed either by gassing (as in the case of the Jewish and Gypsy children) or by phenol injections (as in the case of the Polish children from the region round Zamość).

The absence of the relevant camp documents makes it practically impossible to establish the number of children registered in *KL Auschwitz* or the number of children there were in the camp at any particular period. But it has been established on the basis of fragmentarily surviving documents that the Nazi authorities were holding about a thousand children under 14 years of age in *KL Birkenau* in the summer and autumn of 1944. From August 1944 several hundred Polish children were brought to this camp from Warsaw following the outbreak of the Rising. Most of them remained there until January 1945, i.e. until the final evacuation, when the boys were evacuated on foot to Wodzisław and thereafter transported in open waggons to the Mauthausen concentration camp. [16]

When the camp was liberated on 27 January 1945, it was found to contain Polish and Russian children, and Jewish children from various countries. Some of them were too young to know their own surnames and to this day are still seeking their parents and relatives.

Besides children there were also in *KL Auschwitz* young prisoners aged between 14 and 18, whose number it is impossible to determine in

---

[16] Account of the former prisoner of *KL Auschwitz*, Ignacy Mrożewski. APMO. Zespół "Oświadczenia", t. 68, k. 103.

the absence of sources. All that can be said, by way of example, is that in the second half of 1944 — probably because of the sudden increase in the need for labour — juvenile prisoners were sent to the numerous subcamps of *KL Auschwitz III*, where they were employed even in such arduous work as coalmining (e.g. in the Fürstengrube mine). In the subcamp at Trzebinia during this period juveniles constituted over 14 per cent of the prisoners employed. Out of 813 prisoners employed 19 were aged 14-15 and 101 were aged 16-17.

6. QUARANTINE

Newly arrived prisoners were isolated and kept in quarantine in order to prevent the spread of infectious diseases in the camp. Such at least was the theory. Depending on current needs various places were set aside for keeping prisoners in quarantine: blocks, huts, even tents holding several hundred persons apiece (two such tents were used for prisoners in quarantine in *KL Auschwitz III — Monowitz*). In 1943 one of the construction sectors in *KL Birkenau* (BIIa) was set aside for quarantine purposes. There in 16 stable huts several thousand prisoners were kept at a time. New arrivals at the women's camp were also kept in quarantine.

The time spent in quarantine was a shattering experience for every prisoner, for it was then usually that the new arrival first became acquainted with the laws governing the prison community in Nazi concentration camps, where the SS man responsible for a block (*Blockführer*) exercised unlimited authority, aided by trusties in the block (*Blockführer*) *Blockältester* (block senior) and their subordinates (*Stubendienst*).

The rigorous daily regimen, beginning with a brutal awakening in the morning and the prisoners being driven from their straw pallets, and continuing with exercises (described as "sport"), lasting for hours on end, learning how to fall in on the *Appellplatz,* taking off and replacing caps at the word of command, "learning" how to sing various German songs and learning the correct pronunciation of a number of typical German phrases (e.g. reporting to an SS man), filled the entire period spent in quarantine.

The primitive facilities and overcrowding, the dirt and impossibility of observing personal hygiene, combined with the rampant terror, had a disastrous psychological effect on the prisoners, especially on those held in quarantine at Brzezinka where the mass extermination installations were. The appalling consequences of being kept in quarantine in BIIa are revealed in the notes and documents saved from destruction by Dr. Otto Wolken, a former inmate employed as a doctor in the clinic.[17]

The number of prisoners kept in quarantine in sector BIIa varied on average from about 4,000 to 6,000. In the period from September 1943 to November 1944, 4,023 prisoners were transferred from quarantine to the camp hospital in view of illness or their poor state of health Apart from this, during the same period 1,902 deaths were noted, while 6,717 prisoners, whom the SS considered as too emaciated to work, were selected for the gas chamber.

Prisoners released from the camp also had to pass through quarantine before leaving *KL Auschwitz*. This concerned above all the *Erziehungshäftlinge*, as the number of prisoners of other categories who were released was small. Released prisoners detained in quarantine were examined by SS doctors. Excessive emaciation, overly impaired physical condition, ulcers, swellings, hunger oedema or suspicion of a contagious disease ruled out the possibility of a prisoner's being allowed to leave the camp. If their health did not improve, prisoners intended for release were detained in the camp, and many of them were never released.

Prisoners leaving the camp attracted universal attention because of their general appearance and emaciated state, encountering spontaneously expressed sympathy and help from the Polish civilian population. The Czech prisoner Antonin Čenek recalls:

"When we found ourselves alone at the station, little girls came up to us giving us bread and even milk to the weaker looking among us. We were surprised and touched at this help organized by the Poles... Returning home by train, we encountered other moving scenes. Our Polish travelling companions gave us everything they had with them."[18]

7. LIVING AND SANITARY CONDITIONS

One of the causes of the epidemics and contagious diseases prevailing in *Kl Auschwitz* was to be found in appalling living conditions which, however, varied during the different periods of the camp's existence and also in each of its three parts.

---

[17] Protocol of the examination of 24 April 1945 of former prisoner of *KL Auschwitz* Otto Wolken. APMO. *Akta Krakowskiej Okręgowej Komisji Badania Zbrodni Niemieckiej w sprawie karnej b. komendanta obozu koncentracyjnego Oświęcim-Brzezinka Rudolfa Hössa* (Documents of the Cracow Regional Commission for the Investigation of German Crimes in the case of the former commandant of the concentration camp Oświęcim-Brzezinka, Rudolf Höss), t. 6, k. 5 and *passim*.
[18] APMO. Zespół "Oświadczenia", t. 22, k. 149.

In the main camp (*KL Auschwitz I*) twenty brick buildings formerly used as barracks — of which six were two-storied, the remainder single-storied — were set aside as prisoners' quarters in 1940. These buildings, measuring 45.38 m. by 17.75 m. each, because of their lack of sanitary installations, were unfit to accommodate the several hundred prisoners each building had to hold.

The existing buildings were therefore extended with the addition of another floor and the construction of eight new blocks was begun. Although from August 1941 the blocks were numbered 1-28, this did not mean that all the buildings were used to accommodate prisoners. Some were used for storing prisoners' clothing and linen, the personal effects taken from prisoners, then there were the bathhouse, delousing chamber, camp offices, canteen, etc. Prisoners from the blocks to which a new floor was being added had to be accommodated in other blocks, thus adding to the general overcrowding in the whole camp. The new stories were not completed until the spring of 1943.

The number of prisoners living in one block varied and depended on the overall number of prisoners in the camp. The arrival in the autumn of 1941 of over 10,000 Soviet POWs (for whom nine blocks were set aside) and in March 1942 of several thousand women prisoners (for whom ten blocks were set aside) worsened the already bad living conditions.

Throughout the first year or so of the camp's existence the inmates of *KL Auschwitz* slept in rows on straw mattresses laid out in the various rooms. These mattresses had to be gathered up at reveille and piled up in a corner of the room. The result was the rapid disintegration of the straw in the mattresses and the raising of great clouds of dust when they were laid out at night and stacked up in the morning. In the rooms (known as *Stuben*), which were five metres wide, the prisoners slept on mattresses in three rows, packed to capacity. They could only sleep on one side. Because of the lack of space, the trusties in the evenings crammed the prisoners in by force to sleep. If one of them rose in the night to answer a call of nature, by the time he returned there would no longer be a vacant space.

The disastrous living conditions were well known to the camp command. Excellent testimony to this is furnished by an event connected with Himmler's first visit to *KL Auschwitz* on 1 March 1941. His arrival having been announced, appropriate preparations were made in the camp. The agenda was to include the "visiting" of one of the blocks which served as prisoners' living quarters. The choice fell upon Block 6 (later Block 14). First of all, prisoners who were visibly in bad shape were removed, then in the whole block, which was then still one-story, three-tiered wooden bunks were installed. A suitable number of blankets was also issued. Of course the beds had to be made in the military fashion, with the edges of the paillasse and blanket clearly visible. The preparations also extended to the prisoners, whose external appearance was supposed to bear witness to the good order prevailing in the camp. Naturally only as many prisoners were left in the block as there were mattresses, so as to create the impression that each prisoner slept separately.[19]

Everything went according to plan. Himmler and his entourage "visited" the block that had been prepared. No sooner had the SS dignitaries left the camp, however, than the former state of affairs was restored: the bunks were removed and the straw mattresses once again spread out on the floor.

The first three-tiered wooden bunks were delivered to *KL Auschwitz* at the end of February 1941 and in the following months they were gradually installed in the blocks used for prisoners' living quarters.[20] One such bunk, measuring 80 cm. wide by 200 cm. long and 225 cm. high, with three straw mattresses, was theoretically intended for three prisoners. In practice two or more prisoners slept on the one mattress. After the completion of the additional floors on the blocks, several hundred three-tiered wooden bunks were installed in each. According to an inventory of 25 January 1943 [21] twenty-one blocks were set aside at that time for prisoners' living quarters (including Blocks 24 and 25 which were only partially used for living quarters). At that time, for example, in Block 2 there were 234 bunks and 702 mattresses for 1,193 prisoners, so that almost half had to sleep two to a mattress. Separate iron beds were available only to trusties, for whom separate but not large quarters were set aside in the blocks.

Because of the overcrowding prevailing in *KL Auschwitz I* wooden huts of the type used for stables were introduced for a transitional period, and cellars and lofts were also used for living quarters. The number of cubic metres of sleeping space available in the brick-built blocks came to about 2,900. Thus if there were about 1,200 persons per block, each prisoner would have about 2.5 cubic metres of air.

Besides the three-tiered wooden bunks, each block contained the following furnishings; coal-fired stoves, about fifteen wooden cupboards, a few wooden tables and several dozen primitive stools. The above-mentioned itmes were installed successively. Each inhabited two-story block in the main camp was administratively divided into two parts: the

---

[19] Account of former prisoner of *KL Auschwitz* Erwin Olszówka. APMO. Zespół "Oświadczenia", t. 72, k. 130.
[20] Report of the head of the Camp Employment Section, *SS-Hauptsturmführer* Heinrich Schwarz. APMO. Sygn. D-AuI-3a/1, nr inw. 29720.
[21] APMO. Sygn. D-AuI-4/34, nr inw. 161197.

ground floor (e.g. Block 1) and the upstairs floor (Block 1a). Each constituted an independent administrative unit, except that in most of the blocks the upstairs floor consisted only of two large rooms, while the downstairs was usually divided into smaller rooms. Sanitary facilities, usually to be found only on the ground floor, were shared and consisted of latrines (22 toilet seats and urinals) and a washroom with earthenware gutters over which 42 taps were installed. It should be emphasized that all these amenities were installed only after the setting up of the camp. In the summer and autumn of 1940 the needs of several thousand prisoners were served by only two wells, from which water for washing was drawn, and a provisional field latrine. After latrines were installed in the blocks, access to them was limited by various orders issued by the trusties.

In *KL Auschwitz II (Birkenau)* two kinds of barrack huts were used for housing prisoners: brick and wooden. The brick huts constructed in great haste in sector BI (later the women's camp) were built on marshy soil and not made adequately proof against damp. These huts, 36.25 m. long by 11.40 m. wide and 5.80 m. high (with a surface area of 413.25 m^2 and a cubature of 1,235 m^3), possessed seventeen permanently closed windows, two ventilators and one door on either side of which were two rooms: one for the *Blockälteste*, the other for storing bread. In each of the huts 60 sleeping compartments were built, each with three tiers, constituting a total of 180 sleeping places measuring four square metres on each of which in turn four prisoners were to sleep — according to the guidelines laid down by the SS authorities. Such a density (over 700 persons to a hut) worked out at only about 1.7 cubic metres of air per person. These huts possessed practically no heating, although two iron stoves were installed in each for the sake of appearances. Instead of a floor there was originally just the bare earth, which was later replaced by a layer of bricks laid out flatwise or a thin layer of concrete. Sanitary installations were lacking. Not until 1944 was a small space set aside for washrooms and WCs. The camp was liberated before they could be completed, however. Initially these huts did not have electric light either.

The other type of prisoners' living quarters at Brzezinka was constituted by the wooden stable huts known officially as *Pferdestallbaracken, OKH-Typ. 260/9*, which were erected from prefabricated elements supplied to the camp. These huts measured 40.76 m. long by 9.56 m. wide and were 2.65 m. high (and hence with a surface area of 389 m^2 and a cubature of 1,248 m^3) and had no windows but merely a row of skylights running along the top at both sides. The walls were formed from thin, ill-fitting boards, and the roof, which was also the ceiling, was composed of a layer of planks covered with tar paper. The roof was supported by the outer walls and two rows of pillars, dividing the hut widthwise into three parts. At each end of the hut was a double door (or rather gate).

The interior was divided into 18 compartments originally intended to serve as stalls for 52 horses.

In every such hut part of one of the compartments near the entrance was set aside for the prisoner performing the function of block senior, while at the back of the hut by the rear entrance containers for faeces were placed. In the remaining fourteen compartments were three-tiered wooden bunks or plain boards measuring 280 cm. by 185 cm. and 200 cm. high on which fifteen prisoners each were to sleep, making a total of 400 persons per hut. A chimney flue running almost the entire length of the hut completed the furnishings. These huts contained of course no sanitary facilities, and the density assumed "in theory" allowed for three cubic metres of air per person.

All the figures given above regarding both the brick and the wooden huts should be treated as only a rough guide. In reality the number of prisoners in a hut was considerably higher and occasionally approached a thousand. The situation in this respect was constantly changing in view of the dispatch to the camp of transports numbering as many as several thousand people. On those occasions the wooden bunks might have to hold 45 instead of 15 people, as a result of which the boards would break and the prisoners fall to the ground.

In the brick huts the bunks occupied by the prisoners were covered by a thin layer of straw (although it was not rare for prisoners to sleep on bare boards), while in the wooden huts the bunks or boards were covered with paper mattresses stuffed with so-called wood wool. Blankets were issued as coverings.

The damp prevailing in the huts, the leaking roofs and the soiling of the straw and pallets by prisoners suffering from dysentery aggravated the already bad living conditions, the more so as the regulations forbade the opening of the doors at night for ventilation purposes. The huts were infected with insects of all kinds, and the rats that roamed the camp attacked prisoners in their sleep and gnawed at the bodies of the dead. The situation was exacerbated by the chronic lack of water for washing and the absence of appropriate sanitary installations.

For the first fifteen months or so in sector BI of *KL Birkenau* water was to be found only in the kitchen huts and the prisoners were denied access to it. Because of the lack of facilities for washing, the prisoners had to remain dirty and unwashed for months on end, and had to perform their natural functions in primitive field latrines that were totally exposed. Thus it is not surprising that in these conditions and given such overcrowding various epidemics of contagious diseases should break out time and time again, literally decimating the prisoners. This state of affairs was well known to the German central authorities, who instead of radically improving the prisoners' living conditions and sanitary situation merely regretted the impossibility of increasing the number of prisoners in the concentration camps.[22] The order issued on 19 August 1942 requiring the commandants of concentration camps to see to it that Jewish prisoners washed their feet, so as to lower the sick rate and raise their productivity[23], borders on irony (it is not known why this order should apply only to Jews, who at that time constituted about 50 per cent of the prisoners in *KL Auschwitz*).

Sanitary conditions only improved somewhat after the building of bathhouses with saunas and installations for the disinfecting of clothing. One such building was erected in sector BIa, BIb and BII respectively. In 1943 huts containing latrines and washrooms went into service in sector BI. These buildings, made of brick and measuring 4.50 m. by 36.25 m. and 2.50 m. high, had either drainage gutters and 90 water taps each (in the case of the washrooms) or waste pipes covered with a single slab of concrete pierced with 58 holes to serve as lavatory seats (in the case of the latrine huts). Thus in 1943 in sector BI for sixty-two huts occupied by women prisoners there were only ten sanitary huts: four for ablutions, four containing lavatories and two with wash basins on one side and privies on the other. The washrooms and lavatories could however only be used a few minutes before leaving for work in the morning and in the evening after returning from work. Because of the resultant crowding and jostling the female trusties had to "regulate" the traffic with shrieks, beatings and abuse.

In sector BII of the Birkenau camp stable huts were used for the installation of sanitary facilities. In sector BIIa for sixteen huts there were only three huts fitted out with wash basins and lavatories, while in each of the remaining sectors (BIIb, BIIc, BIId and BIIe), consisting of thirty-two huts apiece, six sanitary huts were built (three with wash basins, three with privies). The time allowed to make use of these facilities was, as in sector BI, very curtailed, and if the number of prisoners is taken into account (anything from five to twenty thousand in each sector), it can be seen that making use of these facilities involved a great deal of difficulty. Even after the bathhouses went into service prisoners were taken to them very seldom. They had to strip in their block or hut whence — regardless of weather conditions — they were chased to the bathhouse. Many a prisoner paid for this kind of bath with his life.

The living and sanitary conditions in *KL Auschwitz III (Monowitz)* and in the scores of branch camps were similar to those described above.

---

[22] APMO. Zesp. *Sammlung von Erlassen*, sygn. D-RF-9/WVHA/8/1, p. 10.
[23] APMO. Zesp. *Sammlung von Erlassen*, sygn. D-RF-9/WVHA/8, p. 40.

8. CLOTHING

Prisoners arriving at the camp were issued upon registration with special prison clothing made of coarse cloth with blue-grey stripes which made prisoners clearly distinguishable even at a distance and undoubtedly made concealment difficult in the event of escape. Male prisoners received a shirt, long drawers, a blouse and trousers. There were summer and winter outfits (*Sommeranzug* and *Winteranzug*), differing only in thickness of material. In winter "coats", made from thicker striped material but without lining, were issued. For footwear the prisoners were issued with clogs of the Dutch type, made from a single piece of wood, or clogs with leather uppers. The dirty, lice-ridden and ill-fitting uniforms with their tendency to stiffen in the rain and the clogs which hampered movement constituted an additional torment for the prisoners.

The difficulties which existed right from the outset in supplying *KL Auchwitz* were responsible for the fact that in the cold and even snowy autumn of 1940 the prisoners were, it is true, issued with winter clothing but not with clogs. They had to walk about and work barefoot, and also stand barefoot for hours on end during roll calls. In these conditions many of them caught cold, which hastened the emaciation of the organism and consequently brought about an increase in the mortality rate. The "winter" clothing did not protect prisoners from the cold, especially during the exceptionally severe winters that then prevailed. In order to protect the body against loss of heat and frostbite, many of them placed paper taken from empty cement bags under their blouses, although they could be severely punished for doing so. Not until 24 September 1941 was an order issued allowing prisoners to inform their relatives that they could send warm underclothes and jerseys to the camp.[24]

The difficulty, increasing from year to year, in obtaining supplies of the material from which camp uniforms were made forced the SS authorities to issue permission for civilian clothing to be worn in the concentration camps. A circular of 9 February 1943[25] allowed the clothing taken from Polish and Russian civilians and stored in the camp to be used for this purpose, and a circular of 26 February of the same year ordered that specially marked civilian clothing be issued generally to prisoners employed inside the camp.[26] From then on the striped camp uniforms were to be issued only to prisoners employed outside the camp, and hence

---

[24] *Ibid*, p. 18.
[25] APMO. Zesp. *Sammlung von Erlassen*, sygn. D-RF-9/WVHA/8/1, p. 20.
[26] *Ibid*, pp. 23—24.

in places where civilian clothes could aid escape by making identification of prisoners more difficult.

Another circular of 26 May 1943 [27] ordered that all prisoners hand in their caps for the duration of summer after which they would be reissued. The most drastic order was that of 7 November 1944, according to which only one kind of striped uniform was to be issued, the issue of striped coats or warmer clothes to prisoners working or simply present inside the camp was forbidden, and the increased use of civilian clothing was enjoined.[28] It is true that the same order mentions that the prisoners may wear comforters (*Leibbinde*) and sweaters, but practice in the Nazi concentration camps showed that such items were unavailable to prisoners.

In *KL Auschwitz* practice was considerably ahead of the orders under discussion, as already in the spring of 1942 the uniforms of the liquidated Soviet POWs were being used in the camp, having been issued to newly arrived and registered women prisoners. In the same way the shoes, clothes and underwear of persons who perished in the gas chambers were used. Civilian clothing, as already mentioned, was specially marked with stripes applied with oil paint or pieces of striped material sewn on the back. The only prisoners who continued to wear striped uniforms were those employed outside the camp or who worked alongside civilian workers (e.g. prisoners employed in the subcamps or at the IG Farben branch at Monowice). In accordance with binding regulations, prisoners transferred to other concentration camps were also dressed in striped uniforms.

The overcrowding prevailing in the huts of *KL Auschwitz*, the lack of sanitary installations, the various disorders that plagued the prisoners such as starvation-induced dysentery, and above all the impossibility of maintaining personal hygiene, meant that the clothing worn by the prisoners was torn, dirty, lice-ridden, often soiled by urine or faeces — in short it was disgusting and stank. The only prisoners who could wear clean uniforms were those who in the course of their work came into close contact with SS men, for the latter were terrified of the lice which were the bearers of typhus.

Initially at *KL Auschwitz* there was no laundry, and the facilities installed later were inadequate, laundry was sent to Bielsko to be cleaned. The result of the insufficient number of laundries and their low capacity, as well as the lack of appropriate equipment for disinfecting lice-ridden clothing was that prisoners went for weeks and months without a change of linen. The half measures applied in consequence turned out

---

[27] *Ibid*, p. 43.
[28] *Ibid*, pp. 79—80.

to the disadvantage of the prisoners, such as the famous delousing (*Entlausung*), during which prisoners of both sexes had to remain naked outside the huts all day, while the huts were disinfected by Cyclon B, and their clothing and underwear were steeped in vats containing a solution of Cyclon. It is not hard to imagine how such operations ended for the emaciated and the ill, especially when they were conducted in bad weather. If the prisoners got wet at work or during roll call, they went to bed in wet clothing and dried it with their own body warmth during sleep. The lack of water (even for drinking) made it impossible for the prisoners to do their own laundry.

Footwear was a separate problem which particularly affected those prisoners who had to cover considerable distances during the day. The ill-fitting clogs caused painful chaffing of the feet, which, exacerbated by vitamin deficiency and general exhaustion, resulted in the appearance of suppurating sores which refused to heal and were an indirect cause of death in the case of thousands of prisoners. When SS doctors made their selection sores on the lower extremities were one of the things that qualified a prisoner as unfit for work, which meant death by a phenol injection through the heart or in the gas chamber.

9. FOOD

Prisoners in the camp received three meals daily: in the morning, at midday and in the evening. The nutritive value of these meals depended above all on the dietary norms binding in the Nazi concentration camps, which norms changed several times during the period of *KL Auschwitz's* existence. On the basis of these norms weekly and daily menus were drawn up, in which the food components and calorific value of the products envisaged for consumption were specified. Such were the principles, but the reality was quite different.

The food stores and kitchens were in the charge of SS personnel. As the depositions and accounts of former prisoners reveal, the SS men removed the more valuable food products such as meat, margarine, sugar, cereals, flour and sausage from the stores, so that the amount of food available for preparing the meals was already less than that laid down in the established norms.

Documents from the SS Institute of Hygiene at Rajsko, to which samples of the food and meals issued to prisoners were sent after 1943, reveal that for example the soup was lacking in 60-90 per cent of the amount of margarine envisaged in the official recipe, the bread was sour and hard to digest, and the sausage contained barely half of the fat as that eaten by the SS men, although it was produced by the same butcher.[29]

The serving of meals and food constituted a separate problem. In accordance with the system prevailing in the Nazi concentration camps, the serving of food was the business of trusties. They collected from the cookhouse vats of soup, "coffee", "tea" and other food products which they proceeded to divide among the prisoners. The corrupt trusties were recruited — especially in the early period of the camp's existence — from among common criminals of German nationality, whose first concern was to see to the needs of themselves and their friends. They reduced portions with impunity, especially of the more nutritious items such as bread, sugar, sausage and margarine, retaining the surplus thus created for their own use. Thus instead of the regulation 1,700 calories for those engaged in lighter work and 2,150 calories for those engaged in heavy work, the prisoners of *KL Auschwitz* in fact received an average of about 1,300 calories daily in the case of those engaged in lighter work and 1,700 calories in the case of those engaged in heavy work.

In the morning the prisoners received only a half litre of black coffee (made from a coffee substitute) or of a herbal brew known as "tea". These liquids were generally unsweetened.

The accounts of former prisoners and surviving menus[30] reveal that so-called soups "with meat" were issued four times a week, and meatless or "vegetable" soups three times a week. It should be explained that the "fresh vegetables" mentioned in the camp food norms consisted simply of turnip cabbage. Thus the basic soup components were potatoes, turnip cabbage and a small number of other additives such as hulled barley, millet, rye flour and a food extract called "Awo". After 1942 various products found in the baggage of those killed in the gas chambers were used to enrich the soup. One portion of soup measuring about three quarters of a litre possessed a value of about 350-400 calories. The soup was foul tasting and watery, and frequently new arrivals, not yet reduced by hunger, ate it with extreme distaste. The nutritive value as well as the taste was impaired when it was consumed cold, and this happened very often, for example when prisoners returned to camp from work late in the evening or at night (this particularly affected the prisoners employed by IG Farben).

---

[29] The German doctor Hans Münch, employed in the SS Institute of Hygiene at Rajsko near Oświęcim during the occupation, in 1947 prepared a number of articles based on the documents of the Institute, dealing *inter alia* with the quality of the food issued to the inmates of *KL Auschwitz*. APMO. Sygn. "Opracowania" (Münch), 103, t. 35.

[30] One such menu has been preserved among the documents concerning the sub-camp at Trzebinia, a branch of *KL Auschwitz*. APMO. Zespół "Trzebinia", t. 3/2, k. 12.

For supper the prisoners were given about 300 grams of bread and something extra in the shape of about 25 grams of sausage or margarine, or a spoonful of jam or cheese. These products were frequently stale or even mouldy. The food value of supper came to about 900-1000 calories. The bread issued in the evening was also intended to do for the morning, but in view of the rampant hunger in the camp the prisoners who could bring themselves to divide their bread and save a piece for breakfast were few. The majority ate their bread immediately, desiring to appease their hunger if only momentarily.

Special extra rations for those engaged in heavy labour (*Schwerarbeiterzulage*) were issued consisting of bread, margarine and sausage, according to the current obligatory norms. These too were issued in reduced amounts.

Given such hunger rations, most prisoners after a few weeks in camp began to exhibit symptoms of exhaustion, which led in consequence to people being reduced to the state of "Moslems".* Thousands of starved prisoners in the last stages of emaciation strove at every opportunity to get something to eat, unable to restrain themselves from rummaging in the refuse bins outside the kitchens.[31] The eating of raw peelings and rotting cabbage turnip or potatoes, instead of appeasing hunger pangs, brought on a disease tragic in its consequences — hunger-induced dysentery.

Like other Nazi concentration camps, the various divisions of *KL Auschwitz* possessed camp "canteens". Prisoners could make purchases in the canteen only at narrowly specified times if they had in their account *Reichsmarks*, either deposited at the moment of registration or sent by postal order by their families. In fact the canteens played no positive role in view of the assortment of goods they offered. They sold neither bread nor any other wholesome food. From time to time it was possible to buy in the canteen pickled beetroot, salted snails, mineral water, cigarettes, shaving implements, toothbrushes, camp notepaper, postage stamps and other items of minor value. Thus the extract from camp regulations printed at the head of every sheet of camp notepaper (including such information as the fact that food parcels might not be sent "as the prisoners can buy everything in camp") was a cynical attempt to mislead public opinion and conceal the fact that the prisoners were starved. It was only the difficult situation on the battlefronts and the necessity of making maximum use of the prisoners' labour that induced the central SS authorities to raise in a circular of 29 October 1942 the ban on sending

---

* Prisoner in extreme state of emaciation, often clad only in a blanket.
[31] APMO. *Zbiór rozkazów garnizonowych KL Auschwitz* (Collection of garrison orders of KL Auschwitz), sygn. AuI-1/132.

food parcels to the inmates of concentration camps.[32] This of course improved the lot only of those prisoners whose families were in a position to send them food parcels. Soviet POWs, Jewish inmates or those whose families were in liberated territories could not take advantage of this convenience.

From the autumn of 1942 food parcels began to arrive in *KL Auschwitz*, and in view of the lack of restrictions any number could be sent. Such parcels did at least enable some of the prisoners to stave off death by starvation, but it did not improve the situation of all prisoners, especially not that of the Jews.

In addition to parcels sent by relatives, from 1943 onwards parcels began to arrive in *KL Auschwitz* from the International Red Cross. These parcels were addressed personally, and the prisoner had to confirm receipt on a special form which was later returned to the sender. This operation had great psychological significance but in fact it did not play a major role, as the International Red Cross did not possess a sufficient number of addresses of prisoners in the Nazi concentration camps and regulations required that the prisoner's name, camp number and the name of his camp be specified on the parcel. In any event the arrival of the first parcels from the International Committee of the Red Cross testified to the fact that the inmates of *KL Auschwitz* were not as isolated as the SS authorities would have liked and, uneasy about this, the camp command began an investigation aimed at establishing how the addresses of prisoners were finding their way abroad (some were sent out by the resistance movement inside the camp). The matter must have been of interest to the SS central authorities, as a circular of 1 August 1944[33] empowered the commandants of concentration camps to requisition all parcels sent from abroad or by the Red Cross. The contents of the parcels were to be passed on to the camp kitchens. This order was probably intended to make it impossible for prisoners to sign the receipts which were a proof of the prisoner's presence in the concentration camp. This did not prevent the commandant of *KL Auschwitz* from giving the delegate of the International Committee of the Red Cross, who on one occasion in the autumn of 1944 visited the camp, an assurance that the parcels were still handed over individually, and that the division of collective parcels among the prisoners was carried out by trustees elected by the prisoners themselves and the *Judenältesten*.[34] This was of course a lie, as there were no

---

[32] APMO. Zesp. *Sammlung von Erlassen*, sygn. D-RF-9/WVHA/8, p. 52.
[33] APMO. *Höss Trial*, t. 12, k. 141.
[34] Report of the visit in *Comité International de la Croix Rouge en faveure des civil détenus dans les Camps de concentration en Allemagne (1938—1945), I — Visite au Commandant du Camp d'Auschwitz d'un délégué du CICR (Septembre 1944)*, Geneva, April 1947, pp. 91—92.

"elected trustees" among the inmates of *KL Auschwitz*, and the collective parcels sent by the International Red Cross found their way not to the prisoners' cookhouse but to the larders of the SS.

The starving prisoners strove by various means to appease their hunger by getting additional food. Usually the only way was that known as "organization", i.e. pilfering it when engaged in such tasks as tending vegetables or delivering them to the SS stores. Particularly sought after were fresh vegetables and fruit which were not in the camp menu at all. Despite the ruthless punishment meted out to prisoners caught in the act of "organizing", the practice spread not only in *KL Auschwitz* but in all the concentration camps. Food obtained in this "illegal" fashion and even various objects "organized" from the storehouses containing the effects of those gassed were later bartered by the prisoners on the camp's "black stock exchange".

10. THE PRISONER'S DAY

About the discipline, punishments and daily schedule of the camp the prisoner found out through his own, often tragic experience. The advice given to new arrivals by acquaintances, friends or simply well-wishers enabled the former to adjust to the climate more readily and so avoid unpleasantness.

All activities in camp were carried out at a word of command or a signal. Prisoners who did not understand the commands (which were issued in German) or were too slow in carrying them out, were liable to beating and harassment by the SS and trusties.

At about four o'clock in the morning the sound of the gong rang out for reveille. Hustled, cursed and beaten, the prisoners had to get up as fast as possible. Where there were three-tiered bunks and straw mattresses, they had to be turned down with blankets military fashion. The slightest unevenness could cost the culprit dear. After reveille very little time remained for answering the call of nature, "washing", joining the queue for "breakfast" and the consumption of same. In individual blocks or huts where there were several hundred prisoners, all these activities took place in feverish haste, many prisoners could not press their way through to the water, and the coffee often ran out before everyone was served.

At roll call the prisoners fell in rows of ten to facilitate counting by the SS. The length of time of any roll call depended on how soon the presence of all prisoners could be established. After roll call at the command to form work squads (*Arbeitskommandos*) the prisoners made for designated spots in the camp, whence the squads departed for work. While marching out of the camp they were played to by camp orchestras which existed in all three parts of *KL Auschwitz*. Once outside the gates each group was joined by SS guards who supervised the prisoners at work.

Effective working time, as regulated by internal ordinances of the commandant's office of *KL Auschwitz*,[35] was eleven hours (from 6 a.m. to 5 p.m.), with a half-hour break for lunch. Considerably longer hours were worked by prisoners employed for example in the camp kitchens and stables. Some of the prisoners had to march anything up to about fifteen kilometres a day to reach their places of work (e.g. those employed on the site of IG Farben, before their transfer to the future *KL Auschwitz III* at Monowice).

In the initial period of the camp's existence, work had to be performed on the double. The SS guards and prisoner overseers drove prisoners relentlessly with shouts and beatings. The terror of the prisoners — especially the women — were the SS dogs, specially trained to attack people and capable of causing serious injuries with their fangs. Some SS guards desiring to get an extra few days' leave, would order a prisoner to go beyond the guarded perimeter and then shoot him down with a machine gun burst. Upon the squad's return to camp the SS man would report to his superiors that he had shot a prisoner "attempting to escape", and if he could prove that he had acted showing "presence of mind", he would either receive a commendation or a few days' special leave. So it was not surprising that many prisoners perished at work, their comrades having to carry their bodies back to the camp.

Upon returning to the camp in the evening the prisoners, worn out with labour and harassment, had to brace themselves as they passed through the gate for yet another effort: they had to march in even ranks to the beat of a march played by the camp orchestra, to make it easier for the SS men to count them. At the gate returning prisoners were also searched. Those caught carrying anything at all — even a piece of turnip — could expect severe punishment for "sabotage" and violation of regulations.

After evening roll call came supper which was followed at about nine o'clock by lights out, after which prisoners were forbidden to leave their quarters. Those who broke this rule were fired on by the SS guards in the watchtowers. Occasionally the sound of shots breaking the night silence would mean that one of the prisoners, spiritually broken, was trying to "go into the wire". In camp jargon the expression "to go into the wire" meant to commit suicide by throwing oneself into the elect-

---

[35] APMO. *Zbiór rozkazów garnizonowych KL Auschwitz* (Collection of garrison orders of *KL Auschwitz*), sygn. D-AuI-1/40, 43.

rified wire of the camp fence. The guards were under order to stop anyone approaching the fence and usually just shot at them.

Apart from work, punishments and harassment, the prisoners' most irksome and hated experiences included the roll calls which occasionally lasted a whole day, if, for, example, it was found that a prisoner had escaped. After the escape of the prisoner Tadeusz Wiejowski on 6 July 1940, a punitive roll call was ordered which lasted nineteen hours. This roll call is recalled by the former prisoner Henryk Król as follows:

"The night was appalling... By the small hours everyone was shuddering with cold... The rays of the rising sun only brought temporary relief. Soon the heat beating down from the heavens increased our suffering. One after the other we fainted. Those who fainted had water poured over them. During the night an unfortunate incident occurred. ...an interpreter, the prisoner Baworowski, at one point stepped out of line and asked the SS man in charge for permission to answer a call of nature. He was refused. The SS man ordered him to step into line. After a while a smell reached our nostrils. Baworowski had been unable to contain himself and had soiled his trousers. When the SS man realized who had committed this 'crime', he ordered Baworowski to take off his underpants, make a bundle of them and hold it in his teeth. He also ordered him to squat and bark. The SS man's action revolted all the prisoners, giving us a foretaste of what awaited us in the camp." [36]

After another escape in November 1940 the prisoners were kept on the *Appellplatz* from midday until night time, after which the bodies of 120 who had either died or fainted were removed from the square. During this roll call snow fell, and the prisoners were dressed only in thin camp uniforms, without shoes, caps or coats.

In 1941 during roll calls — usually the evening roll call — as punishment for the occurrence of escapes, a dozen or so prisoners would be singled out and sentenced to death by hunger. The victims were chosen from among the prisoners in the escaper's block.

For the women prisoners of *KL Auschwitz* particularly nerve-wrecking were the so-called general roll calls at which not only were their numbers checked but selections were made of the sick and unfit for work for liquidation in the gas chambers. "General roll calls" could last for over 12 hours, during which time the women had to remain outside the huts. Two such roll calls took place for example in the women's camp at Brzezinka on 7 and 28 February 1943.

For the prisoners, worn out by heavy labour, even Sundays and feast days were not days of rest. Apart from work on these days so-called delousing (*Läuseappelle*) was carried out.

---

[36] APMO. Zespół "Oświadczenia", t. 76, k. 199.

Among the methods of terror used by the SS authorities was an extensive system of punishments which were frequently inflicted on prisoners. The most frequently applied included banning the sending or receiving of mail, punishment drill, being made to work during leisure time, making prisoners do without "dinner" on specified days while performing their normal duties, whippings (often inflicted publicly, with the prisoner required to count each stroke in German), the "pillar" (suspending a prisoner by his hands tied behind his back), relegation to a penal company, and detention in the cells of the camp prison.

Each of the punishments mentioned, except, of course, the ban on mail, besides causing physical pain and humiliation, in many cases hastened death or even directly caused it. *

On the subject of punishments, care should be taken in distinguishing those inflicted with the retention of certain formalities, i.e. those of which a record remains in the form of a written application for permission to inflict punishment (*Strafmeldung*) and confirmation on a special form (*Strafverfügung*), and those inflicted by SS men at their pleasure and of which the only evidence was on the body of the victim.

Given the constant peril and minimal — in practice — chances of survival, many prisoners saw escape as their only hope. On the basis of the fragmentary documents which remain it has been established that 667 prisoners escaped from *KL Auschwitz (I, II and III)* and its numerous branch camps, of whom 270 were caught.

11. CONTACT WITH THE OUTSIDE WORLD

Given the complete isolation of the inmates of *KL Auschwitz*, the only official possibility of contact with loved ones was by correspondence. The regulations laid down that a prisoner might write and receive two letters a month. All letters sent and received were of course subject to close censorship by a group od SS men employed in the *Postzensurstelle*, which in the camp's organizational structure came under the camp command (*Abteilung I*).

Prisoners' correspondence had to be conducted in the German language. Letters sent by prisoners had to be written on special forms on which the name of the camp and the general rules regarding prisoners' correspondence were printed. Each letter could consist of only fifteen lines. On days when letter writing took place, the block seniors — on the orders of the SS authorities — reminded the prisoners that they had to include the phrase "I am in good health and feel well" (*Ich bin gesund und fühle mich gut*) regardless of their real state of health. The censors

---
* See pp. 97—110.

would cross out sentences which seemed suspicious or even cut out whole passages. In letters sent to the camp it was not allowed to enclose anything, such as photographs. Prisoners arrested under the *Nacht und Nebel* decree * were not allowed to correspond at all, nor were Soviet POWs, most of the Jewish prisoners who were sent to the camp together with their entire families, or prisoners whose relatives were in territories liberated from Nazi rule.

By an order of 30 March 1942 limitations were imposed on the correspondence of Jewish prisoners and prisoners from the eastern territories (*Ostvölker*), who thereafter could only send and receive one letter every two months, while the latter could only send postcards with specially prepared texts (*Karten mit Rückantwort*).[37]

In 1943 Jewish prisoners were forbidden to use the camp notepaper and postcards, in place of which they were issued with postcards without the *KL Auschwitz* letterhead, on which for camouflage purposes the writer could only give the name of the place he was at — which meant nothing — indicating only that it was a labour camp (*Birkenau, Arbeitslager*). Nor were they allowed to give their camp numbers. The cards contained a stamped counterfoil informing the recipient that further correspondence could be conducted only through the Association of Jews in Germany (*Reichsvereinigung der Juden in Deutschland*) in Berlin.[38] The SS authorities hoped in this way to calm the Jewish population of the ghettoes. Direct proof of this was furnished by the "letter-writing operation" (*Briefaktion*) ordered for the beginning of March 1944 and concerning the Jews brought from Terezin (*Theresienstadt*) in Bohemia and held in Sector BIIb of *KL Birkenau*. On 5 March they were issued with postcards and ordered to post-date them (from 25 to 27 March) and send greetings to their families and friends. These prisoners were then liquidated on 9 March in the gas chambers. Their families and friends, on the other hand, were convinced that they were still alive in the "labour camp" of *Birkenau bei Neu Berun*.

The inmates of *KL Auschwitz*, like those of other concentration camps, tried to avoid existing bans by sending letters which evaded the censors for which purpose they made used of contacts with civilian workers while at work. The SS central authorities drew attention to this fact on the basis of reports by their secret agents, and issued a general order on 11 December 1942 to increase supervision, especially of prisoners with communist views.[39]

---

* See p. 49.
[37] APMO. Zesp. *Sammlung von Erlassen*, sygn. D-RF-9/WVHA/8, p. 31.
[38] APMO. *Zbiór listów i korespondentek obozowych* (Collection of letters and camp correspondence), sygn. D-AuI-1/4167, t. 20 (photocopies), p. 15.
[39] APMO. Zesp. *Sammlung von Erlassen*, sygn. D-RF-9/WVHA/8/1, p. 7.

Particular supervision was enjoined upon the camp authorities during the occasional visits made to *KL Auschwitz* by various persons and representatives of institutions. The visitors were shown only living blocks and hospital huts specially prepared for this purpose, and on such occasions the prisoners were served (e.g. in the Fürstengrube subcamp) better dinners.[40] On the other hand no mention of the camp brothels or crematoria was allowed, let alone showing them.[41] The prisoners of course had no possibility of passing on observations or expressing themselves freely with regard to the conditions prevailing in the camp. Thus there is nothing surprising about the fact that the representative of the International Committee of the Red Cross who visited *KL Auschwitz* in the autumn of 1944 was allowed to speak to a few prisoners only in the presence of SS men. The value of the information he received from that conversation may be seen from the fact that he first heard of the existence of mass extermination installations in *KL Auschwitz* and the liquidation of prisoners in them from British POWs in the POW camp at Cieszyn.[42]

12. THE CAMP HOSPITAL

In the evening after the return from work, in front of the doors of the clinic of the camp hospital long queues formed of prisoners desiring medical attention. Among them were many who could barely stand upright, while others lay unconscious on the ground. The prisoner doctors employed in the clinic after a preliminary examination would either give first aid, staunching wounds with paper bandages, or apply for the prisoner to be admitted to the camp hospital. The final decision lay with the SS doctor who was responsible for the state of health of the prisoners in a given sector of *KL Auschwitz*. In the subcamps this function was performed by SS medical orderlies (*Sanitätsdienstgrad* — SDG).

In the early months of *KL Auschwitz*'s existence the camp hospital had no equipment and the work of the prisoner doctors employed in it boiled down to performing the functions of nurses and cleaners. The person responsible for keeping order in the camp hospital, referred to in

---

[40] Account of former prisoners of *KL Auschwitz* Jan Ławnicki and Józef Łabudek. APMO. Zespół "Oświadczenia", t. 60, k. 100 and t. 50, K. 94.
[41] APMO. Zesp. *Sammlung von Erlassen*, sygn. D-RF-9/WVHA/8/1, p. 23.
[42] *Comité International de la Croix Rouge..., I — Visite au Commandant du Camp d'Auschwitz d'un délégue du CICR (Septembre 1.44)*, p. 93.

KL Auschwitz by the abbreviations KB or HKB (*Krankenbau — Häftlingskrankenbau*) was a prisoner peforming the function of "camp hospital senior" (*Lagerältester des HKB*), to whom in turn the block seniors were answerable. Up until 1943 these posts were held exclusively by men and women (in the women's camp) of German nationality, who despite lack of qualifications often themselves decided on the admission of patients, and even interfered in their treatment. By 1941 selections were being carried out in the camp hospital, as a result of which those selected were killed by phenol injections or sent to the gas chamber. For this reason the camp hospital won sombre fame among the prisoners as the anteroom to the crematorium and the waiting room for the gas chamber.

The furnishing of the hospital buildings differed in no way from the prisoners' living quarters. Patients lay on paper mattresses stuffed with the so-called wood wool. The three-tiered wooden bunks made access to the patients more difficult, and made it equally difficult if not impossible to rise. Most of the patients, in addition to their many other ailments, suffered from diarrhoea, so the mattresses were soiled with faeces as well as the pus that oozed from wounds. Prisoners admitted to hospital had their clothing and underwear taken from them. Patients had to lie naked often two to a mattress, covered with dirty and lice-ridden blankets. The stench that reigned in the rooms and huts was indescribable. The groans of the dying and the ravings of the delirious mingled with the cries of those begging for drinking water or help.

The official allocation of medicines was insufficient both as regards variety and quantity. They generally consisted of painkilling tablets (*Schmerztabletten*), aspirin, pyramidon, cough pastilles, coal and tannalbin — for prisoners suffering from diarrhoea. Paper bandages and tissue paper were issued in very small quantities. The lack of preparations for the treatment of scabies was very sorely felt. In this situation the most dedicated efforts of the hospital staff could be of little avail, especially during epidemics of such contagious diseases as typhus and typhoid fever. The insanitary conditions prevailing in the hospitals of the various parts of *KL Auschwitz* and its branch camps, and above all the lack of water and the frequent selections, could not have had a positive effect on the state of mind of those who were sick, so it was only as a last resort that anyone reported to the camp clinic.

The camp hospitals were also used by the SS doctors for carrying out pseudomedical experiments,[*] to which thousands of prisoners in *KL Auschwitz* were subjected. Most of them died or were permanently crippled as a result.

---

[*] See pp. 127—132.

In the offices of the camp hospitals records of the patients were kept and death certificates made out in which fictitious causes of death were entered according to stereotyped formulas supplied by the SS. Before cremation the false teeth were removed from corpses, so as not to waste precious metals. For example the fragmentary surviving reports of the camp dentist (*Leiter der Häftl. Zahnstation des KL Auschwitz*) reveal that in 1942 a total of 16,325 gold and platinum teeth were removed from 2,904 corpses. The e reports concern of course only those prisoners who were previously registered in the camp.[43]

Of the many Nazi concentration camps *KL Auschwitz* was one of those in which right from the start up to the moment of its liquidation exceptionally harsh, and in fact impossible, conditions of survival were created for the prisoners. The overcrowded living quarters, the lack or inadequate number of sanitary installations, the lack of water and means of personal cleanliness, the ill-suited, generally dirty clothing, the meagre rations and inhuman exploitation of the prisoners' labour power led to enormous mortality among them. Those who died of malnutrition, cold, contagious diseases, or who were killed as no longer able to work, were constantly replaced by prisoners from new transports. In the early period of the camp's existence these were Poles, in the following years there were also prisoners from other countries conquered by the Nazis.

On defenceless prisoners deprived of effective medical care criminal experiments were conducted the results of which were meant to serve the implementation of genocidal plans.

Besides the inhuman conditions which hastened the exhaustion of the human organism, the aim in *KL Auschwitz* was to break the prisoners' spiritual resistance. This process was promoted by the entire procedure beginning with the registration of the prisoners, after which they became nameless numbers, right up to the extensive system of prohibitions and punishments. All this was intended to turn the prisoners into creatures without a will of their own, deprived of any possibility of defending fundamental human rights, whose ultimate fate was extermination.

---

[43] The originals of these reports are preserved in the Archive of the State Museum in Oświęcim.

Franciszek Piper

Extermination

I. THE POLITICAL AND RACIST PREMISES FOR EXTERMINATION

During the war an important change occurred in the aims and methods of functioning of the Nazi concentration camps. The moment prisoners of non-German nationality — citizens of the countries occupied by Germany — constituted a majority in the camps, the original aim of putting people in the camps — isolation and "reeducation" or physical extermination of opponents of the Nazi party — ceased to be of immediate concern.

Thenceforward people were put in the camps not so much for their political activity and convictions as for their belonging to a national, social, racial or religious group which was regarded as hostile. From an instrument of internal policy of the Nazi state the camps were transformed into an instrument of wielding power and implementing population policy and extermination plans in the occupied countries. As one of the most important elements in the police apparatus of terror they were to perform on the one hand immediate tasks — above all as regards the crushing of all forms of resistance on the part of the population of the occupied countries (from 1942 they also had to supplement labour shortages in the German armaments industry), while on the other they were to make possible the realization of the fundamental aim of Germanizing Poland and the other countries which lay in the path of the *Drang nach Osten*. This aim, which lay at the root of the German aggression against Poland, Czechoslovakia and the Soviet Union, had inspired the Nazi movement from the moment it came into existence. The programme of the *Deutsche Arbeiter Partei,* or DAP (later renamed the *Nationalsozialistische Deutsche Arbeiterpartei,* or NSDAP) of 24 February 1920 already contains the statement: "We demand lands and territories (colonies) to feed our people and to be settled by our surplus population".[1]

---
[1] Gottfried Feder, *Das Programm der NSDAP und seine weltanschaulichen Grundgedanken*. Munich 1932, pp. 19—22 (quoted in *Powstanie partii hitlerowskiej 1918—1923* by Jakub Banaszkiewicz. Poznań 1968, p. 502).

The direction of the intended expansion was made clear a few years later by Hitler in *Mein Kampf*: "We shall finally break with the colonial and trade policy of the pre-war period and pass on to a new territorial policy. But in speaking today of new lands on the European continent, we are thinking above all of Russia and the adjacent countries subordinate to her."[2]

So that there should be no doubt about the ultimate aim of these intentions, at a secret conference with his military commanders and the foreign minister on 4 November 1937 Hitler declared: "In our case it is not a question of conquering peoples, but solely of gaining land space suitable for agricultural purposes."[3] This notion was developed and supplemented by Heinrich Himmler in July 1942: "Our task is not the Germanization of the East in the old meaning of the word, i.e. by teaching the peoples living there the German language and German law, what we want to achieve is a people of purely German origin living in the East."[4]

It was these concepts which were the cornerstone of the genocidal policy of the Nazi invaders towards the Slav peoples, who were considered a superfluous and undesirable element on the lands they inhabited. Of the 50 million Slavs envisaged for removal as a first priority from the areas of future German colonization, the Poles, being "numerically the strongest and hence the most dangerous of all the alien peoples" (as they were described by Dr. E. Wetzel, the head of the Nazi party's Office for Racial Policy) and at the same time "the nation most given to conspiracy", were to be removed completely with the exception of 15 per cent or so considered to "lend themselves to Germanization".

Setting aside both the general concepts and the detailed plans for the implementation of this task, such as the plan to resettle the Poles in Siberia (the Nazis switched easily from one concept to another depending on current conditions and possibilities, the best example being the so-called final solution to the Jewish question, which was preceded by plans to resettle the Jews in Madagascar), and confining ourselves to an analysis of the facts about everything the Nazis did in Poland, we are compelled to conclude that it was intended to achieve this aim (independently of such means as limiting natural increase and hastening mortality) above all by mass extermination.

A particularly important role in the policy of extermination aimed at depopulating the areas of future German settlement fell to the concentration camps, including, in view of its size and the means at its disposal, the concentration camp of Auschwitz-Birkenau. This camp, intended above all for Poles, soon won for itself grim renown as one of

---

[2] Adolf Hitler, *Mein Kampf*. Munich 1942, p. 742.
[3] Nuremberg Document 386—PS. *Das Urteil von Nürnberg*. Munich 1946, p. 30.
[4] Nuremberg Document 2915—PS. *Ibid*, p. 77.

the most terrible places of torment and martyrdom of thousands of Polish patriots. Despite the influx of prisoners from nearly all the countries of Europe, Poles to the end of the camp's existence constituted one of the most numerous national groups.

Another consequence of the genocidal policy of the Third Reich towards the Slav peoples was the fate of the 12,000 Soviet POWs brought to the camp in 1941 and soon murdered. In 1941 they constituted the second most numerous national group after the Poles.

From 1942 the extermination activity of the Auschwitz camp was radically affected by the decision to concentrate in it the destruction ordered by Hitler of all the European Jews. Preparations for this operation had already been started the year before following an order of 31 July 1941 issued by Hermann Göring in his capacity as Plenipotentiary for the Regulation of the Jewish Question. Former Commandant Rudolf Höss writes of this in his autobiography as follows:

"In summer 1941 — I am unable to give the exact date at this moment — I was suddenly summoned to the *Reichsführer SS* in Berlin directly through the office of his adjutant. Himmler, in a departure from his usual practice, spoke to me without his adjutant present, saying: 'The Führer has ordered the final solution of the Jewish question. We, the SS, have to execute this order. The existing places of extermination in the East cannot cope with operations planned on a large scale. For this reason I have selected Oświęcim for this purpose, both because of its favourable position as regards communications, and because this area can easily be isolated and camouflaged. At first I intended to entrust this task to one of the higher SS officers, but I gave up this idea so as to avoid the difficulties involved in delineating spheres of competence. I am now entrusting you with the execution of this task. It is a difficult and arduous job demanding total devotion no matter what difficulties may emerge. You will get closer details from *Sturmbannführer* Eichmann of RSHA, who will be reporting to you in the near future... After speaking to Eichmann, you will immediately send me the plans of the installations you intend to use. Jews are the eternal enemies of the German nation and must be exterminated. All Jews who come into our hands will in the course of this war be without exception annihilated. If we do not succeed now in destroying the biological forces of Jewry, the Jews will some day destroy the German nation'." [5]

The preparations for the implementation of the "final solution to the Jewish question" were directed by the Reich Main Security Office which was headed by *SS-Obergruppenführer* Reinhard Heydrich, who was personally responsible for executing Göring's order. Heydrich also

---

[5] *Höss Memoirs*, p. 193.

prepared a detailed plan for arresting and deporting to places of extermination over 11 million persons of Jewish origin residing in Europe.

A report on this plan was read by Heydrich on 20 January 1942 at a conference held in Berlin-Wannsee. Those present included Wilhelm Stuckart (representing the Ministry of the Interior), Martin Luther (Foreign Office), Roland Freisler (Justice), Alfred Meyer and Georg Leibbrandt (Eastern Territories), Ernst Neumann (representing the Plenipotentiary for the Four-Year Plan), Josef Bühler (representing the General Government), Gerhard Klopfer (representing the *Parteikanzlei*), Friedrich Kritzinger (representing the *Reichskanzlei*) and representatives of the central offices of the SS: Otto Hofmann of the Race and Resettlement Head Officer (RuSHA), and Heinrich Müller and Adolf Eichmann of RSHA. Also present were representatives of the security police commanders in the General Government.

The plan Heydrich presented envisaged the "combing" of the whole of Europe, from east to west and north to south, in order to pick up all persons of Jewish origin and "evacuate them to the East", by which was meant kill them. According to Heydrich, the operation was to embrace *inter alia* the five million Jews inhabiting the Soviet Union, 2,684,000 Jews from Poland (the General Government and the Białystok region), 865,000 from France, 742,000 from Hungary, 342,000 from Romania and 330,000 from Britain.

In accordance with the decisions taken at this conference, the first transports of Jews from Upper Silesia, Slovakia, France, Holland and other countries began to flow to *KL Auschwitz*.

Another national group whom the Nazis intended for extermination were the Gypsies. Following an RSHA order of 29 January 1943 that all Gypsies in the Reich and the occupied countries be arrested and deported to concentration camps, over 22,000 Gypsies — men, women and children — arrived at the Auschwitz camp. Quartered in a separate part of the camp at Brzezinka, nearly all of them died as a result of hunger and disease, or else were killed. Only a few were shipped out to other camps to be employed in the armaments industry.

During the four years and seven months of *KL Auschwitz's* existence, according to the Extraordinary State Commission of the Soviet Union for investigating crimes committed in the Auschwitz camp and the Supreme National Tribunal in Poland, about four million people from nearly all the countries of Europe, and in some cases even from other continents, died there as a result of the deliberate activity of the Nazi authorities aimed at annihilating the inmates.

They died as a result of inhuman living conditions and work in excess of their strength, as a result of torture and executions, and of pseudomedical experiments; and yet the largest number were done to death in gas chambers specially designed and built for that purpose. Independently of the political, economic and military situation of the German state, regardless of changes in the ways in which the prisoners' labour power was exploited, the goal of extermination assigned to this camp in the early years of the war — the annihilation of entire national, social and racial groups and of all those who in any way at all attempted to resist the invader — was consistently implemented until the moment the camp ceased to exist.

II. METHODS OF INDIRECT EXTERMINATION

1. HUNGER AND DISEASE

In the years 1940-41 in view of the political situation prevailing in Europe it had not yet been decided, even in relation to the Jews, to employ methods of direct mass extermination. This decision only came after the Nazi attack on the Soviet Union. Initially prisoners were killed off by denying them the elementary necessities of life, and the main instrument of extermination was hunger. The amount of food the prisoners received was enough to keep them alive for 3-6 months. Deprived of an adequate number of calories, the organism made up the negative caloric balance from reserves of energy accumulated in its own fatty tissue. After this energy was exhausted, atrophy of the muscle tissue followed combined with impairment of the internal organs and a reduction in the organism's resistance. This in turn led to a high sick rate involving every kind of contagious disease.

Of the numerous diseases that reigned among the prisoners the greatest harvest of death was reaped by a malady completely unknown in normal conditions but universal in the concentration camps: hunger-induced diarrhoea (*Durchfall*). The symptoms of this disease were loss of the digestive functions, extreme exhaustion of the organism and a dramatic drop in body weight. Prisoners reminiscent of skeletons died on the camp streets and in the blocks, were killed *en masse* at work. No more than a few could be admitted to the camp hospital, only the name of which suggested an institution whose purpose was to save human life. The sole privilege enjoyed by those in the hospital was that, having been freed from the obligation to work and the gruelling roll calls, they could die in relative peace.

Another disease, just as frequently encountered and serious in its consequences, being a result of insanitary living conditions, was typhus. This disease, which time after time assumed the proportions of a raging epidemic, lasted in the camp almost without interruption from April 1941 until spring 1944. In periods when it reached particular intensity hundreds and even thousands of prisoners died every month. The most dangerous outbreak was in 1942. The first cases were noted in March in the camp at Brzezinka, and by July the whole camp was in the grip of an epidemic. The number of deaths rose almost daily. In April a total of 2,192 prisoners and POWs died in the camp, in May the figure had grown to 2,982, in June it was 3,688, in July it was 4,124 and in the period 1-20 August, 4,113 prisoners died.

The spreading typhus epidemic constituted a serious obstacle to the exploitation of the prisoners' labour. The interruption lasting from August to October 1942 in the work of the several thousand prisoners employed on the building of the Buna-Werke for IG Farben caused serious losses and delay in the realization of this high-priority investment of particular importance to the German war economy.

This fact, combined with fear of the epidemic spreading to the SS and their families, a fear justified by the increasing number of cases of infection and even deaths among SS men (right at the beginning of the epidemic on 10 May 1942 a garrison doctor *SS-Hauptsturmführer* Siegfried Schwela had died of typhus), finally inclined the SS authorities to take measures to limit the effects and partially eliminate the epidemic.

2. WORK

A tried and effective method of destroying the prisoners in the camp was work. Every prisoner was obliged to work, and if there was no useful work to be done, the prisoners were given pointless tasks. In the first years of the camp's existence the bulk of the prisoners were employed on its extension, e.g. building huts, warehouses, roads, etc. The tools available for this work were of the most primitive kind, such as picks, shovels and crowbars, and there was an almost total lack, not even justified by wartime conditions, of technical equipment. This was only employed on exceptional occasions on very urgent jobs, such as the building of the gas chambers and crematoria. Building material for making extensions to the camp was obtained, among other sources, from pulling down the houses of residents evicted from the area adjoining the camp. For knocking down the walls girders were used as battering rams. This was very dangerous work and cases of people being buried under falling rubble were frequent.

Despite the existence of a motor pool and cart horses, the mass use of prisoners to carry loads, often over considerable distances, and the harnessing of prisoners to so-called *Rollwagen* — large carts used for transporting inside the camp of building materials, food, clothing, faeces from the cesspits or corpses — was a universal phenomenon. In the storage areas and on the building site of the Buna-Werke a shuttle system was used whereby the prisoners transferred from one place to another — from railway waggons to the warehouses, for example — cement bags, bricks, timber, etc., running the gauntlet of SS men and Kapos who beat them with sticks to keep them from flagging.

The same method was used in clamping potatoes and cabbage turnips, which arrived at the camp in large quantities every autumn, as they constituted the staple of the prisoners' diet. They were carried in large wooden crates with handles, which weighed over 150 kilograms when full. Each crate would be carried by two prisoners. This was extremely hard work even for a healthy and well-fed person; for the prisoners it was back-breaking labour. Terrible scenes occurred. Despite the greatest efforts — and everyone realized they were costing him his life — people fell under the crushing load. Anyone who was unable to get up immediately perished under the blows of the overseers' clubs.

A horrible sight was presented by the murdering of those who instinctively remained standing although their torn and bleeding hands were unable to hold on to the handles of the crates. Every so often they would be summoned individually by an SS man or a Kapo and ordered to stoop, after which they would receive a tremendous blow on the back of the neck with a small stool specially prepared for the purpose, the effect of which was instantaneous death. The bodies were thrown into a nearby pit. Terrified the prisoners would run in the direction of the ring of sentry posts surrounding the site, preferring to die from a guard's bullet. About twenty corpses a day were removed from the site.

Seeing this the prisoners became convinced that the authorities were not concerned about the work being done on time at all — it was often completed ahead of schedule — but that the actual aim was to torment and kill. No one was in any doubt that the use of simple means of transport, such as carts or even wheelbarrows, could have changed the work from a killing effort into a hard but bearable one.

"Rationalization" of work stood however in obvious contradiction to the slogan "Annihilation through work" (*Vernichtung durch Arbeit*), formulated for the first time in an agreement between the minister of justice, Thierack, and Himmler in September 1942, although it had been consistently applied for many years. Thus it was that as late as mid-1943, when Germany was faced with an enormous labour shortage, on the building of roads in the camp at Brzezinka the following method of transporting building materials was used: the prisoners were ordered to take off their blouses or coats and put them on again back to front, then lift up the tails and in the receptacle thus created carry earth or gravel to a place several hundred metres distant.

There was no work in the camp which, setting all humanitarian considerations aside, could be held up for reasons of common sense or economic calculation. Suffice it to mention that when in spring 1944 the neighbouring farm attached to the camp at Babice had its horses taken away by the army, women prisoners were harnessed to the ploughs.[6] The picture of women of an alien "race" used as traction power in the fields may be taken as a symbol of Hitlerism, for which the Auschwitz camp, with its gas chambers on the one hand and slave labour on the other, constituted a peculiar testing ground.

As regards lack of any scruples in exploiting the prisoners' labour, private and half-private, half state-owned industrial enterprises were a match for the SS, and their role in the employment of prisoners starting in 1942 (when under the pressure of economic circles Hitler deprived the SS of its monopoly in the employment of prisoners) steadily grew. If in 1942 about 6,000 prisoners were working in industrial enterprises, and in 1943 about 17,000, in 1944 these enterprises were employing over 41,000 prisoners. They were scattered throughout the 28 branches of KL Auschwitz, the so-called subcamps, built mainly in Silesia in the neighbourhood of the works making use of their labour. These enterprises, renting the prisoner's labour at a low (from 3 to 6 marks a day) rate, had guaranteed full freedom in disposing of this labour; they themselves regulated the time, conditions and type of work, and furthermore supervised the prisoners at work, and that not only in a specialist but also in a disciplinary capacity. Although the firms were aware of the harsh conditions prevailing in camp, they demanded the same productivity of the prisoners as of freely engaged workers. In the monthly reports returned to the camp concerning the prisoners' employment, analyses were constantly made of their productivity, which was often assessed on the basis of somewhat illusory criteria at 40-60 per cent of the productivity of the plant's other workers. At the same time what was demanded was not the improvement of the prisoners' living conditions, but increased discipline and punishments. In some branch camps the civilian overseers often exceeded the SS in their ill-treatment of prisoners. Especially in the mines the German foremen beat and even killed prisoners who were unable to fulfil the norm. This was done not only by lower-level employees, but also by members of the mine's management.

---

[6] Account of former prisoners Anna Zdanowska-Wiśniewska and Teresa Wicińska. APMO. Zespół "Oświadczenia", t. 43, k. 49 and t. 47, k. 90.

3. PUNISHMENTS AND EXECUTIONS

The guarantee of the effective functioning of the camp apparatus of terror and violence was absolute obedience on the part of the prisoners. Even the slightest sign of open resistance was met with the severest retaliation.

The regulations of the Dachau concentration camp of 1 October 1933, signed by Theodor Eicke, later inspector of concentration camps, laid down:

"Anyone who assaults a guard or SS man, refuses to obey an order, or at a place of work refuses to work, incites anyone else to do so with a view to fomenting rebellion, or who on the march or at work cries out, calls, stirs up trouble or makes a speech will either be shot on the spot or hanged as a consequence." [7]

Indeed every SS man could kill a prisoner without incurring any responsibility. This kind of behaviour was accepted and supported not only by the camp command, but also by the supreme state authorities. None other than Hitler himself quashed on 29 November 1935 the prison sentences passed on guards of the Hohenstein concentration camp, who, as the Ministry of Justice admitted, "took part in bullying [the prisoners in a particularly harsh and cruel way". [8]

Hitler indeed did not conceal that physical violence and terror are effective means of wielding power:

"I don't," he announced, "want the concentration camps to be turned into sanatoria. Terror is the most effective political weapon. Everyone will think twice before undertaking anything against us as soon as he finds out what awaits him in a concentration camp... I need people who act harshly and are not going to have second thoughts the moment they have to kill someone... Every action has a point to it, so does crime... Conscience is a Jewish figment." [9]

It was in this spirit that the future staffs of the concentration camps were trained and brought up at Dachau — that famous school of killers with the death's head on their caps — by the first inspector and, as Höss described him, true creator of the camps, Theodor Eicke. "For him the prisoners were always enemies of the state, who had to be closely watched, severely dealt with, and in the event of resistance destroyed." [10] This school of Eicke's also produced the cadre of the concentration camp at Oświęcim, which was made up of such men as: the

---
[7] *Der Prozess...* t. XXVI, pp. 291—293.
[8] Nuremberg Document PS 785—788; *Der Prozess...* t. XXVI, pp. 300—327.
[9] Hermann Rauschning, *Gespräche mit Hitler*. Zurich—Vienna—New York 1940, pp. 79, 81, 82, 95, 211.
[10] *Höss Memoirs*, p. 140.

camp commandant Rudolf Höss, a pedantic murderer directing the entire mechanism of extermination from behind a desk; the first *Lagerführer*, Karl Fritzsch, creator of the system of individual terror which lasted up to the end of the camp's existence; his successor, Hans Aumeier, former chief of the special training section at Dachau; and *Rapportführer*, Gerhard Palitzsch, who carried out death sentences.

Regulations governing conduct — in the sense of a register of prohibitions, orders, or punishments, even such as those mentioned above in the case of the Dachau camp — were unknown to the prisoners of *KL Auschwitz*. What was and what was not allowed in the camp was taught with the help of a stick. Here is what a former prisoner, Czesław Jaworski, a doctor arrested by the Gestapo and sent to the Auschwitz camp under suspicion of belonging to an underground organization, has to say on the subject:

"I noticed in the corridor a board with various notices in German affixed to it. I looked for rules concerning our conduct in the camp, thinking they must be formulated in paragraphs and made available for everyone to become acquainted with them. Suddenly I caught sight of the block *Schreiber* [registrar], so I asked him: 'Excuse me, are there any rules binding the prisoners in the camp? I should like to get to know them, so as not to get into trouble.' The fellow looked at me as though I were mad, struck me in the face and said: 'Here's your rules, my learned counsel!' The explanation cost me two teeth." [11]

The most widespread punishment, though not mentioned in any regulation, was the summary beating of a prisoner on the scene of the "crime". The right to beat, and even kill a prisoner, was enjoyed by every SS man and every prisoner to whom a specific function was entrusted, from the camp senior to the block hairdresser. Summary beating and ill-treatment also constituted the essence of a number of so-called regulation punishments, such as: penal work in leisure time, relegation to the penal company, or penal exercises. These punishments were administered on the basis of an SS man's report by the commandant, or by the *Lagerführer* deputizing for him, who issued special punishment orders. On the basis of the 275 reports and 110 punishment orders which have survived it is possible to study the relation between the transgressions committed by the prisoners and the punishments meted out for them.

The commonest causes of the punishment of prisoners included: failure to set out with the *Kommando* to work, avoidance of work, leaving one's place of work without permission, sabotage at work (a concept which covered such things are breaking a concrete pipe during unloading), preparation of meals during work, procurement of food or clothing,

---

[11] Czesław W. Jaworski, *Wspomnienia z Oświęcimia*. Warsaw 1962, p. 46.

barter with civilian workers, illegal posting of letters, and smoking when smoking was prohibited. Punishment reports occasionally throw an interesting light on the relations prevailing in the camp. On 13 June 1944 the head of the subcamp in Jawiszowice, Wilhelm Kowol, reported for punishment the prisoner Lazar Anticoli, born 3 January 1910 in Rome, who had, together with another prisoner, attempted to break into the pigsty to steal the scraps of bread intended for the pigs. For this the *Schutzhaftlagerführer* of *KL Auschwitz III*, Vinzenz Schöttl, sentenced him to 10 Sundays of penal work under supervision.[12]

A frequently applied official punishment was flogging. This was usually carried out publicly during roll call on a special bench constructed in such a way that the prisoner lying on it could not move his legs. The beating was administered with a stick or, less frequently according to the regulations, a whip. The number of strokes, which the rules said should be laid on quickly, could not exceed 25 at a time. In practice, however, it depended on the mood of the SS man supervising the administration of the punishment. The latitude permitted in interpreting the rules concerning this punishment may be seen from the flogging of five prisoners involved in the first escape from the camp, that of Tadeusz Wiejowski. These prisoners were to receive three doses of 25 strokes. After the infliction of the first dose they were put in the cellars of the "Death Block", where they remained for twenty-one days deprived of any medical aid, despite the fact that the wounds they had received were festering and suppurating. After the three weeks were up they were brought out by prisoner orderlies to the *Appellplatz* where they received the remaining 50 strokes all at once. After the execution of the punishment the victims had to be taken to the camp hospital where one of them, Stanisław Mrzygłód, died, and another, Bolesław Bicz, lay unconscious for two weeks.

The prisoner Josef Engel was flogged for attempting suicide. On 2 February 1944 while working down the mine at Brzeszcze-Jawiszowice, unable to bear the hard toil and ill-treatment any longer, he cut his throat with a knife. As a punishment he received 25 blows with a stick. On 25 January 1944 the prisoner Juda Calvo was flogged for selling two gold teeth he had extracted from his mouth for bread smuggled into the camp.

Women were also subject to flogging. One case of female prisoners being punished in this way is recounted by Seweryna Szmaglewska in her memoirs:

"Two hundred women are to be flogged, to receive 25 strokes each. ...In the streaks of light can be seen the procession of women approach-

---

[12] APMO. Collection of reports and punishment orders (*Meldungen und Strafverfügungen*), sygn. D-AuI, II, III-2/284.

ing in slow and orderly fashion the place where each of them lies down under the whip. The stooping figure of Schultz is outlined against the door of the block, the whip in his hand flashing.

"Suddenly confusion breaks out. In the darkness women are trying to slip from the queue waiting to be whipped to the group of women who have already received their punishment. Schultz perceives this, throws down his whip and seizes an emaciated figure wading with difficulty through the mud. He grasps her hips, lifts her high up in the air and hurls her head downwards to the ground. Then, having looked at his swollen hand, he resumes the beating. ...Shrieks, howls and groans re-echo in the darkness of the autumn evening." [13]

Another, equally painful punishment was that known as the "pillar", which consisted in suspending a prisoner by his hands, which were tied behind his back, in such a way that his feet could not touch the ground. This was an extremely agonizing punishment, during which prisoners lost consciousness from the pain. It was also very dangerous because of the consequences which often followed it. Prolonged suspension on the pillar could tear the arm tendons, as result of which the prisoner would lose control of his arms and, as being unfit for work, fall a victim to the selection.

Another very harsh punishment was confinement in the standing cell (*Stehzelle*). Such cells were located in the main camp in the cells of Block 11. Each of the four cells there had a floor area of less than one square metre. The way in was by a low opening covered with a grating and sealed doors. Inside the cell it was completely dark, as even the small opening measuring twenty-five square centimetres, which provided the only ventilation, was covered with a metal lid. Four prisoners were confined to one cell at a time, which made impossible any movement or change of position whatsoever. After a night in such a cell these prisoners were sent out with the others to work the next day. This punishment was often inflicted for several nights at a stretch or even every night for a fortnight.

By an order of the commandant of *KL Auschwitz* such cells were to be built in each of the branch camps. It is known that such cells existed at Brzezinka, Świętochłowice and Wesoła. Detention in these cells, as was the case with other punishments, was used in instances of very minor infringements.

Prisoner no. 60970 received ten nights in the standing cell for going to another block in order to get a second serving of food. Three nights in the standing cell was meted out to prisoner no. 64495 for relieving

---

[13] Seweryna Szmaglewska, *Dymy nad Birkenau*. Warsaw 1945, pp. 195—196. (Eng. edition: *Smoke over Birkenau*. New York 1947).

himself behind a building. Prisoner no. 104909 received ten nights in the standing cell for having taken advantage of the fact that he had taken time off from work to relieve himself, to pick fruit from a nearby orchard. For a similar offence the woman prisoner no. 47332 was punished by five nights in the standing cell.

Prisoners were also confined to cells that were normal except that they were darkened, where they received normal rations every fourth day, being given only bread and water on the remaining days.

An extremely harsh punishment was relegation to the penal company (*Strafkompanie*), which was formed in August 1940. The function of *Blockführer* supervising the company was held in turn by: *SS-Unterscharführer* Gerlach, *SS-Rottenführer* Sternberg, *SS-Hauptscharführer* Otto Moll, and *SS-Unterscharführer* Umlauf. In all about 6,000 persons passed through the penal company, which contained on average at any one time about 150-600 prisoners. They were quartered separately and were not allowed to contact other prisoners or conduct correspondence. They slept on bare boards or the concrete slabs of the floor in nothing but their underwear. In 1940-42 when the penal company was in Block 11 of the main camp, even gravely ill prisoners belonging to it were not admitted to the camp hospital.

In receiving prisoners into the penal company, Otto Moll, later the head of the crematoria and one of the worst criminals which the SS produced, had a habit of asking each individual why he had been sent there. Regardless of the answer, he would then beat each one with a heavy stick, and when the prisoner fell he would kick and trample on him, or loose on him the dog that followed him everywhere about the camp.

The prisoners of the penal company received worse food, although they were employed on the most arduous work, for example in the gravel pits. All work was done on the double. The prisoners had to push barrows laden with gravel up the planks to the edge of the pits at a run. For a moment's rest the SS men and Kapos would beat them mercilessly. If someone fell, they would step on his throat and throttle him. The corpses of those murdered, carried back to the camp by the returning prisoners, were a proof of the zeal of the Kapos and *Vorarbeiter* of the penal company. There was no doubt that if the SS men from the camp command considered the number of corpses to be too small, the next day would bring an even bloodier harvest.

One of the greatest ruffians of the penal company was Ernst Krankemann. He arrived in *KL Auschwitz* on 29 August 1940 in the second transport of German convicts who assumed the functions of block seniors and Kapos in the camp. A barber by trade, he was a short, stout but powerfully built Kapo who could kill a prisoner by splitting his head on the edge of a wall with one blow of his fist. It was he who, seated astride the shaft of a huge roller, urged on from morning to night the priests and Jews yoked to it. Anyone who fell was crushed under the roller. No prisoner whom Krankemann perceived to have gold teeth could hope to escape with his life. To rid themselves of a partner who knew too much, the SS sent him on 28 July 1941 with the first transport of invalids for "treatment" at the euthanasia establishment at Sonnenstein. If he ever did arrive there, however, it was as a corpse, as he was lynched in the railway car by his fellow prisoners, who in this way avenged his victims.

In May 1942 the penal company was transferred to Brzezinka and located in Block 1 of the men's camp. According to a former prisoner, Józef Kret, "the block was reminiscent of a noisome den. Billowing clouds of thick straw dust intensified its normal darkness. In this smoky atmosphere, as in a thick fog, human ants swarmed like clouds of insects." [14]

At Brzezinka the penal company worked on the digging of the central irrigation ditch, known as the *Königsgraben*. The place was notorious for bestial murders. It was there in fact that on 10 June 1942 open rebellion broke out, followed by escapes. Taking advantage of the confusion caused by a sudden downpour, some of the prisoners decided, disregarding the danger from the SS men and Kapos, to seize the opportunity to escape. Momentarily taken aback, the SS came to their senses and opened fire on the prisoners and, together with the Kapos, managed to gain control of the situation. Thirteen prisoners were killed, but nine managed to escape. The remainder were chased back to the camp by the SS under the command of the *Kommandoführer* Otto Moll. The next day in the courtyard of the penal company an improvised investigation was held during which, upon encountering refusal to answer questions, the *Lagerführer*, *Hauptsturmführer* Hans Aumeier, shot seventeen prisoners, and three others were shot by *SS-Hauptscharführer* Franz Hössler. The remaining 320 prisoners had their hands tied behind their backs with barbed wire, after which they were sent off to the gas bunker and killed. Their places in the penal company were taken by fresh prisoners.

The work begun on the digging of the *Königsgraben* was continued. Every day, returning to the camp, the column of prisoners of the penal company dragged behind them a cart laden with the bodies of the murdered. The prisoners of the penal company had to work even after evening roll call when other prisoners had leisure time. For example they were ordered, without being given any tools, to break up large pieces of demolished brickwork. While the work was going on, the Kapo

---

[14] Józef Kret, "Dzień w karnej kompanii" in: *Zeszyty Oświęcimskie*, 1957, no 1, p. 180.

Alfons Göttinger, known as Sepp, a tall, thin man with a long Mephistophelian face, amused himself by lassooing prisoners. He would throw the noose round a prisoner's neck, twist it round several times over his head, and throw the lifeless body into the crate in the corner of the courtyard in which corpses were laid.

Shortly after the creation of the women's camp a women's penal company also came into existence, which at first was located in the village of Budy and later in the camp at Brzezinka. It numbered about 400 women who were employed in cleaning out the fish ponds, damming up streams and similar work. Regardless of the time of year, these women had to work in cold water up to the waist. The hours worked depended on the season, and in summer came to 14 hours a day. Thus there was nothing surprising about their high mortality rate. In October 1942 the German female convicts preforming the functions of Kapos in the course of a single night murdered 90 Frenchwomen who had allegedly been preparing a rebellion. The camp commandant Rudolf Höss, upon arrival on the scene, noted that "the Frenchwomen had been killed with iron bars and axes, some had had their heads cut clean off, others had been killed after being thrown out an upstairs window".[15]

Another of the punishments used in the camp was the drill known in the camp jargon as "sport". It was used either as a form of punitive retaliation, or purely prophylactically during the quarantine that new arrivals had to go through before being put to work. It consisted in a group of prisoners performing on the command various kinds of exercises, such as: marching while singing, running, crawling on elbows and toes, and rolling over ground covered with gravel and broken bricks. These exercises were performed at a brisk pace, regardless of the prisoners' age or state of health. A specialist in thinking up exercises of this kind was *SS-Oberscharführer* Ludwig Plagge. He was capable of drilling the prisoners for hours on end, holding a pipe in his teeth (hence his nickname of "The Pipe" among the prisoners). Those who fell were beaten by Plagge's assistants who forced them to go on. "Stubborn" cases were killed off. This is how the chief of the Warsaw fire brigade, Stanisław Gieysztor, met his death. Because of his bulk (he weighed about 15 stone) he no longer had the strength to run and fell, whereupon *Lagerältester* Leo Wietschorek began to beat him with an iron bar five centimetres thick. Lying on his back and shielding himself from the blows, Gieysztor momentarily seized the bar which infuriated his tormentor even more, to the point where he began to belabour his victim frightfully, and when the latter lost consciousness he suffocated him by ramming the bar into his mouth.[16]

---

[15] *Höss Memoirs*, p. 143.
[16] Statement by former prisoner Michał Kula. APMO, *Höss Trial*, t. 25, k. 5.

A frequently employed punishment was being made to kneel with hands outstretched holding stones.

Among other punishments may be mentioned withdrawal of the right to write or receive letters, deprivation of dinner while working as normal, and being made to work in leisure time.

The maximum penalty applied in the camp was execution. To be sure it was officially maintained that only the *Reichsführer SS*, Himmler, which in practice would have meant RSHA, could decide on whether or not a prisoner was to be executed, but in fact most executions were carried out without any formalities on the orders of the camp authorities. The rules concerning execution were really a fiction intended to camouflage the crimes being committed in the camp.

The execution orders which had once been issued by RSHA had been drawn up at the instance of the camp authorities in connection with disciplinary infringements by prisoners which were considered particularly dangerous, for example in the case of collective escapes. Executions were usually carried out on the orders of the head of the Political Department (the camp Gestapo), Maximilian Grabner, who generally took decisions concerning executions during reviews of the camp cells (the bunker) where prisoners were held for various kinds of disciplinary offences or because they were suspected of illegal activity in the camp. Such a review is described by the SS man Perry Broad, one of Grabner's subordinates:

"Grabner was in the habit — as he used to say cynically — of using every weekend to 'sweep out' the bunker. After briefing, the whole unit had to go to the camp, to Block 11. In fact only three or four officers are needed, but Grabner takes everyone, as he feels good surrounded by a numerous staff. In the orderly room of Block 11 we wait for the *Lagerführer, SS-Hauptsturmführer* Aumeier, to appear. After a delay to underline his importance, the little Bavarian strode into the room. His harsh, screeching voice betrays the drunkard. ...The bunker superintendent and several *Blockführer* are added to the commission which now heads for the cellars to begin the 'sweeping out'. ...The air in the cellar is so stale as to be hardly breathable. ...The superintendent opens the door of the first cell with one of his bundle of keys. ...Aumeier props up against the door a list of the detainees upon whom he and Grabner now pass judgement. The first prisoner gives his name and tells how long he has been in the bunker. The *Lagerführer* asks the *Rapportführer* briefly the cause of detention. In cases where the prisoner was detained by Department II, the deciding voice belongs to Grabner. Then the two camp dignitaries decide if it is to be punishment report 1, or punishment report 2. ...With a blue pencil Aumeier marks a thick cross, so that everyone can see, by the name of a given prisoner. ...it was no longer a secret to anyone what punishment report 2 meant." [17]

Those condemned to be shot were led from the cellars of Block 11 to the washroom on the ground floor where they stripped naked and awaited execution. In a neighbouring room women, also naked, waited to be shot. In the first years of the camp's existence, when the prisoners did not yet have their numbers tottooed on the arms, each of the condemned had his camp number written on his chest with an indelible pencil. Up to the end of 1942 the condemned had their hands tied with wire, but later this was abandoned as cases of resistance were rare. In the face of inevitable death the prisoners behaved with calm and dignity. They were shot singly or in pairs in the back of the head. The place of execution was the yard between Blocks 10 and 11, which was sealed off by two walls. Here there was a wall, specially painted black, built of wood, sand and insulating board. At the foot of this wall sand was sprinkled to soak up the blood of the victims. Regardless of the time of year, the latter were shot naked and barefoot, first the women, then the men. The still bleeding bodies were then taken by van to the crematorium. As the vans passed along the camp streets, they would leave trickles of blood behind them.

Thus perished many leaders and organizers of the camp underground, who had previously been placed in the cells by the Political Department. On 25 January 1943, following a selection in the bunker, 51 prisoners were taken out and shot. Among them were Polish officers who had formerly held high rank: Colonel Jan Karcz, former head of the cavalry department in the ministry of military affairs, Colonel Karol Kumuniecki and Captain Edward Göt-Getyński. On 11 October 1943, 54 prisoners were shot after a selection in the bunker, among whom were a number of distinguished Polish military, political and community leaders accused of organizing a military conspiracy in the camp. They included the well-known lawyers Wacław Szumański of Warsaw and Józef Woźniakowski of Cracow; the pre-war conservative politician and publicist, Jan Mosdorf; Lieutenant-colonel Teofil Dziama, former deputy commander of the First Air Regiment in Warsaw; Colonel Janusz Gilewicz and Captain Tadeusz Paolone-Lisowski. The former prisoner Ludwik Rajewski writes:

"The first to go before the screen [i.e. the wall of death] were Colonel Dziama and Captain Lisowski-Paolone. They went as became soldiers. Dziama asked the executioners carrying out the death sentence not to shoot him in the back of the head but straight in the face, as befitted

---

[17] *Auschwitz seen by the SS. Höss, Broad, Kremer* (hereafter *Auschwitz seen by the SS*) Oświęcim 1972, pp. 138—139.

a soldier. ...Lisowski cried out: 'Long live a free and indep — ...!' these were his last words." [18] *

Every so often during roll call the names of anything up to several dozen prisoners would be called out with the order to report to the camp office in Block 24. These included prisoners in whose files the Gestapo, in sending them to the camp, had entered the phrase "return undesirable". After their personal data were checked in the camp office, these prisoners were taken off to the execution wall and shot. As in the case of prisoners shot after reviews of the bunker, the cause of death given in the death certificates was a common disease. Sometimes such prisoners were even entered fictitiously in the hospital register beforehand.

On the order of the Security Police and SD Commander executions were also carried out in the camp of hostages who had either been specially brought to the camp for the purpose, as in the case of 40 Poles shot on 22 November 1940, or who were already in the camp in this capacity. They were shot in retaliation for the activities of the resistance movement in their places of residence. The execution on 27 May 1942 of 168 actors, artists and former officers of the Polish army arrested in a Cracow café following an attempt on the life of a high-ranking Luftwaffe officer had such a retaliatory character.

Following acts of sabotage in Silesia, 56 prisoners from the region were executed on 18 August 1942. For the activity of the resistance movement in the Lublin area, about 280 prisoners brought from Lublin and its environs were shot in the camp on 28 October 1942.

Every few weeks a summary court (*Polizei-Standgericht*) of the Gestapo headquarters in Katowice sat in Block 11 and dealt with Poles from Silesia accused of illegal political activity hostile to the occupying power. They also included persons arrested for possessing a radio, passing on current political information, etc. These persons men and women, sometimes even children, were not formally prisoners of the camp but remained at the disposal of the Katowice Gestapo. The trial which was to decide their further fate was the conclusion of a long period of investigation during which the most refined tortures were used to extract information and confessions. The preliminary to torture was a frantic beating with a whip and a kicking on every part of the body. If the explanations given failed to satisfy those conducting the investigation, or if the prisoner refused to give testimony (which often might implicate friends or family), beating on the so-called seesaw was employed. The prisoner's hands were fettered and he was then ordered to embrace his

---

[18] Ludwik Rajewski, *Oświęcim w systemie RSHA*. Warsaw—Cracow 1946, p. 112.

* In Polish: *Niech żyje wolna i niep-*. The finished sentence would undoubtedly be "Long live a free and independent Poland" (Tr. note).

bent knees under which an iron bar was slipped and secured in such a way that the prisoner was suspended head down, thus enabling his tormentors to beat him on the buttocks and sexual organs. The beating was done with such force that the body carried out a rhythmic swaying motion, sometimes even making a complete revolution around the axis of the bar. When the victim cried out, his face was covered with a gas mask.

Another method of extorting testimony was the pouring of hot water into a person's mouth or nose by means of a special funnel, as a result of which the victim choked. Those interrogated also had their fingernails pulled out, needles driven into the most sensitive parts of the body, women had wads soaked in petrol inserted into the vagina and set alight. Not surprisingly, therefore, the victims confessed to all charges, and the sitting of the summary court was only a formality. Its sentences nearly always ran as follows: "Following investigations by the state police, it has been found that the Pole... violated the legislation of the German state by... the summary police court of the Secret State Police in Katowice sentences him to death." [19] In a small number of cases prisoners were sentenced to a term in a concentration camp. The records of the sessions of the summary court have not survived. The documents of the camp resistance movement, which did all it could to document the criminal activities of the camp authorities, reveal that in the course of six sittings of the summary court (2 September 1943, 22 October 1943, 29 November 1943, March 1944, 29 September 1944 and 30 October 1944) out of 580 persons sentenced 556, including 76 women, were sentenced to death, the remaining 24, who included one woman, being sentenced to detention in a concentration camp.

The same system of tortures was used by the functionaries of the Political Department during interrogations of camp inmates.

KL *Auschwitz* was also used as a place for executing civilians, members of underground organizations and partisans — men, women and children brought here by the police exclusively to have their death sentences executed. These persons were not entered in the camp records but shot immediately upon arrival at the camp. One of many such executions is described by a former prisoner, Dr. Bolesław Zbozień:

"Once — I don't remember the exact date — we met Palitzsch on a street of the Auschwitz camp. He was hustling a man and woman on ahead of him. The woman had a small child in her arms, and two older children aged perhaps about four and seven respectively were walking beside her. The whole group was making for Block 11. Together with my companions I managed to run to Block 21. There, standing on a table

---

[19] *Auschwitz Seen by the SS*, p. 149.

in an upstairs room we looked down on the courtyard of Block 11. The scene which was played out before our eyes will remain in my memory to the end of my life. The woman and man put up no resistance when Palitzsch positioned them against the wall of death. The whole thing took place in the greatest calm. The man held the child on his left by the hand. The second child stood between them and they also held its hands. The smallest child the mother held to her breast. Palitzsch first shot the baby in the head. The shot shattered the head... causing immense bleeding. The baby quivered like a fish, but the mother hugged it all the more tightly to herself. Palitzsch then shot the child standing in the middle. The man and woman... continued to stand motionless like statues made of stone. Later Palitzsch tussled with the oldest child which wouldn't let itself be shot. He turned the child over on the ground and standing on its back shot it in the base of the skull. Finally he shot the woman, and at the very end the man. It was monstrous... Afterwards, although many executions were carried out, I did not watch them." [20]

Another witness of such an execution was the former prisoner Franciszka Gulba, who had been sent as a punishment to Block 11:

"One evening a dozen or so persons were brought to Block 11... The group was made up of men, women and children... They were placed in the cellars of Block 11. ...About noon the next day the men were brought out first from the said group. They were led out in pairs to the courtyard of Block 11. Their hands were tied with wire behind their backs. The block senior led them out and took the condemned men up to the 'wall of death'. The execution was carried out by *Rapportführer* Palitzsch. In the intervals before the next group was brought up, he would sling his carbine over his shoulder and with perfect calmness smoke cigarettes, strolling about the courtyard. Finally a woman and a child were led up — we assumed it was a mother and her daughter. The mother... held the daughter by the hand. Both were stripped to their shifts. Palitzsch first shot the mother. When she slumped to the ground, the child threw herself weeping on the body of the lying woman, crying out in despair: 'Mama! Mama!' Palitzsch shot at the girl but evidently missed, as the child continued to embrace the mother's body and shake it. The block senior came running up and held the girl so that Palitzsch was free to take aim. In a moment the child was dead. We saw such executions almost every day." [21]

Executions by shooting were secret. While they were in progress and while the bodies were being removed to the crematorium no one was allowed to leave the block. The windows of the neighbouring Block 10

---

[20] APMO. Zespół "Oświadczenia", t. 70, k. 159—160.
[21] APMO. Zespół „Oświadczenia", t. 70, k. 46—47.

were specially boarded up, and the windows of Block 11 were partially walled up. Before executions prisoners were transferred from the rooms giving out on the courtyard to rooms on the other side of the block.

In the case of particularly renowned and bold escapes from the camp the recaptured prisoners were executed by hanging. As opposed to executions by shooting, these executions were public. Their aim was to terrorize the prisoners and convince them of the senselessness of any attempt at escape. They were carried out during roll call, so that everyone should be present. There were two special mobile gallows kept in the courtyard of Block 11. Makeshift gallows were also erected when necessary. It was on such a gallows — a rail fastened to three upright posts — that on 19 July 1943 twelve prisoners of the surveying party were hanged, having been accused of assisting in the escape of three of their colleagues; on 6 December 1943 nineteen prisoners in the subcamp of Neu-Dachs at Jaworzno were hanged, being suspected of preparing an escape by digging a tunnel; and in July 1944 the Pole Edward Galiński was hanged, having been caught making a joint escape with the Jewess Mala Zimetbaum, who was also executed.

A source of particular horror in the camp was execution by starvation. In the case of a prisoner escaping, the camp commandant or *Lagerführer* would choose during roll call ten or more prisoners from the block in which the escaper had lived or the commando in which he had been working, and they would then be locked up in one of the cells in the basement of Block 11. There, receiving nothing to eat or drink, they would die in the course of a few days, at the longest a fortnight, in terrible agony. On the basis of the register of prisoners in Block 11 a few dates have been established when "selections" of this kind were made. For example on 23 April and 17 June 1941 ten prisoners each were picked out and starved to death following escapes. During one such "selection" conducted at the turn of July and August 1941 the Franciscan Father Maximilian (Rajmund Kolbe),* a Polish missionary who had been well known in Catholic circles before the war, stepped forward and asked the *Lagerführer*, Karl Fritzsch, to be included in the group intended for death instead of one of those chosen, Franciszek Gajowniczek. After surviving nearly two weeks in the bunker of Block 11 and the deaths of most of his companions, Father Kolbe was killed on 14 August with a phenol injection.[22] Father Kolbe's heroic act was probably the reason for the discontinuing of "selections" for death by starvation. Later the punishment of death by starvation was

---

[22] Accounts by the former prisoners: Bruno Borgowiec, Maksymilian Chlebik, Franciszek Gajowniczek and others. APMO. *Materiały o Ojcu Kolbe*. Sygn. Mat. 605/47a.

* beatified in 1982 (Ed. note).

applied only in relation to individual prisoners for disciplinary infringements.

Besides the 12,000 Soviet POWs registered in *KL Auschwitz*, political officers and other Soviet POWs, who had been weeded out of the POW camps by the *Einsatzgruppen*, were sent there for summary execution following an order by the chief of the Sipo and SD. These prisoners were not registered but done to death immediately upon arrival at the camp. The first such group of about 300 prisoners, mostly political officers of the Red Army, arrived at the camp in July 1941. In the space of a few days they were murdered at work in the gravel pit beside the camp kitchen. The prisoners at the bottom of the pit were fired at by SS men standing on the rim. If any of them failed to die from the bullets of the SS, he was beaten to death by the Kapos with sticks, shovels and picks.

In view of the practice of executing in the camp civilians and prisoners not entered in the camp files, the falsification of documents and the fact that most of the camp records were destroyed, it is impossible to establish even approximately how many persons were executed in the camp. It has been estimated that at least 20,000 people were killed at the Wall of Death alone.

III. METHODS OF MASS EXTERMINATION

1. LETHAL INJECTIONS

The political situation in Europe, Germany's military successes and the conviction that the Soviet state would soon collapse, heightened the Nazi authorities' feeling of impunity and encouraged them to speed up the extermination operation in the camps. Because the previously used methods of extermination had turned out to be inadequate, it was decided to kill prisoners by lethal injections and in gas chambers, which had previously been used in Germany in the so-called euthanasia institutes for killing the mentally handicapped. These were specially adapted bathhouses where, thinking from the appearance of the installations that they were going to be bathed, the patients were gassed by carbon monoxide introduced through the water pipes.

Concentration camp inmates were initially weeded out for killing in the euthanasia institutes by special medical commissions applying the criterion of fitness for work. Often, too, the transports of invalids and the chronically sick, who were allegedly being sent away to lighter work or for treatment, had other unwanted prisoners added to them.

In *KL Auschwitz* the first selection of this kind was made on 28 July 1941. Following it 575 prisoners were gassed at the euthanasia centre at Sonnenstein in Saxony.

A continuation of this action — designated by the cryptonym "14 f 13" — was the liquidation of the sick by phenol injections through the heart which was begun in August 1941. Selections of the sick were conducted by the SS doctors Friedrich Entress, Erwin von Halmersen, Heinz Thilo, Edmund König, Josef Mengele and Bruno Kitt. The phenol injections were usually administered by the SS orderlies Josef Klehr (who since 1965 has been serving a life sentence in the Federal Republic of Germany) and Herbert Scherpe, and the prisoners Alfred Stesel and Mieczysław Pańszczyk who had been taught the technique. Prisoners intended for "the needle" had to report to Block 20. There they were called in individually to the clinic and placed in a chair, whereupon two prisoners designated for the purpose would seize the victim's arms and a third would bind his eyes with a towel. Then Klehr would drive the needle trough his heart and inject the phenol in the syringe. The corpse would be thrown into the neighbouring washroom and the next prisoner would be immediately summoned. In some periods several dozen, or even more prisoners would be killed in this way every day. For example in the space of four months in 1942 (August, September, November, December) 2,467 persons were killed with phenol injections.

2. THE GAS CHAMBERS AND CREMATORIA

More or less at the same time as the first transport of the sick was sent from the camp to the euthanasia institute at Sonnenstein and killing by means of phenol injections was begun, there arrived at the camp, as mentioned earlier, large groups of Soviet prisoners of war who had been sent for immediate execution at the order of the chief of the Security Police and SD. Because the numbers in the transports being sent for execution were increasingly large, the *Lagerführer* Fritzsch decided to use for their liquidation the gas Cyclon B which had been previously used in the camp for disinfection purposes.

On 3 September 1941 another transport of about 600 Soviet POWs was herded off to the cellars of Block 11 (where 250 patients selected from the camp hospital had also been put) into which, after the windows had been blocked by having earth heaped up over them, gas was introduced. After it was discovered the following day that some of the occupants of the cellar were still alive, the dose of gas was doubled and the cellar closed again. On 5 September the prisoners of the penal company and the orderlies of the camp hospital were summoned and taken to the courtyard of

Block 11, where they were told that they would be assigned to special work about which they were to tell no one on pain of death. They were then ordered to don gas masks and taken down to the cellar where the corpses of the gassed lay. Thence they had to carry them up to the courtyard, strip them of their military uniforms and then transport them to the crematorium. Because for the duration of the gassing it had been necessary to remove all prisoners from the block (which contained the camp jail and housed the penal company) and thereafter spend a long time ventilating all the rooms, the next group of POWs was gassed in the morgue beside the crematorium. This was a spacious chamber, which had once served as an ammunition bunker, with a floor space of 65 square metres. And here is a description of how the liquidation of the transport of 900 prisoners went:

"While the transport was being unloaded, a few holes were made in the ceiling of the morgue. The Russians had to undress in the anteroom, after which they went perfectly quietly into the morgue, as they had been told they were to be deloused. The transport filled the whole morgue to capacity. Then the doors were locked and gas sprinkled through the shafts. I don't know how long they took to die, but for a long time there was a kind of murmuring. After the gas was thrown in, some of the prisoners shouted: 'Gas!', after, which a loud roar broke out and they began to press against the doors from the inside. However the doors withheld the pressure. Not until a few hours later was the chamber opened and ventilated." [23]

Later transports of POWs were liquidated in the same way. The commandant of *KL Auschwitz*, Rudolf Höss, responsible for preparing the mass extermination of the Jews in his camp, having established the effectiveness of Cyclon B, concluded that it was a better means of the mass poisoning of people than the carbon monoxide used in the euthanasia institutes. He soon told Adolf Eichmann of RSHA of this during one of the latter's visits to Auschwitz in connection with the preparations for beginning the "final solution to the Jewish question". The two decided that this gas would also be used in the extermination of the Jews.

The first transports of Jews arrived at the camp from Silesia at the beginning of 1942, probably soon, after the conference at Berlin-Wannsee. At first these people were killed, like the Soviet POWs, in the morgue beside the crematorium. The transports arrived by rail at the unloading ramp near the camp, whence they were escorted by the SS to the courtyard of the crematorium. In the meantime, all approach and transit roads were cleared and closed and it was forbidden to venture out onto them. After undressing the victims were led into the morgue-cum-gas chamber.

---

[23] *Höss Memoirs*, pp. 150—151.

They were told they were going to have a shower, after which they would receive a meal and be assigned to work. The moment the gas was introduced, in order to drown out the screams and groans of dying people, the motor of a lorry kept specially standing by for this purpose was switched on.

Initially the process of killing and ventilation of the gas chamber lasted several hours. Later, after the installation of ventilators, this period was shortened to about an hour. After this time had elapsed, the prisoners of the crematorium squad proceeded to burn the corpses. All this took place in the deepest secrecy, with participation limited to the minimum number of SS men from the camp command and the Political Department. Among those who took part in these actions were Maximilian Grabner, Franz Hössler, and the disinfection expert Adolf Theuer.

The modest capacity of the crematorium, which could cope with 340 corpses in the space of 24 hours, and the difficulty of keeping the whole action a secret, resulted in the operation being transferred to Brzezinka, which had been the original intention. A dwelling house belonging to one of the evacuated inhabitants of Brzezinka, which Eichmann had already singled out during his first visit, had its windows walled up, its doors strengthened and sealed by screwing them in place, and shafts drilled in the walls. The entrance door bore the inscription "To the Baths", and on the inside of the exit door, which opened out into open countryside, the inscription "To Disinfection" was emblazoned. This completed the gas chamber known as bunker 1.

Transports intended for gassing were directed to the unloading ramp of the goods station at Oświęcim, whence they were led off to the bunker. From July 1942 incoming transports began to be submitted to selections. After the train was sealed off by a cordon of SS guards, the waggons were opened, the occupants told to get out and the sorting out process started immediately. The men were stood in one column along the ramp, the women and children in another. This procedure was accompanied by the weeping and cries of people who, uncertain of their fate, were afraid of being parted from one another. The people had to approach the SS doctors in turn, who decided on the basis of their external appearance on their fitness for work. With a movement of his hand the doctor directed some to the right, some to the left.

Depending on the current need for labour and the breakdown of a transport according to age and sex, anything up to 30 per cent, consisting of young, strong and healthy people, would be sent to the camp, while the rest — the sick, cripples, mothers with children, pregnant women and persons with a weak physical constitution, were doomed to die. With the help of stepladders they were loaded into waiting lorries and carried off to the bunker. If there was not enough room in the lorries for everyone, the remainder were led on foot across the meadows where later the huts of construction sector III of the camp at Brzezinka were to stand. The escorting SS men tried not to be provocative, on the contrary dispelling fears with false information about the fate that awaited them. People must have been reassured by the outward appearance of the secluded cottage, especially in spring when the trees of the surrounding orchard were in bloom. Upon arrival, the people were told of the baths and disinfection that awaited them and ordered to undress in two huts reserved for this purpose, then they were led into the house. Individuals suspecting a trick, whose behaviour might evoke panic, were discreetly led behind the building and shot in the back of the head with low-calibre weapons.

The chamber, which was divided into two compartments, could admit 800 people at a time, and if the need arose considerably more could be crammed in. Those who nevertheless could not be fitted in were shot immediately. After the doors were shut, bolted and screwed fast, specially trained SS disinfection experts introduced the gas Cyclon B in the form of small lumps of diatomite soaked in prussic acid. Death of the people inside the gas chamber occurred after a few minutes as a result of internal "suffocation", caused by the halting by the prussic acid of the process of exchange of oxygen between the blood and the tissues. Those standing near the shafts died almost instantly; those who shouted, the old, the sick and children also died a quicker death. In order to ensure that no one remained alive, the gas chamber was not opened until half an hour had elapsed. In periods when the pressure of incoming transports was particularly intense, the gassing time was shortened to ten minutes. Most of the corpses were found near the door through which the victims had tried to escape from the spreading gas. The corpses, which covered the entire floor of the chamber, had their knees half-bent, and were often cloven together. The bodies were smeared with excrement, vomit and blood. The skin had assumed a pink hue.

Following ventilation of the gas chamber, the corpses were removed, loaded onto iron waggons and transported by a narrow-gauge railway for a distance of several hundred metres and there buried in deep pits.

After the mass extermination action had already begun, Eichmann brought an order from Himmler to shear the hair of the female corpses and to remove all gold teeth from the victims. The hair was sold at half a mark per kilogram to German textile firms to use in the manufacture of haircloth. One such firm was Aleks Zink of Roth near Nuremberg. The gold teeth on the other hand were melted down into bars in the SS hospital building in the main camp, which bars were then sent to the *SS-Sanitätshauptamt in Berlin.* Rings earrings and other jewelry were also removed from the corpses.

All the personal belongings that people had brought with them had to be left at the unloading ramp. The owners were told that their things would be sent on to the camp separately. These belongings, gathered up by prisoners of a special commando (the *Aufräumungskommando* known in the camp jargon as the "Canada" commando), were loaded onto waiting lorries and taken to special warehouses which initially occupied five, and towards the end of the camp's existence thirty, huts. There they were gone through, sorted, cleaned and disinfected, before being sent off to be sold or for industrial processing. Besides articles of everyday use, such as clothing, shoes and linen, people brought with them jewelry, watches, works of art, and money. Doctors brought medicines and whole sets of medical instruments. Almost all these items were dispatched with the knowledge and approval of the ministry of economy to various institutions in the Reich. Some of them were distributed to the population of bombed German towns, some to *Volksdeutsche* settled in the General Government, and some sold at low prices in work establishments. Valuables were negotiated abroad to gain necessary foreign exchange used for the purchase of raw materials essential to the German economy. A small proportion of these things were put on show in the camp "museum" in Block 24 of the main camp, where visiting SS dignitaries were taken.

In the summer of 1942, in view of the intensified influx of transports, a second gas chamber was brought into commission, which, like bunker 1, consisted of a converted dwelling house. This chamber, which was called bunker 2, contained four compartments in which it was possible to gas 1,200 people at a time. It was this chamber which was used to show Himmler during his two-day visit to the Auschwitz camp in July 1942 the whole gassing procedure, from the reception of the transport and the selection at the ramp to the clearing out of the bunker. Also present were the *Gauleiter* and *Oberpräsident* of Upper Silesia, *SS-Brigadeführer* Fritz Bracht, and the HSSPF from Wrocław, *SS-Obergruppenführer* Ernst Schmauser.

Shortly after this visit there arrived at the camp *SS-Standartenführer* Paul Blobel of Eichmann's department, who since June 1942 had been engaged in removing all traces of the mass executions in Poland and the Soviet Union, with orders to dig up all the graves and burn the corpses contained in them. Commandant Rudolf Höss, accompanied by *SS-Untersturmführer* Franz Hüssler of the Employment Department and *SS-Untersturmführer* Walter Dejaco, went to Chełmno on the Ner to acquaint themselves with the technique of burning bodies. Upon inspection of the experimental installations existing there (one of the methods tried was the destruction of large numbers of bodies with the help of explosives) it was decided that the fastest and most effective method of destroying corpses was burning in the open air.

Towards the end of September 1942 in the Auschwitz camp the bodies of the newly gassed began to be burned on pyres on which layers of 2,000 corpses each alternated with layers of kindling. At the same time the exhumation and burning of bodies already buried in the pits was started. The fire was kept going by pouring on the corpses the waste products of refined petroleum or methanol as well as by the fat of the burning bodies themselves.

All auxiliary activities, such as removing the bodies from the gas chambers, cutting off the hair, pulling out the gold teeth and burning the corpses, were done by the prisoners of the special squad, or *Sonderkommando*. They were chosen chiefly from among Jewish prisoners of the countries from which current transports were arriving. Their number varied with the size and frequency of transports for extermination. In order to isolate them from the other prisoners, the members of the *Sonderkommando* were quartered separately — in the main camp at Oświęcim in the cellars of Block 11, and at Brzezinka in a block specially set aside for them, and from mid-1944 over the crematoria. In the event of refusal to carry out this work they were killed at once. On 22 July 1944, 435 young Greek Jews were gassed for refusing to work in the *Sonderkommando*.

According to an order of Eichmann's these prisoners were supposed to be liquidated after every major action. In fact they were liquidated at intervals of a few months, while specialists such as stokers, mechanics and overseers were spared.

The first *Sonderkommando* — numbering about 80 prisoners — which had been employed to bury the bodies of those gassed in bunkers 1 and 2, were liquidated in August 1942. The second — numbering some 150-300 prisoners — which had been employed in these same bunkers from September to the end of November 1942 and had also burned 107,000 corpses buried earlier in mass graves — was gassed on 3 December 1942 in the gas chambers attached to crematorium I.[24]

Both the gas bunkers and the burning pits were treated as temporary expedients. They functioned until the four specially designed gas chambers and crematoria went into service.

Work on the latter had begun in July 1942 and continued at an accelerated pace until the middle of the following year. Several hundred prisoners on day and night shifts were employed on them. The first to be completed — on 22 March 1943 — was crematorium IV, the next — cremato-

---

[24] The psychological ordeal of prisoners detained to the *Sonderkommando* is described by a former member, Załmen Lewental, in *Wśród koszmarnej zbrodni — notatki więźniów Sonderkommando odnalezione w Oświęcimiu* (Amidst a Nightmare of Crime. Notes of Prisoners of Sonderkommando, found at Auschwitz) in: *zeszyty Oświęcimskie*, 1971, Special Issue II (hereafter *Amidst a Nightmare of Crime*): pp. 133—135.

rium II — was ready on 31 March, followed by crematorium V on 4 April and crematorium III on 25 June. Crematoria II and III, identical in construction, possessed five three-door furnaces with two generator hearths in each furnace. Crematoria IV and V, on the other hand, had one eight-door furnace. Before the crematoria were officially commissioned, on 4 and 5 March 1943, in the presence of high-ranking SS officers from Berlin, representatives of the camp authorities and engineers and employees of the firm Topf und Söhne, a test of crematorium II was held. Prisoners of the *Sonderkommando*, who had been acquainted with the functioning of crematorium installations by a Kapo brought from the Buchenwald crematorium, August Brück, on the morning of 4 March lit burners of the generators and maintained the fire in them until four o'clock in the afternoon. Next, in the presence of the members of the above-mentioned commission who, watch in hand, were following the course of the test, three corpses were placed in each retort (a total of 45 bodies). Because, contrary to expectations, it took as long as forty minutes to burn them, orders were given for the ovens to be heated for a fortnight. Ultimately, as is revealed by a letter from the SS construction department (*Zentralbauleitung der Waffen SS und Polizei Auschwitz*) to *Amtsgruppe C* of SS-WVHA dated 28 June 1943,[25] the capacity of the individual crematoria over a twenty-four hour period was established as follows:

Crematorium I — 340 bodies
Crematorium II — 1440 bodies
Crematorium III — 1440 bodies
Crematorium IV — 768 bodies
Crematorium V — 768 bodies

Thus in all the crematoria it was possible to dispose of a total of 4,756 bodies in the space of twenty-four hours. This was a theoretical capacity assuming the smooth functioning of the crematoria without any technical breakdowns and taking account of the time needed for current maintenance, deslagging the hearths, etc. In practice the capacity was twice as high. In crematoria II and III, 5,000 corpses were disposed of every twenty-four hours, and in crematoria IV and V up to 3.000.[26]

Henceforth bodies were burned in the open only when there was an influx of particularly large transports and the crematoria were unable to keep pace with the work of extermination. In view of the unlimited capacity of the burning pits the number of bodies cremated depended in prin-

---
[25] *SS im Einsatz. Eine Dokumentation über die Verbrechen des SS*. Kongress-Verlag. Berlin 1960, p. 269.
[26] Deposition of the former *Sonderkommando* member Stanisław Jankowski *Amidst a Nightmare of Crime*, p. 48.

ciple on the numerousness of the transports and the capacity of the gas chambers, which was theoretically estimated at 60,000 over a period of 24 hours, taking account of gassing time and the time needed to remove the bodies. The highest daily number of gassed and cremated actually achieved — in 1944 during the extermination of the Hungarian Jews — was 24,0000. At that time bunker 2 was reactivated, the old burning pits reopened, an additional five large pits were dug around crematorium V, and the railway onto which the transports were shunted was extended right up to the crematoria themselves.

Each of these up-to-date crematoria was surrounded by a barbed wire fence, possessed a separate entrance, and was concealed on the camp side by a wicker fence. Neatly tended flower beds gave the whole place an innocent appearance.

The gas chambers and undressing rooms attached to crematoria II and III were underground. On the walls of the spacious undressing room were, apart from appropriate notices, numbered pegs to hang clothes on with benches under them, while the gas chamber had piping and imitation shower sprays. People entering the chambers — first women with children, followed by men — were led up to the opposite wall, behind a cordon of SS men standing in front of it. As the gas chamber filled up, the latter withdrew towards the door. In this way 3,000 people would be crammed into a gas chamber with a floor space of 210 square metres — 30 metres long by 7 metres wide and 2.4 metres high.

In crematoria IV and V, for reasons of economy, the gas chambers had not been built underground but on the surface. Each of these chambers had been originally divided into three, later into four, compartments, containing 1,500, 800, 600 and 150 people respectively. As in the bunkers, the gas shafts in the gas chambers attached to crematoria IV and V were in the side walls. In the gas chambers attached to crematoria II and III the gas was introduced through openings in the ceiling which led into special pillars made of thick wire netting and with a movable core, which reached to the floor. The SS disinfector opened a tin of Cyclon B and threw its contents into a special separating cone thanks to which the lumps of diatomite distributed themselves evenly inside the core of the mesh pillar, which hastened the process of gassing. From 6 to 12 kilograms of gas would be introduced into the gas chamber at a time (in the years 1942-43 19,652.69 kilograms of Cyclon B were delivered to Auschwitz by the firm Tesch und Stabenow). Through a special spyhole in the door the SS doctor supervising the gassing could observe the interior of the chamber. One of the few persons besides the SS doctors and crematorium personnel to witness a gassing was the camp commandant Rudolf Höss. Here is what he has to say on the subject:

"Through the spyhole in the door one could see how those persons standing nearest to the shafts fell dead immediately. Nearly a third of the victims died instantaneously. The others began to huddle together, scream and gasp for air. Soon however the screams turned into a death rattle, and a few minutes later all were lying down. By the time twenty minutes at the most had passed, no one was moving." [27]

After the ventilators were switched on and the gas removed from the chamber, the doors were opened and the corpses dragged out and raised in an electric goods elevator to the crematorium building which was at ground level.

Next, after the hair had been cut off and the gold teeth removed, the corpses were dragged up to the ovens and laid on special trolleys which were then pushed inside. The period of cremation lasted about 20 minutes. The ashes and remains of bones were ground down in special grinders and thrown into rivers or carried away in lorries to the village of Harmęże where they were thrown into fish ponds, scattered in the swamps or used to fertilize the fields of the camp farms. The gold teeth extracted from the corpses were melted down on the spot in a special melting pot installed in crematorium III and in some periods the daily haul came to as much as 12 kilograms. The crematorium roofs, warmed by the ovens below, were used for drying the hair of the murdered victims.

All these auxiliary operations were carried out by the prisoners of the *Sonderkommando* under the supervision of SS men. In the years 1942—45 the post of crematorium chief was held consecutively by: *SS-Hauptscharführer* Otto Moll (sentenced to death after being tried at Dachau and executed on 28 May 1946), *SS-Hauptscharführer* Hirsch, *SS-Unterscharführer* Steinberg, *SS-Scharführer* Buch and *SS-Oberscharführer* Erich Muhsfeld (sentenced to death by the Supreme National Tribunal in Poland and executed on 22 December 1947). The *Sonderkommando* attained its largest complement — of about 1,000 prisoners — in the early summer of 1944 during the peak period of the extermination of the Hungarian Jews. On 30 August 1944, 874 prisoners worked in two shifts in the four crematoria at Brzezinka.

As the number of transports sent to the camp for extermination fell in the late summer of 1944, it was decided to liquidate gradually the members of the *Sonderkommando*. In September about 200 of them were sent from Brzezinka to the camp at Oświęcim where they were gassed by a ruse in a chamber thitherto never used for this purpose. Despite the fact that this took place in close secrecy, news of the fact reached the surviving members of the *Sonderkommando* who began to prepare for resistance. When an attempt was made to liquidate a second batch on 7 October a rebellion broke out during which several hundred prisoners were either

---

[27] *Höss Memoirs*, p. 209.

killed fighting or murdered. By 9 October 1944 the *Sonderkommando* numbered only 212 prisoners. The next day fourteen of them were arrested and placed in the bunkers of Block 11 in the main camp. Among them was one of the organizers of the rebellion — Jankiel Handelsman of Radom. The remaining 198 prisoners were employed in crematoria II, III and V. Crematorium IV, damaged during the rebellion, was out of order at this time.

In the last period of the camp's existence the prisoners of the *Sonderkommando* were used to remove traces of the crime. In October 1944 they were employed in pulling down the walls of the burned out crematorium IV, and in November, after the mass extermination had been halted, they dismantled the technical installations of the gas chambers and the ovens in crematoria II and III, which were then blown up. On 26 November of the some 200 prisoners of the *Sonderkommando* 100 were chosen and allegedly sent to *KL Gross-Rosen* — their later fate remains unknown. On 5 January 1945 six members of the *Sonderkommando* were dispatched to *KL Mauthausen* where they were shot, 30 remained to man the last functioning crematorium V and 70 were employed in clearing out and filling in the burning pits.[28]

The prisoners of the last two groups left the camp on 18 January 1945 setting off on foot, together with other evacuated prisoners, under an SS escort in the direction of Wodzisław Śląski. Barely a dozen of them survived the war. They included: Alter Feinsilber, otherwise known as Stanisław Jankowski, who arrived in camp on 27 March 1942 from Drancy, receiving the camp number 27675. In November 1942 he was assigned to the *Sonderkommando*. He escaped during the evacuation of the camp in January 1945 in the region of Rybnik; Szlama Dragon, who arrived in camp on 7 December 1942 from the Mława ghetto, receiving the camp number 80359. He was a member of the *Sonderkommando* from 10 December 1942. He escaped in the region of Pszczyna during the evacuation of the camp; and Henryk Tauber, who arrived in camp on 19 January 1943 from the Cracow ghetto, was a member of the *Sonderkommando* from February 1943, and escaped during the evacuation of prisoners in January 1945.

These prisoners gave the Polish courts lengthy depositions concerning the details of the mass extermination in the gas chambers.[29]

Furthermore, after the war in the vicinity of the crematoria five ma-

---

[28] Manuscripts by an Anonymous Author and Chaim Hermann published in: *Amidst a Nightmare of Crime*, pp. 116, 161—170 and 184.
[29] Depositions of Jankowski, Dragon and Tauber. APMO. *Höss Trial*, t. 1, k. 3—28; t. 11, k. 103—121, 122—150; Jankowski's deposition was also published in: *Amidst a Nightmare of Crime*, pp. 30—66.

nuscripts of members of the *Sonderkommando* were found buried, signed by Załmen Gradowski, Załmen Lewental, Chaim Herman, a prisoner called Lejb and an Anonymous Author. Together with the depositions of the prisoners, they constitute an invaluable, and at the same time shocking testimonial to a crime. [30]

In addition to the persons of Jewish origin brought for extermination in the mass transports, throughout the period of the camp's existence more or less numerous groups of Poles — members of the resistance, partisans, hostages — and Soviet POWs were added to the transports and killed in the gas chambers along with them. This is dealt with in the deposition of Alter Feinsilber (Stanisław Jankowski):

"Besides this, in the same room of corpses two or three times a week a so-called 'roll-out' was held, i.e. groups of anything up to 250 people (varying as to age and sex) who, after undressing, were shot. These were people from outside the camp, i.e. they were not Auschwitz prisoners. They had been arrested by the Gestapo in various localities and were brought to the crematorium to be shot without being entered in the camp books. Only in a few cases did the 'roll-outs' embrace Auschwitz prisoners as such. I would like to point out that the shootings were carried out personally by that same Quackernack. For the duration of the shooting he would remove all the Jews [i.e. of the *Sonderkommando*] to the coking room and carry out the shooting in the presence of the Poles and Germans employed in the crematorium. Because the coking room was only a dozen metres away, we Jews heard the shots and the thuds of people falling and their cries. With my own ears I heard those who were being shot crying out that they were innocent, I heard the cries of children and Quackernack replying: 'More of our people are killed at the front'. Then we were summoned to the room in which the shooting had been carried out, from which room we Jews took the still warm, bleeding bodies to the crematorium ovens. We carried out thirty human corpses an hour. Quackernack stood gun in hand, bespattered and dripping with blood. Also present besides Quackernack at shootings of this kind were the Auschwitz *Lagerführer* Schwarz and the commandant of the whole camp together with a retinue of SS... Every week 10-15 Russian prisoners of war, who had been held a few days beforehand in the bunkers of Block 11, were shot by the crematorium oven. They were not entered in the camp books, they were not registered at all, so the numbers killed could not even be established on the basis of the camp documents. I observed these shootings for the period of a year at Oświęcim, and later the same was repeated

---

[30] Manuscripts by Gradowski, Lewental, Herman and the Anonymous Author were published in: *Amidst a Nightmare of Crime*, pp. 67—184. manuscript by Lejb in: *Zeszyty Oświęcimskie* 1972, no. 14, pp. 15—62.

at Birkenau, except that at Birkenau a larger number of Russian POWs were killed weekly." [31]

Of the gassing of Polish resistance members brought from outside the camp another member of the *Sonderkommando* writes in a memorial found after the war:

"Some time before the end of 1943 the following incident took place. 164 Poles from the surrounding district were brought in, including twelve young women. All were members of a secret organization. At the same time several hundred Dutch Jews — prisoners from the camp — had been brought for gassing. A young Polish woman delivered a very short but fiery speech to all those present, stripped naked, denouncing Nazi crimes and oppression and ending with the words: 'We at this moment are not dying, we shall be immortalized by the history of our nation, our initiative and spirit are alive and flourishing, the German nation will pay as dearly for our blood as we are able to imagine, down with barbarism in the shape of Hitler's Germany! Long live Poland!' Then she addressed herself to us Jews, to the *Sonderkommando:* 'Remember, you are bound by the sacred duty of avenging us innocent ones. Tell our brothers, our people, that we went consciously and full of pride to meet our death.' Then the Poles knelt to the ground and recited a prayer in an attitude which made an enormous impression, then they rose and all together sang the Polish national anthem, the Jews sang *Hatikwa*... With profoundly moving sincerity they thus expressed their final feelings and hope and faith in the future of their people. Then they sang the Internationale together. While they were singing the van marked with a Red Cross arrived, the gas was thrown into the chamber, and they all perished..." [32]

Throughout the period of the camp's existence the gas chambers and crematoria were also used to dispose of thousands of registered prisoners of all nationalities who under the "euthanasia" programme begun in July 1941 were considered incurably ill. The constant selections made in the camp hospitals meant that prisoners went to them only as a last resort, for a longish period in hospital or an infectious disease were enough to qualify someone "for the gas".

The selections were made not only in the camp hospitals but also among the healthy. In the main camp at Oświęcim selections took place, for example, in the camp baths between Blocks 1 and 2. One participant in these selections was *Rapportführer* Oswald Kaduk, sentenced in the Federal Republic of Germany in 1965 to life imprisonment. Often drunk to the point of being unable to stand upright, he would review the prisoners fi-

---

[31] *Amidst a Nigthmare of Crime*, pp. 41—43.
[32] Manuscript by the Anonymous Author in: *Amidst a Nightmare of Crime*, pp. 110—111.

ling past him while seated on a stool with a bottle of liquor at his feet. Here is an eyewitness account:

"Selections in the sick blocks were an everyday affair. On the other hand an incredible panic gripped the prisoners when after evening roll call *Lagersperre* was announced and there arrived at the baths a group of SS men including *Lagerführer* Baer, the *Arbeitsdients, SS-Untersturmführer* Sell, and Kaduk... At a sign from the block senior we set off at a brisk trot in single file so that the eyes of the SS could rest for a moment on each of us. We had to be very careful, as the boards under the out-of-order showers were unevenly laid, which meant that it was easy to sprain an ankle and fall. Tripping or falling meant that one was immediately placed among those doomed to die. The SS devoured us with an avid gaze. They were looking for victims. The more the better. After the inspection, during which we ran the entire length of the bathhouse, we fell in in the avenue of birches near the wire. The block senior again counted the number of prisoners. Of our block six of our comrades remained in the bathhouse, doomed to the gas chamber or a phenol injection. We experienced terrible moments. The effect on some was to make them lose all their energy, while others were seized with euphoria. Back in the block Adolf could not believe that he had passed the ordeal. He tried to run across the room at the same speed as he had in the baths, and tripped where there was no obstacle. He kept touching his swollen legs, stroking them lovingly and repeating over and over: *'Mein Gott, mein lieber Gott. Wie habe ich das fertig gebracht?'* (My God, how did I manage it). He then walked naked about the room as if to reassure himself that he was still among the living. He rejoiced like a child receiving an unexpected present and made everyone admire him for looking like a young god. In October that same year we had to go once again through such a test of strength and nerves. This time Adolf did not come back with us..."[33]

Selections in the women's camp were usually made while the commandos were returning from work or during the so-called general roll calls. For this purpose the women walking in their heavy clogs were ordered to run for about fifteen meters. Those who ran too slowly were plucked from the ranks by SS men with the crooks of their walking sticks and placed to one side. In the event of the gas chambers being busy, they were put in Block 25, which was isolated from the rest of the camp. It had barred windows and the only entrance was a permanently guarded gate in the wall that surrounded the courtyard. The weeping and wailing of women waiting for death could be heard, as they stretched their arms out through the grating in supplication, begging for a mug of water. But no one was allowed even to approach this block. The loading of the

---

[33] Franciszek Stryj, *W cieniu krematoriów*. Katowice 1960, pp. 225—226.

victims as they pleaded for their lives onto lorries was done with the greatest brutality. Defending themselves desperately, the women were swung by their arms and legs and hurled into the lorries. The dead were thrown in together with the living.

In the men's camp at Brzezinka, the same function was filled by Block 7. There the seriously ill were assembled, not only from that camp but also from the main camp. The block held on average 1,200 prisoners. A litre of soup had to be divided up between from three to five prisoners. Bread was almost never issued. For whole days at a time the inmates would be made to stand in front of the block, and often even at night as well. They were beaten and murdered by drunken SS men. When the lorries came to take them to the gas chambers, Dantesue scenes took place. The immates tried to hide, anywhere at all, until the lorries went away. They were found buried under refuse, under the straw on the bunks, in every nook and cranny of the block. When they were finally hustled onto the lorries, some became apathetic while others tried to escape on they way by leaping from the moving vehicle. There were times when the doomed victims sang patriotic songs and hymns. A profoundly moving impression was made on the other prisoners by a transport of Frenchwomen singing the *Marseillaise* with strong voices as they were driven to the gas chamber. Such scenes became fixed in the memory of many prisoners, as each day they followed the lorries with their eyes until they disappeared through the gates of the crematorium, where the final act in the tragedy was played out. This fate was intended to remain forever the secret of the executioners, and so no doubt it would have been were it not for the miraculous survival of a handful of former members of the *Sonderkommando*. Of the final moments of those selected for death the former prisoner Dr. Miklós Nyiszli, who on the orders of Dr. Menegele carried out post mortems in a specially equipped dissecting room in crematorium II, writes:
"From my room two large grated windows screened with green mosquito netting look out onto the courtyard. Every day, about seven in the evening, a lorry drives through the crematorium gate. It brings some seventy to eighty men or women for liquidation. The day's batch selected from the camp. They come here from the huts and the hospitals. They are for the most part inmates of the camp of many years or at least many months standing, who have no illusions as to their lot. When the lorry drives in through the gate, the whole courtyard becomes filled with the dreadful cries of those awaiting death. Those chosen for death know that there is no escape from the shadow of the crematorium chimney. They no longer have the strength even to jump from the lorries. The SS guards shout and urge them on. The NCO driving the lorry loses patience. He gets back behind the wheel and starts the motor. The back of the lorry begins to rise slowly and spills people onto the ground. The sick, half-dead,

fall on their heads, faces, on top of one another, onto the concrete. A terrible cry is raised to the heavens, they writhe convulsively on the ground. A terrible scene... The *Sonderkommando* is already tearing the victims' clothes off and piling them up in the courtyard. They carry the unfortunates into the boiler room where in front of the hearth *Oberscharführer* Muhsfeld is waiting for them. Today it is his turn. He is wearing rubber gloves and holds a gun in his hand. They place before him people who — one after the other — fall to the ground dead, making room for the next. In the space of a few minutes Muhsfeld has 'bumped off' all eighty — that was what he used to say: *umgelegt*. Half an hour later all that remained of them was a handful of ashes." [34]

In the periods when epidemics were raging in the camp, not tens but hundreds of prisoners were killed in the gas chambers. On 29 August 1942 the newly appointed garrison doctor Kurt Uhlenbrock ordered the gassing of all those suffering from typhus, including those reconvalescing in the camp hospital. On that occasion 746 prisoners were taken from the hospital and killed in the gas chambers.

On 11 and 12 July 1944 during the liquidation of the family camp BIIb at Brzezinka at first about 3,000 and next about 4,000 people were killed. On 2 August, in connection with the liquidation the Gypsy camp at Brzezinka, 2,897 Gypsy men, women and children were gassed. This was the last batch of the over 20,000 Gypsies brought to the camp since February 1943. Apart from a few who had been released or sent to other camps, all the rest had died of hunger and disease.

Death in the gas chambers was also the lot of many former residents of the Zamość region who had been brought here following the evictions which had initiated the liquidation of the last area where Poles who had been removed from other parts of the country had been allowed to settle, which area had previously been the General Government.

Gassing was also the fate of prisoners from the branch camps for whom visiting SS doctors, following inspections of the sick bays, did not see any hope of a speedy return to work. In this way Dr. Horst Fischer, (acting) camp doctor for *KL Auschwitz III*, between November 1943 and January 1945, se'ected between 1,300 and 1,600 prisoners in the subcamps of *Neu-Dachs* at Jaworzno, *Eintrachthütte* at Świętochłowice, *Janina-Grube* at Libiąż and *Jawischowitz* at Jawiszowice. Selections in the subcamps were also made by SS orderlies authorized by him. The number selected at any one time ranged from a dozen to a hundred. In the largest subcamps, such as *Buna* at Monowice or *Neu-Dachs* at Jaworzno, it

---

[34] Miklós Nyiszli, *Pracownia doktora Mengele, Wspomnienia lekarza z Oświęcimia*. Warsaw 1966, pp. 96—97. (Eng. edition: *Auschwitz. A Doctor's Eyewitness Account*. New York 1960).

might even come to several hundred. For example on 18 January 1944 in the subcamp of *Neu-Dachs* 254 prisoners were selected, of whom by 3 February four had died, three had been crossed off the selection list, and the remaining 247 had been gassed in *KL Auschwitz II*.

In the largest of the Auschwitz branch camps, *KL Monowitz*, attached to the IG Farben works, in the years 1942—43 selections were carried out regularly once a fortnight, more rarely thereafter. As a result of them in the period between November 1942 and December 1944 over 8,000 prisoners were transferred mainly to *KL Auschwitz II* at Brzezinka, the rest to *KL Auschwitz I*.

The place of those selected was taken by fresh arrivals of strong and healthy prisoners. The firms employing prisoners regarded this kind of constant turnover as a way of maintaining a proper level of productivity. Indeed productivity was dealt with by relevant clauses of contracts concerning the hiring out of prisoner labour. In a contract dated 26 April 1944 between SS-WVHA and the firm of Ost-Maschinenbau GmbH of Sosnowiec, it is clearly stated in clause 4: "Sick prisoners will be taken back to the concentration camp at Oświęcim should their illness prove not to have a transient nature and no return to work can be expected." [35]

An additional guarantee of the system of labour turnover functioning effectively was the principle of financial calculation used. Most firms paid the camp only for the days actually worked by the prisoners. Thus if a prisoner fell ill, the state treasury, on whose behalf the camp was paid, bore a loss. The removal of those who were sick and unfit to work from the subcamps was in the interests of both sides.

There were instances of representatives of the firms themselves taking part in selections, pointing out prisoners for removal from the subcamp. Sometimes they made their own vehicles available to the camp for this purpose. One such case was testified to by Stanisław Pluta, who was employed as a driver in the refinery at Trzebinia:

"On the order of my dispatcher I took my lorry to the camp at Trzebionka, where 15 sick or emaciated Jewish prisoners were loaded onto it. I took these prisoners and an escort of SS men to the concentration camp at Brzezinka. After setting them down at the camp, I took on a dozen or so other healthy prisoners from Brzezinka whom I took to the camp at Trzebionka." [36]

The prisoners selected were generally killed straight away in the gas chambers or kept for a while in provisional accommodation in the men's

---

[35] Voivodship State Archives in Katowice. Zespół *Berghütte*, sygn. 25—11, pp. 6—6a.
[36] Akta Okręgowej Komisji Badania Zbrodni Hitlerowskich w Krakowie (Documents of the Cracow Regional Commission for the Investigation of Nazi Crimes), sygn. Ds 18/67.

hospital at Brzezinka. In his memoirs the former prisoner Juliusz Ganszer writes of this as follows:

"One day they brought us [at the hospital camp at Brzezinka — F.P.] a whole group of gaunt and haggard prisoners from the surrounding mining camps. They were locked up in the *Waschraum* where they were kept for three nights and two days. The block senior of the *Waschraum* was Staszek Paduch. Heedless of the risk he was running, together with me he got a barrel of soup to them. In our block there were a lot of Poles who received parcels, so there was soup left over. As we rolled the barrel towards the *Waschraum* which Paduch had opened, our nostrils were assailed by a stale stench. The doomed naked inmates were heating the cold concrete shower room with the warmth of their bodies. Some were praying aloud, others were making speeches. They all fell upon the soup. The next day they were all taken away to be gassed." [37]

Throughout the almost five years of the camp's existence about 4,000,000 people lost their lives as a result of disease, execution and mass gassing, including 340,000 of the over 400,000 men, women and children registered in the camp.

IV. AT THE SOURCES OF NEW CONCEPTS IN EXTERMINATION

1. STERILIZATION EXPERIMENTS

The Auschwitz camp was not only a huge "death factory", it also fulfilled the function of a laboratory for the development of new crimes that would embrace not millions but tens of millions of people. Because the capacity of the gas chambers and crematoria did not, as it transpired, correspond to the scale of the intended murders, medical science was called upon to help. Professor Carl Clauberg and Dr. Horst Schumann were entrusted with the task of developing, on the basis of experiments conducted on prisoners, methods of mass sterilization of those nations which the Nazis had marked down for biological extermination. The chief of Himmler's personal staff, Rudolf Brandt, testified as follows during the trial of the Nazi doctors at Nuremberg.

"Himmler was extremely interested in the development of a secret and rapid method of sterilization which could be used against the ene-

---

[37] APMO. Zespół "Wspomnienia", t. 2, k. 379.

mies of the German Reich, such as Russians, Poles and Jews. It was expected that in this way the enemy could be not only defeated but also destroyed. The labour of sterilized persons could be used by Germany while their fertility would have been removed. Mass sterilization was a constituent part of Himmler's racial theory. For this reason a particularly large amount of time and labour was devoted to these experiments." [38]

This is also confirmed by the former commandant of the Auschwitz camp, Rudolf Höss, who testified at his trial in Warsaw:

"From my conversations with Clauberg and the RSHA functionaries Thomas and Eichmann, I know that Himmler intended to use Clauberg's methods to liquidate and destroy biologically the Polish and Czech nations. He took the view that both these nations should be removed from the territories they occupied, which in his opinion belonged organically to the German living space." [39]

Originally Himmler proposed that Clauberg conduct his experiments at the women's concentration camp at Ravensbrück. However at the request of Clauberg, who during the war had been conducting a gynaecological clinic at Chorzów, he was allowed to use *KL Auschwitz* for this purpose, where since 26 March 1942 a women's section had also been in existence. The experiments, begun in 1942 and initially conducted at Brzezinka, were continued in the main camp at Oświęcim in Block 10 which had been specially vacated for this purpose.

The aim of Clauberg's experiments was to find a quick and reliable method of mass sterilization of women. An essential premise of these experiments was the provision that the persons sterilized should not be aware of the fact. The technique of the sterilization operation consisted in causing inflammation of the woman's generative organ producing scabbing and occlusion of the oviducts. Clauberg's task was to try out the chemical substances which lent themselves best to this purpose and which could be introduced into the oviducts under the guise of, for example, conducting a gynaecological examination.

Clauberg chose for his experiments female prisoners between the ages of 20 and 30 who had already had children. The preliminary phase of the experiment was to establish the patency of the oviducts. Clauberg would place the woman being experimented on in a gynaecological chair, introduce a contrast medium into the oviducts and follow its progress by X-ray. In the event of a positive result he would introduce an indeterminate substance similar to formalin to the oviducts, which caused in-

---

[38] Jan Sehn, *Zbrodnicze eksperymenty sterylizacyjne Carla Clauberga*, in: *Zeszyty Oświęcimskie*, 1958, no. 2, p. 8.
[39] APMO. *Höss Trial*, t. 21, k. 136.

flammation. He would then conduct renewed tests every week or fortnight. Usually after six weeks had elapsed all women showed occlusion of the oviducts, and hence sterility.

Clauberg's assistants were the SS sanitary orderly Binning and Dr. Johann Gebel, a representative of the concern Schering-Werke which made the chemical substances used for infecting and incidentally took advantage of Dr. Clauberg's experiments to try out new contrast media. These extremely painful tests were sometimes accompanied by violent haemorrhaging from the reproductive tract and even brought about collapse.

The first stage of his experiments was summed up by Clauberg in a letter to Himmler of 7 June 1943:

"If my research continues to yield such results as it has so far, and there are no grounds for supposing it will not, it will not be long before I am able to report that one experienced doctor in an appropriately equipped clinic and assisted by a staff of ten medical auxiliaries... will most likely be able to sterilize in the course of a day several hundred or even a thousand persons." [40]

In the prisoner employment statistics of *KL Auschwitz* for 1943 prisoners subjected to experiments appear under the heading of *Häftlinge für Versuchszwecke*. For example on 1 May 242 female prisoners (excluding nursing personnel) figured under this heading, while on 1 June there were 225 and on 1 October, 394. Fluctuations in the number of women destined for experimental purposes (e.g. on 2 June 225 persons were listed and on 3 June only 136, a loss of 89) and the depositions of former prisoners indicate that some of the women subjected to experiments died or were killed, after which post mortems were carried out. According to Alter Feinsilber (Stanisław Jankowski), who was employed in the cremation of bodies in crematorium II: "Every week the dissected bodies of women arrived from Block 10." [41]

The aim of the experiments conducted by Dr. Horst Schumann was identical: the development of methods of quick mass sterilization. By contrast with Clauberg, who carried out experiments exclusively on women, Schumann experimented chiefly on men. Schumann's method consisted in depriving people of their generative capacities by strong irradiation with X-rays of the testicles in the case of men, and of the ovaries in the case of women. In the course of the experiments the time and intensity of the irradiation were altered in order to obtain optimal indices, while at the same time in the case of some persons both genital organs were irra-

---

[40] Nuremberg document NO-212; Reimund Schnabel, *Macht ohne Moral. Eine Dokumentation über die SS.* Frankfurt/Main 1957, p. 274.
[41] *Amidst a Nightmare of Crime*, p. 43.

diated and in the case of others only one. In order to establish the efficacy of this treatment the irradiated organs were removed by operation and subjected to laboratory tests. The experiments conducted by Schumann from November 1942 to April 1944 did not yield the expected results. On the other hand the burns suffered as a result of the irradiation and castration operations left the persons subjected to experiments to extensive and painful sores which were slow to heal. Few prisoners survived these experiments. Some died as a result of their injuries, while others were killed by phenol injections or by gassing as unfit to work. After submitting to Hitler's chancellery in April 1944 a report on the results of his experiments, Schumann transferred his work from Block 30 of the women's camp at Brzezinka (BIa) to *KL Ravensbrück* where he continued his experiments on Gypsy children.

2. OTHER PSEUDOMEDICAL EXPERIMENTS

If the premises of Clauberg's and Schumann's experiments are to be sought in the Nazi policy of exterminating alien peoples held to be hostile, the experiments of another medical criminal, Dr. Josef Mengele, were inspired by a pro-natal policy conducted in relation to the German people. Dr. Mengele had to find an answer to the question of how to increase the fertility of the German population to a degree corresponding to the needs of the large-scale plan to settle the occupied territories of eastern Europe with Germans. He was interested in the problem of twins and the physiology and pathology of dwarfism. His experiments were carried out on monozyggotic twins (mainly children), dwarfs and persons crippled from birth, who were sought out among the transports arriving at the camp.

The course of the experiments conducted by Dr. Mengele can be divided into two stages. Stage one embraced every kind of test to which a living human being can be subjected, i.e. of the organs of sight and hearing, of the blood, every conceivable measurement of the skull, and of height. On the orders of Mengele the woman prisoner Dina Gottliebová of Prague made comparative sketches of heads, auricles, noses, mouths, hands and feet. Blood transfusions between twins were also carried out and X-ray photographs taken. Stage two involved comparative analyses of internal organs carried out during post-mortems. The low likelihood of both twins dying simultaneously would make such analyses impossible in normal circumstances. In the camp hundreds of such comparative analyses were carried out by Dr. Mengele on twins whom he killed for this purpose with phenol injections. In the conduct of his experiments Mengele collaborated with the *Institut für Rassenbiologische und Anthropologische Forschungen* (Institute for Race-biological and Anthropological Research) in Berlin whither he sent the more interesting anatomical specimens for closer analyses. The findings returned from Berlin were kept together with the entire documentation of the experiments in files which were kept for each individual.

Other experiments were also conducted in the camp. In the years 1941-44 Drs. Helmuth Vetter, Friedrich Entress, Edward Wirths and Fritz Klein carried out on prisoners pharmacological experiments, the purpose of which was to try out new medicines not yet brought into general use. They bore such cryptonyms as "B-1012", "B-1034", "3382", or names like "Rutenol".

These experiments were carried out chiefly on persons suffering from typhus, consumption or phlegmon, and more rarely from erysipelas, trachoma or other diseases. They were conducted not only on persons who were already sick, but on healthy people who had been specially infected, for example by intravenous injection in the case of typhus. The medicines to be tested were administered in the form of tablets, granules, injections or enemas. Some of them caused vomiting or bloody diarrhoea. Frequently the experiment contributed to the death of the patient, as none of the preparations used showed any healing properties, while some were downright harmful. Despite the decidedly negative results, the doctors experimenting on behalf of the pharmaceutical firms continued their tests, while at the same time withholding other, well-known and effective medicines. The correspondence between the commandant of the camp and the pharmaceutical firm of Bayer concerning the sale of 150 female prisoners for experimental purposes has survived. After the setting of a price of 170 marks a head (the camp had originally asked for 200) the deal was finalized, as can be seen from a letter from Bayer to the commandant of *KL Auschwitz*, which contains the passage: "We have received a consignment of 150 women. Despite their emaciated state we consider them appropriate. We shall keep you informed of the course of the experiments." A later letter contained the information: "Experiments have been completed. All the persons died. We shall soon be getting in touch with you concerning a new consignment." [42]

Another doctor who carried out experiments in the camp and who, like Mengele, killed his victims, was Johann Paul Kremer. He conducted research into yellow atrophy of the liver. Even when a patient suspected of this disease was already stretched out on the dissecting table, he would question him about the details of his condition before killing him.

In 1944 a doctor called Emil Kaschub carried out experiments in the camp for the Wehrmacht. He would rub toxic substances into the upper

---

[42] Nuremberg document NI-7184 (quoted in Jan Sehn, *Obóz koncentracyjny Oświęcim-Brzezinka (Auschwitz-Birkenau)*. Warsaw 1964, pp. 80—84.

and lower limbs of healthy prisoners, as a result of which painfully suppurating sores would appear. The results of his observations, documented with photographs, were supposed to furnish comparative material to aid in unmasking persons trying to evade military service by self-inflicted injuries.

Also for the Wehrmacht, the SS doctors Victor Capesius, Bruno Weber and Werner Rhode tried out on prisoners the effects of an unknown liquid which caused the death of some of the prisoners who drank it. The idea in this case was to find a drug which, by making them lose control over their behaviour, would induce POWs to betray military secrets.

Dr. Eduard Wirths conducted tests and operations on women suspected of having tumours.

Prisoners of the Auschwitz camp were also used to furnish anatomical exhibits. In 1943 the camp authorities delivered to the anatomical institute at Strasbourg, whose director was Professor August Hirt, 115 specially selected prisoners (79 Jews, two Poles, four prisoners from Central Asia and 30 Jewesses) in order to supplement the collection of skeletons being assembled there.[43]

The gas chambers and crematoria were the most durable buildings to be erected in the concentration camp of Auschwitz-Birkenau. They also, together with the planned Crematorium VI, which was to exceed all its predecessor in size and capacity, were an indication of the camp's intended development. In order to obliterate the traces of the crimes committed, the Nazis blew them up. But to this day the reinforced concrete ruins constitute a grim memorial to the four million victims of Nazi genocide.

---

[43] Note by *SS-Standartenführer* Wolfram Sievers to Adolf Eichmann of 23 June 1944. APMO. Proces przeciwko członkom załogi SS oświęcimskiej przed Najwyższym Trybunałem Narodowym w Krakowie (Trial of the Members of the Auschwitz Camp Staff Before the Supreme National Tribunal in Cracow). Hereafter *Proces załogi*, sygn. Dpr.—ZOp/1a, t. 37, k. 27.

Barbara Jarosz

The Resistance Movement in and around the Camp

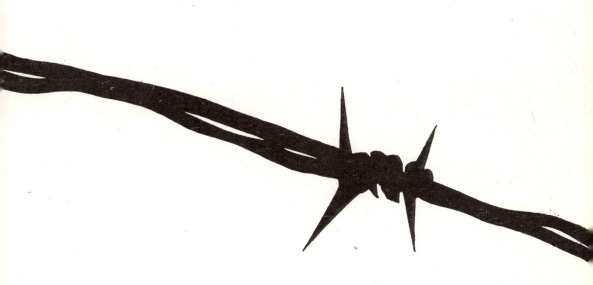

1. THE CONDITIONS IN WHICH THE CAMP RESISTANCE MOVEMENT WORKED

The Auschwitz camp was not only a place where prisoners were exterminated, it was also a place of struggle. Due to the specific conditions of the camp this struggle, which was waged by the resistance movement, differed from that waged on the other side of the barbed wire. The methods used by the SS — terror, hunger, terrible living conditions, hard labour, the constant threat of death, lack of contact with relatives — were intended to break the prisoners physically and mentally, to turn them into automata without a will of their own. Many prisoners however refused to yield and retained their human dignity. Never losing hope of regaining their freedom, they managed to oppose the criminal actions of the camp authorities by working to rescue their fellow prisoners and to expose and document the crimes committed in the camp.

Thanks to the activities of the camp resistance organization, the truth about *KL Auschwitz* was known even under the occupation not only throughout Poland but also abroad, despite the Nazis' efforts to shroud their crimes in total secrecy. For this purpose they developed a complete system of isolation. In adapting the military barracks situated in the outskirts of Oświęcim for a camp, they took into account many factors, such as the barracks' out-of-the-way location in the fork of the Soła and Vistula, outside the built-up area, making it easy to cut off from the outside world.

The camp was surrounded by a barbed-wire fence, and in addition around the camps at Oświęcim and Brzezinka a cordon of watchtowers was created, thus forming what was known as the closed area (*Sperrgebiet*). This area could only be entered by persons holding special passes issued by the camp commandant. This order also affected SS men of the camp staff and the members of their families.

Another very important element in the system of isolation was the eviction of the inhabitants of the area surrounding the camp.*

Following the escape of Tadeusz Wiejowski on 6 July 1940, the HSSPF in Wrocław, *SS-Obergruppenführer* Erich von dem Bach-Zelewski issued on 18 July an order to conduct "in the immediate future with the parti-

---

* See pp. 19—21.

cipation of the SD and the security police an action aimed at clearing the entire area within a radius of five kilometres around the camp of suspect, work-shy rabble", [1] the motive for the issuing of such an order was the attitude of the local population, which had been described by Rudolf Höss as "fanatically Polish" and who were always ready to help the prisoners.

The order was carried out. All the inhabitants within a radius of five kilometres of the camp were evicted. Some of the buildings they left behind were demolished, the remainder were set aside as living quarters for the members of the SS staff and their families. Thus in addition to the barbed-wire fence and concrete wall, the system of watchtowers and the cordon of guard posts, the camp was further isolated by the belt of the SS estate (*SS-Siedlung*).

The Polish inhabitants of the neighbouring villages were also evacuated, their farms being taken over by *Volksdeutsche* imported from Romania. The area thus evacuated, measuring some 40 square kilometres, was called the camp zone of interest (*Interessengebiet*). It was filled to overflowing with SS units, gendarmerie and Gestapo.

Only some of the original inhabitants were left — the families of miners, railwaymen, craftsmen and other specialist workers — who were to constitute the labour force in German industrial enterprises and farms. These people were not very many, but they showed great patriotism and courage by risking their freedom and even their lives throughout the entire occupation to take active part in the resistance movement. Liaison between the local Polish population and the prisoners lasted throughout the period of the camp's existence. There also arose in the region adjacent to the camp political organizations and partisan groups which occupied themselves with getting help to the prisoners and contributed to the emergence and development of the resistance movement inside the camp.

2. THE EMERGENCE OF A CLANDESTINE MOVEMENT INSIDE THE CAMP

The activities of the camp resistance movement assumed various forms at various periods. In fact one may speak of its manifestations from the moment the first transport of prisoners arrived. In this initial period the activity of the resistance movement consisted in mutual assistance and the establishment of contacts with the population of the area adjacent

---

[1] APMO. Documents concerning the escape of Tadeusz Wiejowski, sygn. D-AuI-1/13, k. 25.

to the camp. This was possible because many prisoners went to work outside the camp, while on the site of the expanding camp various German firms employed Polish civilian workers. By these illegal channels the prisoners began to pass information to the outside. It is true that to begin with such information concerned only the prisoners' personal affairs, for example a prisoner's family would be informed of his whereabouts, or requests would be made for food and medicines. In the course of time the scope of the information smuggled out was broadened. Loose contact with civilians solidified into fixed contact routes along which travelled letters and goods. The latter included documents, copies of orders issued by the camp authorities, plans etc. To the camp by return post were sent food, medicines and explosives.

The emergence of permanent contact routes was undoubtedly connected with the development of clandestine organizations within the camp, in which many prisoners worked who before their arrest had represented various socio-political orientations.

The first organizations began to arise in the camp as early as the second half of 1940. In the autumn a group of the Polish Socialist Party (PPS) was formed. Its organizers and leaders had been active on the left of the party in the inter-war period. They were Stanisław Dubois (in the camp he was known by the name of Dębski and was shot on 21 August 1942) and Norbert Barlicki, who died in camp on 21 September 1941. Other members of the group were Adam Kuryłowicz, a PPS member, and Konstanty Jagiełło, a member of the Red Pioneers (Scouts) *. Later the group was also joined by peasant activists and communists, such as the Polish Communist Party (KPP) members Julian Wieczorek (died in camp 9 January 1943), Juliusz Rydygier and Stefan Bratkowski. This group was very cohesive and developed lively political activity and organized aid for fellow prisoners. Through the intermediary of civilian workers and organizations operating in the area adjacent to the camp it established liaison with organizations in Cracow and Warsaw, whither information from the camp was sent.

The professional soldiers were very active. In October 1940 Cavalry Captain Witold Pilecki (in camp under the name of Tadeusz Serafiński) organized a group which assumed the name of Military Organization Union (ZOW). The organization was based on the system of five-member cells. Its members included Edward Ciesielski, Lieutenant Kacperski, Captain Henryk Bartosiewicz and Cavalry Captain Włodzimierz Makaliński. The work of the group consisted mainly in organizing food, warm clothing, keeping up the prisoners' morale and spreading news from the outside.

---

* A mainly working-class youth organization (1926—39) which was under the ideological influence of the Polish Socialist Party.

Reports on the situation inside the camp were sent to Warsaw via escapers, such as Lieutenants Wincenty Gawron and Stefan Bielecki, who on the orders and with the help of the organization escaped from the camp on 16 May 1942, and Lieutenant Stanisław Jaster, who together with three other escapers succeeded in getting away by lorry on 20 June 1942.

Witold Pilecki, who was brought to the camp on 22 September 1940 having deliberately let himself be caught during one of the Gestapo's street round-ups in Warsaw, also escaped from the camp. The purpose of his escape was not to save his own life but to take out documents concerning Nazi crimes, to give the world an eyewitness account of the truth about the camp and to prepare with the help of the underground organizations a plan for recapturing the camp and liberating the prisoners. Before escaping from the camp he entrusted the leadership of his group to Major Zygmunt Bończa-Bohdanowski (shot at the Execution Wall on 11 October 1943) and Captain Henryk Bartosiewicz.

In February 1941 Colonel Kazimierz Rawicz (in camp under the name of Jan Hilkner and sent to *KL Mauthausen* in August 1942) founded the Union of Armed Struggle (ZWZ). The leadership was composed of Air-Force Colonel Teofil Dziama (shot in camp on 11 October 1943), Captain Tadeusz Paolone (in camp under the name of Lisowski, shot on 11 October 1943), Bernard Świerczyna, hanged in camp on 30 December 1944 following an unsuccessful escape attempt, and Captain Alfred Stössel.

In the wake of these organizations other military groups arose, such as that of Colonel Aleksander Stawarz (shot in camp on 16 June) and that of Cavalry Captain Włodzimierz Koliński. In spring 1942 in sector BIb at Brzezinka Colonel Jan Karcz organized a group to which belonged Czesław Ostańkowicz, Władysław Ostrowski, Janusz Krzywicki and Stanisław Grudziński, among others. The main aims of the group were to save prisoners in the hospital from the selections, extending protection to the prisoners in the penal company and organizing additional food. When Karcz was shot on 25 January 1943, the leadership of the group was assumed by Ostrowski. In March of the same year some of the members of this organization were sent in a transport to *KL Buchenwald* and the group practically ceased to exist.[2]

In autumn 1941 right-wing groups also became active, composed of former sympathizers of the National Democrats and the National Radical Camp, and created on the initiative of Professor Roman Rybarski (died in camp 6 March 1942) and the journalist Jan Mosdorf (shot in camp on 11 October 1943).

Towards the end of 1941 the ZWZ initiated a merging operation. Leadership of the new organization was assumed by Colonel Rawicz. The

---

[2] Account of Czesław Ostańkowicz. APMO. Zespół "Oświadczenia", t. 49, k. 65.

supreme organ was the Committee which was composed of several persons representing individual political and military groups. Besides Rawicz and Pilecki, the Committee included Rybarski as chairman, Dubois as vice-chairman, and Mosdorf representing the youth group. The Committee functioned until August 1942, i.e. until Rawicz's transfer to *KL Mauthausen*. Thereafter the command was assumed by Colonel Juliusz Gilewicz (shot in camp on 11 October 1943). Until October 1942 all groups, with the exception of that of Karcz and Koliński, subordinated themselves to a joint command. The organizational structure of the combined forces underwent a change. The old system of five-member cells was abandoned in favour of a division into battalions, companies and platoons, which had areas of operation assigned to them. The overall commander of the organized forces was Major Bończa-Bohdanowski, while the commander of the 1st Battalion was Captain Stanisław Kazuba, the commander of the 2nd Battalion was Captain Gött-Getyński, the commander of the 3rd Battalion was Captain Tadeusz Paolone, and the commander of the 4th Battalion was Captain Julian "Trzęsimiech."[3]

In 1943 the camp authorities launched a series of offensives against the resistance movement, as a result of which the military leadership was smashed. Scores of military and political activists were killed in mass executions (on 25 January 1943, 51 prisoners suspected of illegal activity directed against the SS were shot, and 54 on 11 October). Despite this resort to bloody repression, the SS authorities did not achieve their aim.

Two new centres of the resistance movement arose. One, of a left-wing character, was born in the main camp. It was composed of former members of the PPS, communists and persons without party affiliation, embracing both old and newly arrived prisoners. Its members included Józef Cyrankiewicz, Tadeusz Hołuj, Ludwik Rajewski, Stanisław Kłodziński, Adam Kuryłowicz and Lucjan Motyka. The second clandestine centre arose at Brzezinka. In 1943 there existed there a left-wing group which maintained contact with the organization at Oświęcim. In the hospital in sector BIIf a clandestine cell was organized by Dr. Alfred Fiderkiewicz. Its members included Henryk Korotyński, Tadeusz Borowski and Andrzej Kobyłecki. The group's main task was to save the sick inmates, especially important political leaders and academics. Attempts were made to get them additional food and medicines. Moreover propaganda work was carried on. Political information gained about the situation at the front was spread among the prisoners to give them courage and sustain their morale. Preparations were also made for self-defence in the event of an uprising breaking out in the camp or of an attempt by the SS to liquidate all the prisoners. In sector BIId a left-wing group was ac-

---

[3] Recollections of Witold Pilecki. APMO. Zespół "Wspomnienia", t. 1, k. 111.

tive, whose members included Konstanty Jagiełło, Zygmunt Balicki, Wincenty Rutkiewicz and Dawid Szmulewski. There was also in this sector a military group commanded by Aleksander Żytkiewicz, the leadership of which included Jan Dmochowski, Zygmunt Idziak, Stanisław Raczkowski and Zygmunt Majewski.[4] The members of these organizations were employed in various work commandos, which enabled them to move about all over the camp. They thus managed to maintain liaison between the cells in the men's and the women's camp. They passed food, medicines, letters and documents.

In the women's camp too there arose in summer 1943 an underground organization. The first group of five comprised Stanisława Rachwałowa, Antonina Piątkowska, Helena Hofman, Wiktoria Klimaszewska and Zofia Bratro.[5] Later other women prisoners joined: Anna Pawełczyńska, Maria Mazurkiewicz, Wanda Marossanyi, Maria Maniak and Wanda Jakubowska. The women maintained constant contact with the organization in the men's camp, to which they passed on information and documents. In spring 1944 the women's organization passed under the command of Żytkiewicz, and when in the middle of that year Żytkiewicz was transferred to Gross-Rosen his place as leader was taken by Colonel Władysław Smereczyński who had arrived from Majdanek.

Apart from the Polish underground, in the winter of 1942/43 national resistance groups arose in the camp. One of the first was an Austrian group which came into existence in 1942. Though small, it was very cohesive and active. It was mainly composed of communists, social democrats and former members of the International Brigades who already had a certain amount of experience and political sophistication — acquired in other camps or in the Spanish Civil War — when they came to *KL Auschwitz*. The core of the organization was composed by Ernst Burger, Hermann Langbein, Alfred Klahr (in camp under the name of Ludwig Lokmanis), Rudolf Friemel, Ludwig Vesely, Heinz Dürmayer and Ludwig Soswinski. They were particularly active in the camp hospital where many of them worked.

From 1942 a French group also existed. It was started by Georges Varennes, a communist and a schoolteacher by profession, who began to organize self-help among the French inmates. After his death at the end of 1942 his place at the head of the organization was taken by Roger Abada, Eugène Garnier and Roger Pelissou.[6] On 27 January 1943 there ar-

---

[4] Accounts of Aleksander Żytkiewicz and Zygmunt Idziak. APMO. Zespół "Oświadczenia", t. 67, k. 7 and t. 52, k. 23.
[5] Accounts of Zofia Bratro and Wiktoria Klimaszewska. APMO. Zespół "Oświadczenia", t. 15, k. 30 and t. 15, k. 1.
[6] Accounts of Roger Abada and Eugène Garnier. APMO. Zespół "Oświadczenia", t. 31, k. 120—136.

rived at the camp the first transport of French women political prisoners, who included Danielle Casanova, Marie Polizer, Raymonde Salez and Yvonne Blech. They joined in the work of the underground and established contact with the men's group. The women's organization was headed by Danielle Casanova (died in camp of typhus on 10 May 1943) and Marie Claude Vailland-Couturier.

A Belgian cell headed by a communist named Berliner collaborated with the French group.

The Russian group was both numerous and active. Its activities covered both Oświęcim and Brzezinka. The core of the organization in the main camp was constituted by Captain Viktor Ivanov, Pilot Officer Valentin Sitnov and Colonel Kuzma Kartsev. The group was headed by Alexander Lebedev and Fyodor Skiba. The group was represented in Brzezinka by Professor Ivan Mironov, Pyotr Mishyn, Mikhail Vinogradov, Vladimir Soroko and, from 1944, General Dimitri Karbyshev (who arrived at Oświęcim on 9 April 1944 from the camp at Majdanek and in the autumn was evacuated to Mauthausen where he died in February 1945) and Vladimir Degtarev. Women were also active. The organization was joined by Nina Guseva, Anna Trynda, Zhenya Sarycheva, Nina Kharlamova, Dr. Lyubov Alpatova and others.

In 1943 a German group arose composed of members of the Social Democratic and Communist parties and other anti-fascists who had spent years in German concentration camps. This group collaborated closely with the Austrian group. Its organizer was Bruno Baum. The German group included Karl Lill, Alfred Ponthius and Rudolf Göbel at Oświęcim, Horst Jonas at Brzezinka, Kurt Posener, Stefan Heymann and Ludwig Wörl at Monowice, and Orly Reichert, Judith Dürmayer and Gerda Schneider in the women's camp.

There was also a Czech group represented both at Oświęcim and Brzezinka. Its members included Emil Panevič, Dr. Jan Češpivy, Dr. Miloš Nedvěd, Igor Bistric, Karel Beran, Erich Kulka and Ota Kraus. Among the women should be mentioned the communist Hertha Sosvinská, Věra Foltýnová, Vlasta Kladivová, Zdenka Nedvédová and Dr. Sláva Klein.

The smallish Yugoslav group was composed mainly of former women partisans. It was organized by Norka Vuksaovič.[7] Other members of the group were Stefka Štibler, Jelena Vasiljevič, Zora Raković and Nada Čalič.

There was also a Jewish group in the *Sonderkommando*, whose leaders were Załmen Gradowski, Jankiel Handelsman and a man called Kamiński. It was composed of prisoners who worked in the crematorium and at the burning pits. This was one of the most endangered groups. In order to rid

---

[7] Account of Tadeusz Hołuj. APMO. Zespół "Oświadczenia", t. 37, k. 33.

themselves of witnesses to their crimes the SS camp authorities liquidated every so often the members of the *Sonderkommando*. To save itself this group raised on 7 October 1944 a rebellion during which one of the crematoria was destroyed. The rebellion ended, however, in a bloody massacre of the participants.*

The activity of all the national groups consisted above all in making it possible for the camp inmates to hold out, in providing material help in the form of medicines, food, clothing, in saving them from extermination, in organizing escapes and in collecting information about the situation in the camp.

It was in the interests of the camp resistance movement to coordinate the activity of the various national and Polish groups. From the beginning of 1943 at the initiative of the Austrian group negotiations were begun with the aim of combining into a general international organization. At a secret session in May 1943, a joint organization was formed under the name of the Oświęcim Fighting Group, or GBO (in Polish *Grupa Bojowa Oświęcim,* in German *Kampfgruppe Auschwitz).* It was headed by a Chief Committee whose members were Józef Cyrankiewicz, Tadeusz Hołuj, Ernst Burger and Hermann Langbein. When on 25 August 1944 Langbein was evacuated to the Neuengamme concentration camp, his place was taken by Heinz Dürmayer and Ludwig Soswinski, and after an unsuccessful escape attempt by Burger (who was hanged in camp on 30 December 1944) Bruno Baum joined the committee.

The basic organizational unit was the cell, and cells existed in the various commandos. The cells were combined in groups. Meetings of the leadership were held in the cellar of Block 4 where Ernst Burger was the registrar, or in the internee hospital, where there were many members of the organization and inmates collaborating with them.

The international organization was not joined by the Polish military groups. Not until 1944 was agreement and cooperation achieved, resulting in the creation of a joint Camp Military Council (RWO). In the coordinating group of the RWO the GBO was represented by Lucjan Motyka and Heinz Dürmayer, and the military group by Bernard Świerczyna and Mieczysław Wagner. The RWO was intended to deal with military matters, prepare cadres, form combat groups and assign them particular tasks. The activity of the GBO embraced only the main camp and Brzezinka. In Monowice there existed a separate organization with its own leadership whose members were Leon Stasiak, Stefan Heymann, Kurt Posener and Piotr Machura. There was however contact between the two organizations.

---

* See p. 119.

3. THE RESISTANCE MOVEMENT IN THE CAMP VICINITY

The resistance in the camp was able to exist and carry on its activities thanks to the development of underground organizations in the vicinity of the camp. The Union of Armed Struggle (ZWZ) arose in the winter of 1939 on the initiative of the reserve officers Mieczysław Jonkisz (pseudonym "Mietek"), Stanisław Matuszczyk, Stanisław Krępa-Trojacki (pseudonym "Trojacki") and Lieutenant Jan Wawrzyczek (pseudonyms "Marusza", "Danuta") of the regular army. In the spring of 1940 an Oświęcim Area arose with Alojzy Banaś ("Zorza") as commandant. The headquarters staff consisted of the couriers Stanisław Dembowicz ("Radom") and Antoni Szlachcic ("Laura"), the quartermaster Marian Feliks, the intelligence officer Maksymilian Niezgoda, the chaplain Father Władysław Grohs, the messengers Anna Kubisty and Jadwiga Dylik, as well as Stanisław Krępa-Trojacki and Jan Wawrzyczek. The Oświęcim Area was part of the Bielsko Inspectorate and was divided into four bases: Oświęcim (commander Jan Jakuczek), Kęty (Jan Barcik), Brzeszcze (Rudolf Wittek) and Zator (Roman Zaczyński).

In 1942 the ZWZ was renamed the Home Army (AK). In October that same year, as a result of treachery, the Germans arrested almost the entire headquarters staff of the AK Oświęcim Area. Those arrested were taken to prison in Mysłowice and sentenced to death by a summary court. They were shot in the Auschwitz camp on 25 January 1943. The new commandant of the Oświęcim Area was Józef Górkiewicz ("Górnik"). The quartermaster's department was taken over by Antoni Chowaniec ("Antoni") and intelligence by Franciszek Hoszek ("Beethoven"). Antoni Szlachcic continued to be courier, while the messengers were Zofia Gabryś ("Wera"), Bronisława Dłuciak ("Dzidka") and Waleria Kabaja.

The ZWZ/AK adopted two basic types of activity: one, defined as military action, was the conduct of armed struggle against the occupation forces; the other, defined as civil action, was the provision of assistance for the prisoners. Through the intermediary of Polish civilians employed inside the camp contact was established with the prisoners Stanisław Furdyna, Bernard Świerczyna and Antoni Wykręt. Via this channel information was obtained about the situation in the camp, transports etc. The news was then sent to the headquarters of the Silesian Region in Katowice. The executive organ of the civil action was the Committee for Aiding Political Prisoners in the Camp at Oświęcim. The work of the committee was directed by Helena Stupkowa ("Jadzia"). Those who worked with her included Wincencja Stolarska, Janina Kostecka, Maria Zębata, Michalina Gretka, Janina Kajtoch, Zofia Cicha and Julia Ilisińska. The committee engaged in the smuggling of medicines, food and clothing into the camp and acted as a correspondence channel for prisoners.

Armed struggle in the Oświęcim Area was conducted by partisan detachments. In 1941 the first ("Marusza") detachment arose in the region of Łęki and Jawiszowice under the command of Wawrzyczek. Two further detachments were created in 1942 in the vicinity of Kańczuga and Bielany under the command of Captain Jan Barcik ("Soła") and Sergeant Jan Jamroz ("Maczuga"). These detachments merged in 1943 to form the "Sosienki" detachment under the command of Wawrzyczek. The "Sosienki" detachment was extremely active, organizing escapes from the camp, conducting diversionary and sabotage operations and skirmishing with SS patrols. Scores of escaped prisoners from the camp found shelter in its ranks, including Stanisław Furdyna, Antoni Wykręt, Stanisław Zyguła, Jan Prejzner, Marian Szayer, Wincenty Ciesielczuk and Edward Padkowski. Because in the camp zone the partisans frequently appeared in the uniform of the SS or Wehrmacht, the commander of the SS garrison introduced a special system of control whereby all members of the SS camp staff and auxiliary service had to check one another's papers and give the password of the day.[8]

Besides the ZWZ/AK, the PPS also engaged in wide-ranging activities. In 1940 experienced socialist activists from the inter-war period began to lay the first organizational foundations on which in time strong clandestine centres were to be built. The organizers in Brzeszcze were Piotr Hałoń, Jan Nosal and Władysław Malik, in Oświęcim Jan Krzemień, and in Jaworzno Franciszek Mazur and Franciszek Kobielski. Initially the organization's tasks included political work, hiding people wanted by the Gestapo and carrying out acts of sabotage. When contact was established with the camp at Oświęcim, the main aim of PPS activity became bringing aid to the prisoners. The greatest role in this action was played by the Brzeszcze group, which mobilized whole families to take part in the work, such as the Hałoń, Golczyk, Pytlik, Nikiel, Gach and other families. In 1942 the ranks of the group were strengthened by the addition of young people who had been arrested in April 1940 and imprisoned for more than a year in the Dachau and Gusen camps. They now took over the leadership. Edward Hałoń ("Boruta") became head of the group. The core of the organization was constituted by Władysław Pytlik ("Birkut"), Emil Golczyk ("Jantar"), Bogusław Chmielewski ("Bogdan"), Marian Skubis ("Brom"), Marian Gach ("Alfons"), and the Nikiel brothers: Julian, Tadeusz, Franciszek and Wiktor. In 1944 the organization was joined by Konstanty Jagiełło ("Kostek", "Bezzębny"), Tomasz Sobański and Jerzy Tabeau, all of whom had escaped from the camp. Liaison with the camp was maintained by the couriers Danuta Bystroń and Natalia Szpak. Contacts between the PPS and the camp organization were improved after the

---

[8] *Standort-Sonderbefehl* of 7 November 1944. APMO. Proces załogi..., t. 39, k. 236.

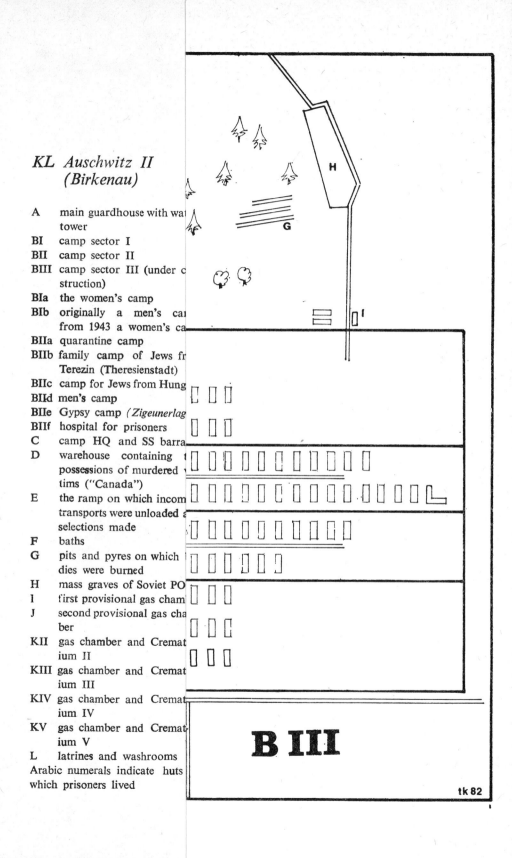

KL Auschwitz II (Birkenau)

- **A** main guardhouse with watch tower
- **BI** camp sector I
- **BII** camp sector II
- **BIII** camp sector III (under construction)
- **BIa** the women's camp
- **BIb** originally a men's camp, from 1943 a women's camp
- **BIIa** quarantine camp
- **BIIb** family camp of Jews from Terezin (Theresienstadt)
- **BIIc** camp for Jews from Hungary
- **BIId** men's camp
- **BIIe** Gypsy camp (*Zigeunerlager*)
- **BIIf** hospital for prisoners
- **C** camp HQ and SS barracks
- **D** warehouse containing the possessions of murdered victims ("Canada")
- **E** the ramp on which incoming transports were unloaded and selections made
- **F** baths
- **G** pits and pyres on which bodies were burned
- **H** mass graves of Soviet POWs
- **I** first provisional gas chamber
- **J** second provisional gas chamber
- **KII** gas chamber and Crematorium II
- **KIII** gas chamber and Crematorium III
- **KIV** gas chamber and Crematorium IV
- **KV** gas chamber and Crematorium V
- **L** latrines and washrooms

Arabic numerals indicate huts in which prisoners lived

establishment of permanent liaison with Edward Hałoń's brother Kazimierz, who was in the camp under the false name of Wrona. Kazimierz Hałoń through the intermediary of the civilian workers smuggled information and documents out of the camp. After his escape on 10 February 1943 this role was taken over by the prisoner Józef Róg. Deliveries to the camp on the other hand included, besides food and medicines, clandestine newspapers, explosives, and civilian clothing and wigs for prisoners preparing to escape. At Brzeszcze prisoners were hidden and looked after until they could be taken over the border to the General Government or to a partisan detachment, and documents were forged. The Brzeszcze PPS was the main intermediate base between the camp and the Regional Workers' Committee of the PPS in Cracow. Towards the end of 1944 the group fell apart. Already in the previous year Edward Hałoń had had to leave the area to avoid arrest. His place as leader was taken by Emil Golczyk, Marian Gach and Władysław Pytlik. In September 1944 they too left for Cracow, and the other members of the organization joined the partisans.

Also very active in the neighbouring villages were the members of the Peasant Party. Interrupted by the outbreak of the war, this party's activity began to reemerge in 1940, assuming new organizational forms. Armed detachments were created which originally bore the name of the Peasants' Guard ("Chłostra"), and from 1941 onwards were called the Peasant Battalions (BCh). The first district commandant of the BCh was Wojciech Jekiełek ("Żmija", "Łysy"). Besides the basic tasks of sabotaging the administrative acts of the occupation authorities and arousing the awareness of the population, the BCh, like other organizations, gave priority to helping prisoners from the camp. The former Peasant Party members found many willing helpers among those who had previously been aiding the prisoners on their own. Among those who made the largest contribution were Helena Płotnicka, Władysława Kożusznik, Irena Kahanek, Anna Szalbut, Zofia Zdrowak, Kazimierz Jędrzejowski, Piotr Jarzyna and Antoni Mitoraj. The first contacts with the camp were established through those prisoners who worked as surveyors or were employed in the market gardens in Rajsko: Kazimierz Jarzębowski, Edward Biernacki, Jan Winogroński and Janusz Skrzetuski-Pogonowski. Women and even children left parcels of food and medicines at night in specially prepared drops.

In 1943 the BCh suffered serious losses. In December 1942 Wojciech Jekiełek had been arrested in Osiek, and Anna Szalbut who had been with him was killed. Jekiełek managed to escape and went to Cracow. The leadership of the organization passed to Kazimierz Jędrzejowski ("Kazek") who was also arrested in October 1943 and taken to the prison at Mysłowice. Sentenced to death by the summary court, he perished in Auschwitz on 26 May 1944. A similar fate befell the devoted Helena Płotnicka. After her arrest in May 1943 she was sent to the camp at Brzezinka, where she died of typhus on 17 March 1944. In order to evade arrest, many individuals had to leave the area surrounding the camp, thus impairing the activity of the BCh.

Despite extremely difficult operating conditions and the particular implacability of the Nazis in combatting the communists, operations to assist the prisoners were also made by cells of the Polish Workers' Party (PPR). Rallying in its ranks the members of such organizations as the Association of Friends of the USSR, Hammer and Sickle etc., the Polish Workers' Party pointed out the necessity of waging armed struggle against the occupation forces and in 1942 created for this purpose its own fighting detachments, known as the People's Guard (GL), later renamed the People's Army (AL).

The partisan detachments which sprang up in the vicinity of the camp helped the prisoners in preparing escapes. For example two successful ecapes were organized in April 1944. The escapers were looked after by the Jarosław Dąbrowski Detachment of the GL, commanded by Stanisław Wałach ("Zdzich").

News of the various exploits of these detachments, not only in the vicinity of the camp but also in the Beskids and Silesia, filtered through to the camp and raised the spirits of thousands of prisoners who no longer felt alone in their struggle. The derailing of trains, the disruption of the road and rail network and the destruction of high-tension pylons disorganized transport and interrupted the work of the factories in which the Oświęcim prisoners were employed. All these actions not only caused material damage to the enemy, but created a sense of ever-present danger, which kept the SS at Oświęcim on edge.

Before May Day 1944 the Central Committee of the PPR called upon the members of its organizations to intensify sabotage actions. As a consequence the camp command issued a special order introducing a state of readiness in the SS guard detachments, additional patrols in the camp and the surrounding area, suspension of leave for members of the camp staff and intensified control of the Polish civilian workers.[9] Such strict orders show that the partisans constituted a force with which the SS had to reckon.

All the organizations operating in the vicinity of the camp, despite political differences, cooperated with one another as regards caring for prisoners. They frequently made use of the same contact routes and the assistance of the same persons or sources from which food, medicines and money for the prisoners were delivered.

---

[9] *Standort-Sonderbefehl* of 29 April 1944. APMO. Sygn. D-AuI-1/99.

Besides political organizations, charitable organizations also took part in actions in aid of the prisoners at Oświęcim. In 1940 the Cracow branch of the Polish Red Cross set up a Section for Aid to Prisoners of War, Evacuees and Political Prisoners. In the same year there arose the Main Shelter Council (RGO). This was a legal Polish organization based in Cracow which existed to help the Polish population of the General Government. It distributed food, clothing and money to the needy and evicted, and also sent parcels to camps and prisons. In March 1943, on the initiative of Teresa Lasocka-Estreicher, Dr. Helena Szlapak, Wojciech Jekiełek and Adam Rysiewicz, a committee called Aid to Concentration Camp Prisoners (PWOK) was created.

4. FORMS OF ACTIVITY OF THE CAMP RESISTANCE MOVEMENT

The activities carried on by the camp resistance movement embraced a wide field, including

(i) the organization of aid to the prisoners in the shape of medicines and food;

(ii) the documentation of the Nazi crimes committed against prisoners;

(iii) the preparing of escapes from the camp;

(iv) sabotage;

(v) political work;

(vi) attempts to get trusty posts fillend by political prisoners;

(vii) the liquidation of informers;

(viii) the preparation of an uprising in the camp.

In the first phase of *KL Auschwitz's* existence the most important task was to obtain additional food and medicines. The food rations issued to the prisoners were insufficient to meet the needs of the organism. Moreover it was not until the end of October 1942 that the central SS authorities allowed food parcels to be sent to the camp. * This order did not however affect all prisoners. Some of their food the prisoners had to "organize" from the warehouses of the SS, the warehouses containing possessions looted from the prisoners ("Canada"), the camp slaughterhouse and the dairy. Considerable quantities were obtained from the outside. The local population left parcels of food and medicines hidden in the places where the prisoners worked. In this action many women distinguished themselves, including Helena Płotnicka and Władysława Kożusznik of Przecieszyn, Maria Górecka and her daughter Wanda of Brzeszcze, Helena Stupkowa of Oświęcim, Janina Kajtoch and Janina Cicha of Babice. The amounts of

---

* See p. 76—77.

food provided ran into tens of kilograms, a fact to which the receipts testify. For example in one day of October 1941 in Andrzej Dusik's shop in Łęki 14.5 kilos of butter, 100 kilos of bread, 10.5 kilos of sugar and 4 kilos of margarine were given out.

The system of rationing introduced by the occupation authorities made the delivery of food to the prisoners difficult. For this reason the political organizations operating in the vicinity of the camp and the charitable organizations of Cracow went into action. In December 1940 the Section for Aid to Prisoners of War, Evacuees and Political Prisoners sent to the camp 1,000 Christmas parcels, and in January 1941 they sent 2,500 parcels. The RGO, PWOK and scouting organizations in Silesia also busied themselves with aid for the prisoners.

The camp organization, realizing that the country had difficulties with food, that food sent to the prisoners was taken from the mouth of the relatives who sent it, decided to seek another source of aid. In mid-1943 lists were drawn up of the prisoners in the camp, giving name, camp number and block, and sent via the contact routes to Cracow and thence to the International Red Cross in Geneva. In a letter smuggled out of the camp dated 20 June 1943 Stanisław Kłodziński wrote:

"It is necessary that our addresses should get to be known abroad en masse, for it is a question of proving to the Germans that the whole world knows about Oświęcim. But the thing must be done on a mass scale, we must send 200 or 300 of our addresses to each country. It is a matter of a mass action, so that they will not be able to call us to account for it. At the same time it would be a good thing also to give the addresses of Germans in the camp, Czechs and others, e.g. Soviet communists. In short the aim is to have the camp suddenly snowed under with international parcels..." [10]

This action produced positive results, and parcels from the International Red Cross began to arrive at the camp. And although most of these parcels were requisitioned by the SS, the fact that the names and numbers of prisoners in the camp were known abroad showed that the secrecy which the camp authorities had so assiduously tried to maintain had been broken. *

Medicines were also delivered to the camp in sizeable quantities. The official allocations of medicaments for the sick were, in the conditions which prevailed in the camp, the proverbial drop in the ocean. Seventy per cent of medicines administered had been illegally supplied. Some of them had been smuggled in by prisoners working in the external commandos. Many smuggled letters have survived containing lists of needed

---

[10] APMO. *Mat. oboz. Ruchu Oporu*, t. I, k. 33.
* See p. 77.

medicines and confirming receipt thereof. For example in a smuggled letter of 31 July 1942 the prisoner Janusz Skrzetuski-Pogonowski confirmed: "I have received about 1,000 ampules of various medicines (Coramine, oligipiratum, calc., gluc. et.). All delivered to the sick bay in KL Au." [11] Another prisoner, Edward Biernacki, writes: "In the months of June, July and August I brought into the camp hospital about 7,500 cm^3 of injections... and 70 series of anti-typhus injections." [12]

Some medicines were sent to the camp by post. In 1944 there passed through the camp sorting house parcels weighing five to ten kilograms addressed to prisoners who were no longer living. By clandestine channels they found their way into the hands of internee doctors. In a smuggled letter of 20 January 1944 Stanisław Kłodziński explains:

"...You send from Ośw. or e.g. from Zator a well-wrapped parcel with drugs addressed to a fictitious name: Häftl. Nr. 71825 Śliwiński Stephan — geb. 12.1.1912 Bl. 25 St. 6 KL Auschwitz Post 2 O/S — and we at our post office collect it without it being checked. In the event of a leak the risk is small. Send such parcels twice a week." [13]

An important transfer point in the smuggling of medicines into the camp was the chemist's shop belonging to Maria Bobrzecka in Brzeszcze. Certain amounts were also delivered by chemists in Oświęcim town, Kęty, Chrzanów and by the RGO.

The requirements for food and medicines were enormous. It was impossible to deliver by illegal routes parcels for the thousands of persons detained in the camp. Nevertheless even that modest assistance in the conditions of the time had enormous significance and saved the lives of many prisoners.

Another and very important form of the resistance movement's activity was the gathering of evidence of the crimes committed by the SS and sending it out of the camp. The most important documents sent from the camp included:

(i) the bunker books, containing the names of prisoners detained in the cellars of Block 11 and information about their fate, which were sent out by the block registrar Jan Pilecki;

(ii) the morgue books, i.e. lists of the camp numbers of prisoners who died or were killed by phenol injections;

(iii) lists of women prisoners who died or were gassed, containing about 10,000 names;

(iv) three photographs taken illegally in camp in summer 1944, showing

---

[11] APMO. *Mat. oboz. Ruchu Oporu*, t. I, k. 5.
[12] *Ibid*, t. I, k. 10.
[13] *Ibid*, t. II, k. 58.

women being herded to the gas chamber and the burning of bodies on pyres;

(v) plans of the crematoria and gas chambers, stolen in 1944 from the office of the *SS-Bauleitung* by women prisoners employed there: Krystyna Horczak (Poland) and Věra Foltýnová and Valéria Vlanová (Czechoslovakia);

(vi) numbered charts of transports of male and female prisoners brought to the camp. Copies of the original transport lists were made by prisoners working in the reception office of the Political Department.

Besides documents, reports were also smuggled out of the camp in which exact figures were given concerning the number of prisoners confined in the camp, the number of transports arriving and departing, the names of prisoners who were shot, and the names of SS men of the camp staff. Living conditions were described, and dates and routes of escapes fixed. For example, in a letter smuggled out on 16 September 1944, entitled "The Hangmen of Oświęcim", the names and descriptions of a dozen or so of the worst SS criminals were given, with the commandant Rudolf Höss heading the list. The beginning of this letter, addressed to Teresa Lasocka-Estreicher ("Tell") of Cracow, who received most of the correspondence from the camp, read:

"Tell

"We are sending an outline description of the Oświęcim hangmen. All the facts given are authentic beyond all doubt. It is highly desirable that London should announce as soon as possible the passing of death sentences on them." [14]

The data contained in the reports were obtained by prisoners employed in the camp's various administrative offices, in the main registration room, the camp hospital and the offices of the Political and Employment Departments. At the risk of their lives they made copies of documents, plans and reports. The carrying out by the SS of body searches forced the prisoners to find appropriate techniques of concealing and passing on letters. Thus they were concealed in specially prepared candles and inserted in cigarettes, fountain pens, keys, sweets etc. Attempts were made to reduce the format of the letters to a minimum and cigarette paper was often used. Letters containing important information were written in code and signed with pseudonyms: J., Tor., or Cyr. for Józef Cyrankiewicz, and St. or Stakło for Stanisław Kłodziński. Both letters and documents were sent from the camp via permanent contact routes. The role of intermediaries between the organization in the camp and those outside was played by civilians employed inside the camp: Stanisław Mordarski, Józef

---

[14] *Ibid*, t. VII, k. 462.

Cholewa and Franciszek Walisko, as well as Helena Datoń who served in the SS canteen in *Haus* 7. The prisoners passed letters and documents to them, and they in turn delivered them to Brzeszcze. Thence they were forwarded to Cracow by the Kornaś family in Spytkowice or Aniela Kieres in Chrzanów.

In 1944 the organization acquired yet another contact route which led through Maria Stromberger, an Austrian nurse working in the hospital for SS men. Despite the fact that she belonged to the camp staff, Nurse Stromberger became a member of the fighting underground. This route was used to send out larger items — books and documents. Nurse Stromberger either passed them on to Helena Datoń or herself took them to Brzeszcze or Chrzanów. To the camp in turn she brought newspapers, medicines and explosives. Stanisław Kłodziński wrote to Cracow in a smuggled letter of 26 September 1944: "Be in contact with the nurse as frequently as possible — this route is certain and swift — we can always collect." [15]

In summer 1944 an SS man called Frank, the *Blockführer* of Block 5, was also won over. To begin with he gave the prisoners information about the number of guard companies, SS armaments, and new orders issued by the camp command. Later he was entrusted with the function of contact man. In secret messages Frank was called "the ambassador".

"On Friday about 7.30 our ambassador is coming to the same meeting place where he once met Jantar and will bring the plans which, because of their bulk, we don't want to send by the normal channel." [16]

Some of the news that was sent to Cracow was printed on a clandestine press. Others, marked "London", were sent to Britain to be broadcast by radio. Certain items could not be published at once in view of the danger to the prisoners who had provided them.

In view of the approach of the eastern front and the liberation by the Soviet Army of the camp at Majdanek, the SS authorities began to prepare for the liquidation of the camp. Plans were drawn up for removing all trace of the crimes that had been committed. One was known as the Moll Plan, which envisaged the murder of all the prisoners and the obliteration of the camp buildings, especially the extermination installations. The plan was the work of the well-known criminal *Hauptsturmführer* Otto Moll. In order to implement it he demanded motorized SS detachments, artillery, six aircraft and an appropriate number of men to tidy up the site and remove the last traces of where the camp had been. On this occasion the camp organization sent the following report to Cracow:

"Tell

---

[15] APMO. *Mat. oboz. Ruchu Oporu*, t. II, k. 164.
[16] Letter from Stanisław Kłodziński. Smuggled out on 7 September 1944. *Ibid*, t. II, k. 142.

"The matter would be agreed upon completely, as Höss is prepared to furnish these technical means. The thing is held up for the time being because those who are to carry out the order are demanding it in writing, and it is one of these jobs that are done in confidence, without written records. This is at the moment the greatest attempt to remove the traces of crime in the place which has already become a symbol of Nazi crimes. This place is Oświęcim. Send as soon as possible and broadcast by radio." [17]

This information was sent post-haste to London, with an appeal for help. It was published by Reuters, which in large measure frustrated the Moll Plan. The Świt radio station in London, also broadcast an appeal to the entire world to warn Germany of the consequences and not to allow the murder of the prisoners to take place.

Yet another form of the resistance movement's activity was the preparation and organization of escapes from the camp. Prisoners escaping on the orders of the organization had the task of establishing or expanding contacts between the camp organization and the various political groupings operating on the outside. Kazimierz Hałoń, for example, who escaped from the camp on 20 February 1943, strengthened the contacts with the PPS organization in Brzeszcze. Similarly two communists — Dr. Alfred Klahr, an Austrian, and Stefan Bratkowski, a Pole — who escaped from the camp on 15 June 1944, were to establish contact with the PPR organization in Warsaw. There were very many similar cases. Many escapers joined the ranks of the partisans operating in the vicinity of the camp and helped in the organization of more escapes. Often the escapers took with them important documents or plans from the camp, in addition to their value as eye-witnesses in a position to give accounts of the conditions prevailing in the camp and the crimes committed there. The dates when escapes were due to take place were given in letters smuggled out of the camp. For example, concerning Tadeusz Uszyński's ("Cygan") escape of 9 September 1944 the information was sent out: "Wait for friend Bezzębny [Polish for "Toothless"] from the Birkenau joint on the night of Tuesday to Wednesday." [18]

Because escapes led to reprisals against the families of escapers, attempts were made to warn relatives in advance so that they could change their place of residence. In connection with Roman Cieliczko's escape, the following letter was smuggled out of the camp on 14 July 1944: "Please inform Cieliczko Anna, Zakopane G.G., Parkstrasse 935, to leave home immediately, as she may be arrested." [19]

---

[17] Smuggled letter of 6 September 1944. *Ibid*, t. II, k. 140—141.
[18] Smuggled letter of 4 September 1944. APMO. *Mat. oboz. Ruchu Oporu*, t. II, k. 134.
[19] *Ibid*, t. I, k. 38.

All in all about 700 prisoners escaped from the camp, of whom about 400 were recaptured or shot evading recapture.

Besides activity aimed at helping the prisoners, the camp resistance movement also engaged in diversionary operations. Prisoners employed in the various German factories and mines carried out acts of sabotage. For example prisoners working on the dismantling of wrecked aircraft deliberately destroyed parts that were still in good condition, emptied petrol from the tanks, etc. Similarly women prisoners in Rajsko tending the kok-saghiz plant — the roots of which contained 6-8 per cent of high quality rubber — watered it with destructive chemicals and falsified the records of each plant's progress, thus delaying the conduct of experiments on the production of rubber.

The camp organization concerned itself with the political education of the prisoners, the purpose of which was to create international solidarity in the struggle against Nazism. The chief committee of the *Kampfgruppe Auschwitz* prepared a manifesto [20] whose slogans included the following:

(i) it is the duty of every prisoner to fight Hitlerism;
(ii) Hitlerism is the common enemy of all peoples;
(iii) the fight against fascism is a fight for national freedom and democracy;
(iv) this fight is made possible only by solidarity and cooperation;
(v) the main factor of the armed struggle against Hitlerism is the Soviet Union and its Red Army;
(vi) friendship with the Soviet Union is therefore a guarantee of victory and peace.

German propaganda to the effect that the only people in concentration camps were common criminals was also countered. To this a resolution was written in which it was proved that the number of common criminals — who were almost exclusively of German nationality — in the camps did not exceed 5 per cent of the total number of prisoners. The majority, on the other hand, consisted of political prisoners of all countries. The resolution contained the sentence:

"Although we are in slave camps, we people of freedom send news to the free world of our existence, of our uneven struggle for the rights of political prisoners." [21]

In face of the threat of mass extermination, the Camp Military Council began to consider the possibility of raising a general insurrection in the camp in order to free the prisoners. As early as 1942 Colonel Kazimierz Rawicz had worked out a plan for a mass outbreak in and around the camp

---

[20] Filip Friedman and Tadeusz Hołuj, Oświęcim. Bydgoszcz 1946, p. 131.
[21] APMO. *Mat. oboz. Ruchu Oporu*, t. II, k. 87.

and had sent a message to the commander of the Home Army (AK), General Stefan Rowecki, asking for a date to be set when the action should begin. The plan, however, was considered in the situation then existing as too bold and its implementation was not undertaken. The matter was returned to in 1944 in connection with events on the eastern front, which following an offensive by the Soviet Army had shifted rapidly westward. In July Majdanek, the second largest concentration camp on Polish territory, had been liberated with such suddenness that the SS camp authorities had not managed to destroy the mass extermination installations nor to murder all the prisoners. It was feared that the SS, learning from this experience, would try at all costs to conceal the traces of the crimes committed at the Oświęcim camp. In view of the danger of the camp's being liquidated, the leadership of the camp organization made contact with the AK command in Silesia and requested help in the shape of arms and explosives and the organization of diversionary operations outside the camp in order to tie up some of the SS forces and to enable the prisoners to escape. The leadership of the organization emphasized that the liberation or partial liberation of the camp would have enormous importance in view of the international significance of Oświęcim as one of the most sombre symbols of Nazi Germany, that such an operation should not be treated exclusively as help for the prisoners, as from the military point of view the camp represented an enormous reservoir of manpower, part of which would be capable of taking part in an armed uprising.[22] In the camp a report was drawn up containing exact information about the number of prisoners in the camps and subcamps of Oświęcim, and the size of the SS garrison, its arms, technical equipment, etc.[23]

All this information and plans of the camp were passed on to Stefan Jasieński ("Urban") who had been sent by AK headquarters to the area adjoining the camp to study the possibility of conducting hostilities there and establishing contacts with the camp organization. In September 1944 Jasieński was arrested by a German patrol and taken to the camp, where he died.

The plan for an uprising was never implemented, as towards the end of 1944 the camp authorities began to evacuate thousands of prisoners, chiefly Poles and Russians, to other concentration camps situated deep in the Reich, which disorganized the activity of the resistance movement. Nevertheless the *Kampfgruppe Auschwitz* had played an important role in raising the awareness of prisoners who, upon arrival at other camps, joined the organizations operating there.

---

[22] Account of Tadeusz Hołuj. APMO. Zespół "Oświadczenia", t. 37, k. 54—55.
[23] Report of 22 August 1944 by Józef Cyrankiewicz. APMO. *Mat. oboz. Ruchu Oporu*, t. II, k. 98.

★

The camp resistance movement worked in conditions which were particularly dangerous and considerably more difficult than those outside the camp. Many of its members perished. But their heroic effort was not wasted. Thanks to them the lives of thousands of prisoners were saved, and the "Free World", found out while the war was still on of the tragedy being played out in Oświęcim.

The news smuggled out of the camp by the camp organization appeared in the Polish clandestine press, which wrote of the transports arriving at Oświęcim, gave the number of prisoners currently in the camp, the number of those murdered, the names of the executioners and other information about the bestiality of the camp authorities.

Publications about *KL Auschwitz* also appeared abroad. They were based on the accounts of escaped prisoners and on letters and reports smuggled out by the Polish underground. In August 1943 there was published in London a brochure entitled *Obóz śmierci* (Death Camp).

Some news was broadcast over the radio in order to prove to the SS authorities that these deeds were not going to remain a secret and that retribution for their deeds awaited them. The Germans realized that the Allied powers had precise information concerning the mass crimes committed in *KL Auschwitz*. German radio monitors recorded the news broadcast from London. For example there is a note made by the German monitoring authority to the effect that on 15 June 1944 London had broadcast the news of the killing in the gas chambers of Brzezinka on 7 March 1944 of four thousand Jews from Czechoslovakia and of the intention to murder another three thousand persons in the same way by 20 June, and had threatened that those guilty of the murders would be brought to account.[24] The publication of the names of the worst murderers and sadists and the passing of death sentences on them evoked panic among the SS and had an ameliorating influence on conditions in the camp.

Under the occupation the Polish people chose struggle. This struggle was joined by hundreds of prisoners in the concentration camps, who thereby showed that "one can destroy a person physically, but one cannot take away his dignity, nor kill the awareness of the totality of prisoners", as the former Auschwitz prisoner and member of the camp resistance movement, Ludwik Rajewski, wrote in his book.[25]

The prisoners of Oświęcim proved that they were not only passive witnesses and victims, but that they could also oppose Nazism.

---

[24] APMO. *Mat. oboz. Ruchu Oporu*, t. XXIV, k. 3.
[25] Ludwik Rajewski, *Ruch oporu w polskiej literaturze obozowej*. Warsaw 1971, p. 121.

Andrzej Strzelecki

The Liberation of the Camp and Aid to the Freed Prisoners

1. THE LIBERATION OF THE CAMP

The liberation of the Nazi concentration camps and other centres of internment was one of the most glorious achievements of the Allied armies in the last phase of the struggle with the Third Reich. A great many prisoners were saved from impending annihilation, and the enormity of the crimes perpetrated in the camps was revealed. Among the first to be liberated were the camps at Majdanek (23-24 July 1944) and Riga (13 October 1944). *KL Auschwitz's* turn for liberation came in January 1945.

Until the last days before Soviet Army units reached Upper Silesia and the adjacent Oświęcim region, the Nazi authorities had considered two possibilities as regards *KL Auschwitz:* (1) liquidation of the camp in case of unexpectedly rapid advances of Soviet troops; (2) the preservation of the camp as the key link in the Nazi system of genocide and exploitation of the nations of the occupied countries. Taking these possibilities into account, the Nazi authorities, until mid-January 1945, had not been inclined to take steps which would render the further development of the camp impossible or considerably difficult. From August 1944 until mid-January 1945, about 65,000 prisoners who constituted an unnecessary surplus labour force had been eavcuated from the camp. On the other hand, over 65,000 prisoners had been kept at the camp till the last moment, most of them being employed in the Upper Silesian industrial district and other nearby economic centres important for sustaining the military potential of the Third Reich. Also, only preliminary measures had been adopted as regards the removal or covering up of the traces of the crimes committed at the camp. Until the second half of January 1945, one of the Auschwitz crematoria, crematorium V, together with its gas chambers, had been kept ready for use. It had been blown up only shortly before Soviet troops reached Oświęcim.

In the final evacuation of *KL Auschwitz* on 17 to 23 January 1945, close to 60,000 prisoners were sent off from the camp, mainly on foot. A considerable part of them perished either along the evacuation routes or later in the camps inside the Reich.

After the last transports of evacuees had left *KL Auschwitz*, over 8,500 prisoners remained there, chiefly the sick and the emaciated, incapable of being evacuated on foot. According to many sources, the SS was planning to exterminate them as witnesses to the crime and as a sort of unnecessary burden unfit for use as labour force in the camps inside the Reich. Appropriate orders had already been issued. Complying with them, in the last days of *KL Auschwitz's* existence, the SS killed about 700 prisoners, over 300 of whom were burnt in the barracks of the Auschwitz subcamps: *Fürstengrube* in Wesoła near Mysłowice, *Gleiwitz I* in Gliwice, and *Tschechowitz II* in Czechowice [1]. However, most of the prisoners left in *KL Auschwitz* survived until the arrival of Soviet troops. It appears that the prisoners left at the camp avoided death chiefly owing to a coincidence of two factors: relaxation of the discipline in the SS and general disorganization, or even panic, in the ranks of the German troops withdrawing from Oświęcim and Upper Silesia.

The task of freeing Oświęcim fell to the 60th Army of the First Ukrainian Front, which was advancing along the left bank of the Vistula from Cracow toward the Upper Silesian industrial district, as part of an operation, with the participation of other Soviet units, aimed at a partial encirclement of the area and at forcing the German troops to withdraw hastily therefrom. On the order of the Army commander, Col. Gen. Pavel Kurochkin, three Army divisions encircled the German units in Oświęcim. The 100th infantry division of the 106th corps was the fastest, since the first scouts from the division appeared in the eastern part of Oświęcim, in the Auschwitz subcamp of Monowitz at Oświęcim-Monowice, already around 9 a.m. on Saturday, 27 January 1945. On the same day, the 148th infantry division of the 106th corps reached Oświęcim from the north, and the 322nd division of the 28th corps of the 60th Army from the south-east. The Soviet troops entered the town centre in the early afternoon on 27 January 1945. Later, they headed toward the Auschwitz main camp and the camp at Brzezinka (Birkenau), having encountered in the former the resistance of withdrawing German units. They soon broke this resistance and liberated both the main camp and the Birkenau camp around 3 p.m.

The atmosphere prevailing in *KL Auschwitz* at the moment of liberation can be recreated on the basis of recollections and accounts by former prisoners. A woman prisoner has thus described her experiences:

---

[1] The extermination of those 700 prisoners was but a link in the chain of massacres perpetrated in camps and other places of internment which the Nazi authorities were gradually liquidating in the face of advances of Allied troops on the Third Reich. Examples: Malyi Trostinets near Minsk at the end of June 1944 — about 6,500 victims, KL Klooga in Estonia on 19 September 1944 — about 2,200 victims, Łódź-Radogoszcz and Słoński near Kostrzyn in the second half of January 1945 — over 2,800 victims, the complex of eleven camps Kaufering (one of the subcamps of KL Dachau) in April 1945 — over 10,000 victims.

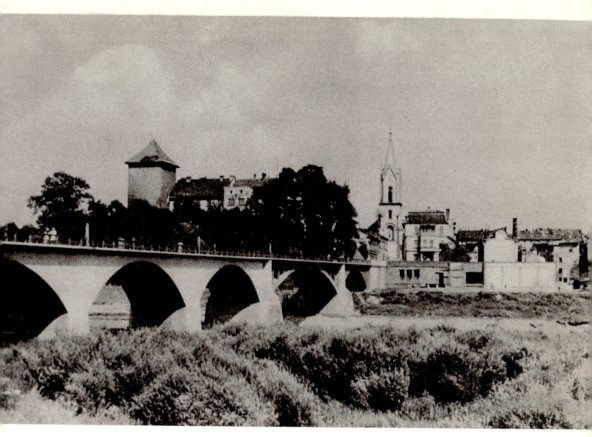

In 1940 in the Oświęcim suburb of Zasole, the Nazis began to build a concentration camp. It was originally intended to hold Poles from Silesia and the General Government as the resistance movement in these territories had intensified.
Photo: General view of the town of Oświęcim during the occupation.

Der Reichsführer SS
- Der Inspekteur der Konzentrationslager -
Az.: 14 a 12/L/Ot.-

Oranienburg, den 21. Februar 1940

Einschreiben.

II c/5 53

Betreff: Häftlingslager im Bereich der Höheren SS- und Polizeiführer.
Bezug : RF SS-Pers.Stab Tgb.Nr. g.R/694/40 Wa/Kp. v. 1.II.40
Anlagen: - 3 -

An den
Reichsführer -SS und Chef
der Deutschen Polizei

Abdr. an:
1.) SS-Gruppenführer P o h l (mit 9 Anlagen)
2.) SS- Gruppenführer Heydrich (ohne Anlagen).

B e r l i n SW 11.

Mit oben angezogener Verfügung hat der Reichsführer-SS die Besichtigung nachstehend aufgeführter Gefangenenlager auf ihre Eignung als Konzentrationslager befohlen:
1.) Polizeigefängnis in W e l z h e i m
2.) Durchgangslager in K i s l a u
   (im Bereich des Höheren SS-und Polizeiführers Südwest)
3.) Lager Frauenberg b/Admont
   (im Bereich des Höheren SS- und Polizeiführers Alpenland)
4.) Lager S o s n o w i t z Ost/O/S.
5.) Lager A u s c h w i t z O/S.
   (beide im Bereich des Höheren SS- und Polizeiführers Südost).
Die Besichtigung ist durchgeführt worden. Das Ergebnis war folgendes:

1.) W e l z h e i m.
Welzheim ist kein Konzentrationslager, sondern seit 1934 ein Hausgefängnis der Geheimen Staatspolizei in Stuttgart und untersteht dieser. Die Bezeichnung "Konzentrationslager" muß irrtümlich erfolgt sein.
Für Konzentrationslagerzwecke ist es ungeeignet.

2.) K i s l a u.
Kislau ist ein Gefangenenlager der Reichsjustizverwaltung unter Bewachung der Justiz und Leitung eines Gefängnisdirektors. Aufnahmefähig für 600 Gefangene. Bis zum Beginn

- 2 -

des jetzigen Krieges wurden durch die Gestapo Karlsruhe auch Fremdenlegionäre in das Lager eingeliefert (gegen Erstattung der Kosten); z.Zt. noch 7 Legionäre in Kislau. Da 1933/34 in der Nähe von Kislau ein Konzentrationslager bestanden hat, wird das jetzige Justizgefangenenlager noch fälschlicherweise als "Konzentrationslager" bezeichnet.
Kislau, ein früheres herzogliches Jagdschloß, ist für Konzentrationslagerzwecke ungeeignet.

3.) F r a u e n b e r g b/Admont.
Frauenberg ist ein vom Landesfürsorgeverband Steiermark eingerichtetes Arbeitslager für Arbeitsscheue und Trunkenbolde. Es besteht aus 5 Holzbaracken und ist aufnahmefähig für 300 Häftlinge.
Die Arbeitshäftlinge sind ausschließlich Steiermärker, die vom Landesfürsorgeverband Steiermark während ihres Lageraufenthaltes für ihre Arbeitsleistung gelöhnt werden(Stunde 27-57 Pfg.,abzüglich Verpflegung).
Die Bewachung erfolgt durch die SA (etwa 20 Mann).
Die Arbeitshäftlinge werden beschäftigt in 2 Steinbrüchen und im Straßenbau. Unweit des Lagers befindet sich ein Moorgelände von ca. 25 - 30 qkm (es soll bis zu 25 m tief sein).Grund und Boden ist jetzt Staatseigentum; früher gehörte es zum Stift Admont.
Frauenberg ist in der jetzigen Gestaltung, ohne größeren Ausbau, für Konzentrationslagerzwecke ungeeignet.

4.) S o s n o w i t z O/S.
Sosnowitz ist nur vorübergehend als Durchgangslager für auswandernde Juden provisorisch eingerichtet; z.Zt. belegt mit 300 Juden. Die Verpflegung dieser jüdischen Auswanderer wird von der Kultusgemeinde Sosnowitz durchgeführt. Die für diesen Zweck mit Stroh ausgelegte Fabrikhalle ohne jegliche Einrichtung, ohne Wasser und ohne Kochgelegenheit ist weder als Konzentrationslager, noch als Quarantänelager verwendbar.

5.) A u s c h w i t z O/S.
Auschwitz, eine ehemalige polnische Artilleriekaserne(Stein- und Holzgebäude) ist nach Abstellung einiger sanitärer und baulicher Mängel als Quarantänelager geeignet.
Ein ausführlicher Bericht ist dem RFSS und Chef der Deutschen Polizei, Gruppenführer P o h l , Gruppenführer H e y d r i c h

- 3 -

und dem Reichsarzt- SS vorgelegt worden. Die noch notwendigen baulichen und hygienischen Untersuchungen in Auschwitz werden z.Zt.durchgeführt. Wenn die vom Chef der Sicherheitspolizei veranlaßten Verhandlungen auf Überlassung des Lagers von der Wehrmacht- es befindet sich, wie bereits gemeldet, noch eine Baukompanie im Lager- zum Abschluß gekommen sind, wird sofort die Ingangsetzung als Quarantänelager von mir durchgeführt werden. Die notwendigen Vorbereitungen habe ich hierzu bereits getroffen.

6.) S t u t t h o f .
Wegen der Übernahme des Lagers Stutthof b/Danzig als staatliches Konzentrationslager ist dem Reichsführer-SS ein ausführlicher Bericht vorgelegt worden. SS-Gruppenführer P o h l und SS-Gruppenführer H e y d r i c h haben die Übernahme befürwortet.

Die Unterlagen der von mir nicht zu besichtigenden Lager im Bereich der Höheren SS- und Polizeiführer Warthe und Rhein habe ich dem SS-Gruppenführer Pohl vorgelegt mit der Bitte um Stellungnahme, ob von ihm an diesen Lagern ein Interesse besteht. Nach Durchsicht der Berichte kommen diese Lager für Konzentrationslagerzwecke meines Erachtens nicht in Frage.

SS - Oberführer.

Photocopy of a letter dated 21 February 1940 from Inspector of Concentration Camps Richard Glücks to *Reichsführer SS* Heinrich Himmler concerning the results of an inspection made of the former Polish army barracks at Oświęcim with a view to establishing a camp there. Glücks affirms that given certain structural and sanitary alterations (pt. 5, pp. 2-3) the buildings are suitable for the purpose of founding a camp.

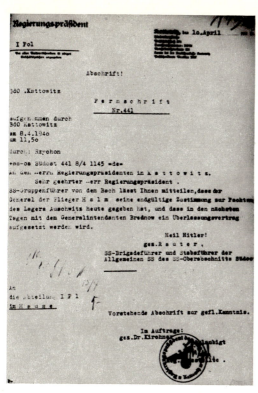

Photocopy of a teletype letter dated 10 April 1940 containing the information that Air Force General Halm has given his final consent to the letting out of the former barracks at Oświęcim for use as a camp.

The first Polish prisoners were employed by the Nazis in pulling down the houses left behind by the Polish residents evacuated from the suburb of Zasole and part of Oświęcim town itself.

The entire area of the camp was surrounded by a double fence of electrified barbed wire, while on the side adjoining the street there was a high wall of concrete slabs with watch towers every few yards.

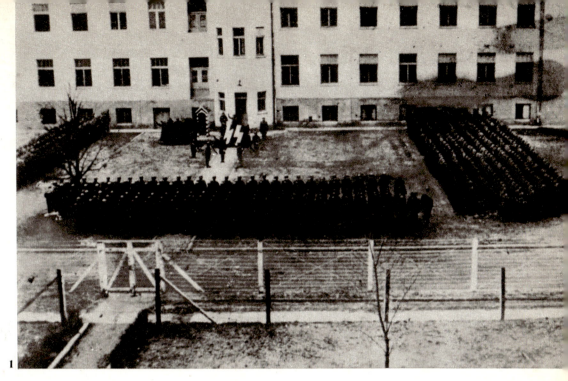

The concentriation camp at Oświęcim, officially known as *Konzentrationslager* (or *KL*) *Auschwitz*, was manned by armed guards from one of the most criminal Nazi organizations, the so-called *Waffen-SS*, who had their quarters in the former buildings of the Polish Tobacco Monopoly, situated near the camp. As the number of prisoners grew, so did the number of SS guards, until in the final stage of the camp's existence there were several thousand of them.

Above: SS camp staff on parade. Below: SS detachment marching in the direction of the camp.

In March 1941 during the first visit of *Reichsführer SS* Himmler to *KL Auschwitz*, a decision was taken to expand the camp to hold 30,000 prisoners. Furthermore Himmler ordered a camp to be built at the village of Brzezinka (later to be called *KL Auschwitz II — Birkenau*), initially intended for 100,000, and later for 200,000 prisoners. At Brzezinka several hundred barrack huts were built, which held scores of thousands of prisoners of various nationalities, as well as Soviet POWs.

Photos: Brzezinka: Huts where prisoners lived (top), main guardroom, and part of the camp.

Under the supervision of the SS, the prisoners, both men and women, carried out arduous tasks connected with the levelling and irrigation of the terrain and erecting various buildings.

The work of building and extending the camp was closely followed by the highest party and government functionaries of the Third Reich, who paid frequent visits to *KL Auschwitz*.
Photo: The first commandant of the camp, Rudolf Höss (third from left), with the *Gauleiter* of Silesia, Fritz Bracht, standing beside him. On the right, only partially visible, is one of the first camp marshals *(Rapportführer)*, Ludwig Plagge.

In charge of all construction work was *SS Sturmbannführer* Karl Bischoff (second from right).

The plan, confirmed by Bischoff, for expanding the camp at Brzezinka envisaged the building of a complex of camps to hold 200,000 prisoners.
Photos: The women's camp, sector BIb (above), the men's camp, sector BIIa — the quarantine camp (left).

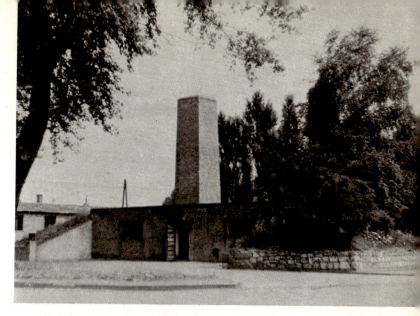

The first crematorium at KL *Auschwitz*, where the bodies of dead prisoners were cremated. It functioned until 1943. From 1941 people were also gassed here with Cyclon B. The photograph shows it as it looks today.

The interior of crematorium I. This was one of the smallest crematoria at *KL Auschwitz*. Its three two-door furnaces were made by the firm Topf und Söhne of Erfurt. After the building of four gas chambers and four crematoria at Brzezinka the crematorium at Oświęcim was used for storing medicines. The photograph shows the former crematorium as it looks today.

Prisoners were also employed on the building of gas chambers and crematoria. Photo: Prisoners engaged in the building of crematorium II or III at Brzezinka.

The Nazi concentration camps, including *KL Auschwitz*, constituted an enormous reservoir of cheap labour. Following a decision by Himmler prisoners of *KL Auschwitz* were employed on the building of the IG Farben works at Monowice near Oświęcim. Later a camp known as *KL Auschwitz III Monowitz* was founded there, to which all the subcamps scattered about Silesia attached to various factories and mines were subordinated.

Photo: *Reichsführer SS* Himmler (first from right) at Monowice.

Photocopy of the first page of the garrison order dated 22 November 1943 on the division of *KL Auschwitz* into three separate camps: *Auschwitz I* (Oświęcim), *Auschwitz II* (Brzezinka) and *Auschwitz III* (Monowice).

Photocopy of a general plan drawn up on 19 February 1942 for the expansion of *KL Auschwitz I*, envisaging the construction of scores of permanent brick buildings for prisoners' quarters and for the SS camp authorities.

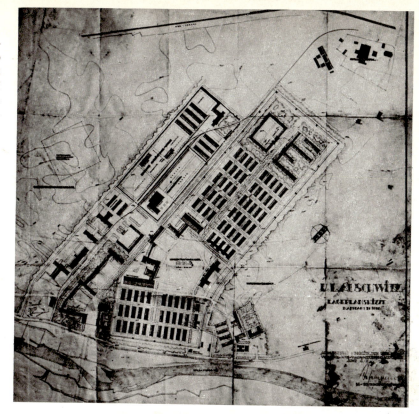

Photocopy of a general plan drawn up on 15 August 1942 for the expansion of *KL Auschwitz II* (Birkenau), envisaging the building at Brzezinka of a complex composed of four construction sectors (*Bauabschnitt I, II, III, IV*) and extermination plants.

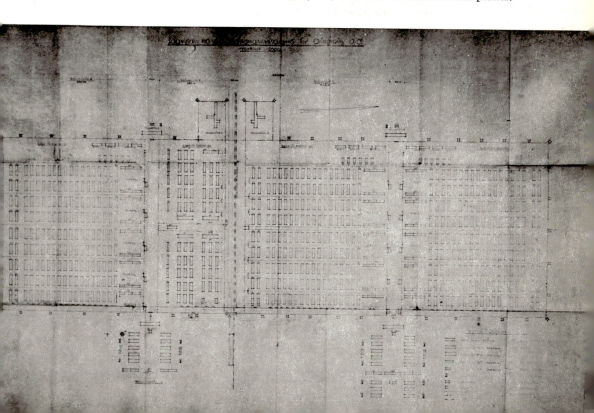

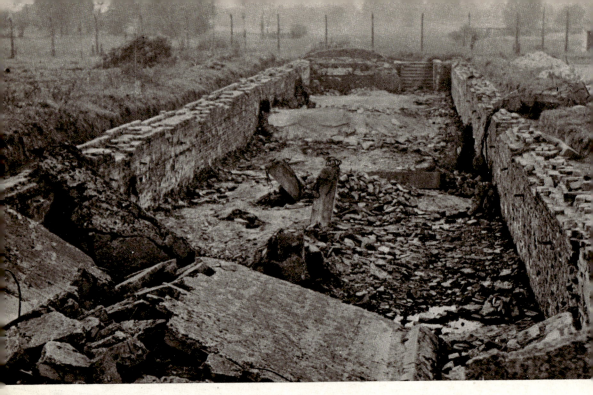

In August 1944 the SS camp authorities, threatened by the summer offensive of the Soviet army, set about removing all traces of the crimes committed.
Photo: Brzezinka: The ruins of the gas chambers and crematorium II.

Upon arrival in camp a prisoner was registered and his name replaced by a number. The basic data concerning every prisoner were contained in the so-called "arrivals' lists" (*Zugangsliste*), which were drawn up every day.
Photo: Photocopy of a list of names of prisoners sent to *KL Auschwitz* on 21 May 1941 by the local Gestapo headquarters in Poznań, Łódź, Katowice, Legnica and Flossenbürg concentration camp. The list is signed by *SS-Unterscharführer* Hans Stark.

KL Auschwitz held prisoners of various nationalities, religious faiths, political convictions and occupations from nearly all the countries of Europe, and even beyond. Photo: A group of Soviet POWs being led into the camp.

The first registered Pole of the group of 728 Polish prisoners brought to the camp from Tarnów jail on 14 June 1940 was Stanisław Ryniak. He received the camp number 31.

After the arrival of a transport persons fit for work were sent to the camp to have their hair shorn, be disinfected and bathe.

Upon arrival at the camp prisoners were photographed in three poses. These photographs were intended to facilitate recapture in the event of escape.

After their personal particulars had been taken down and they had received numbers, which were tattooed on the left forearm, the new arrivals changed into camp garb.
Photo: A group of women prisoners.

Personal belongings brought to the camp were confiscated by the SS and stored in warehouses. Despite the existtence of scores of such warehouses and the constant departures of trains containing clothee belonging to the murdered victims, huge piles of miscellaneous objects grew up in the spaces between the warehouse huts.

Photos: The railway ramp (above) and the warehouses (below) containing confiscated effects and prisoners employed in sorting them.

The interior of a brick-walled hut at Brzezinka. On each of the three tiers slept eight to ten prisoners.

The interior of a wooden hut at Brzezinka.

A latrine at *KL Auschwitz II Birkenau.*

The close cooperation between the SS and the owners of German concerns and industrial plants consisted among other things in the maximum exploitation of the prisoners' labour.
Photo: *Reichsführer SS* Heinrich Himmler (second from right) listens to the information provided by *Oberingenieur* Faust on the building of the IG Farben works at *KL Auschwitz III Monowitz*.

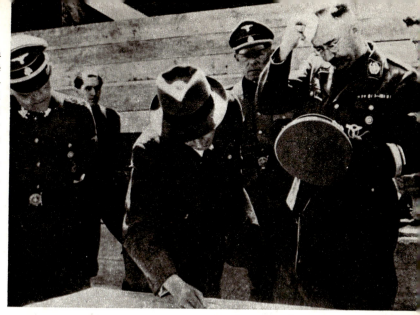

During the building of the IG Farben works the prisoners carried out the heaviest tasks. Preserved documents reveal that about 30,000 prisoners died while engaged on this project.
Photo: A prisoners' work commando leaving for the IG Farben work site.

Leaving for work in the morning or returning at night, the prisoners marched to the accompaniment of the camp orchestra. The idea was to have the thousands of prisoners march through the gate in orderly fashion in order to facilitate counting them.

The frequent visits by members of the SS leadership to the sites of factories being built by German concerns were intended to underline the contribution being made by the SS to the arming of the Wehrmacht.
Photo: (first row from left) *Reichsführer SS* Heinrich Himmler, *Oberingenieur* Faust (with hat) and the first commandant of KL Auschwitz, Rudolf Höss.

Photocopy of a page of the register of sick prisoners in Hospital Block No. 20 in *KL Auschwitz I*. The death of a prisoner is marked by a cross.

With the exception of Soviet prisoners and Jews, prisoners could write letters twice a month to their closest relatives. It was not allowed in this correspondence to write about life in the camp. Letters had to be written on special forms and were censored by the camp authorities.

Photo: Photocopy of the correspondence of the prisoner Mieczysław Pronobis.

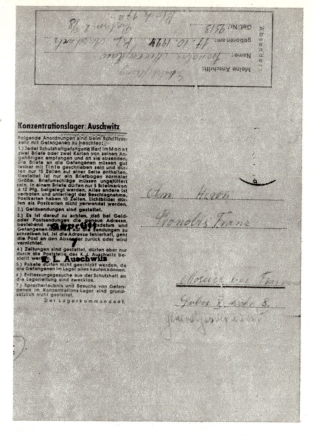

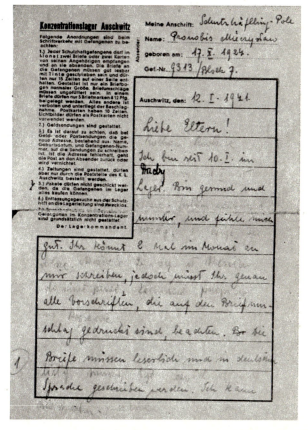

Occasionally prisoners attempted to escape. In most cases they were either electrocuted by the barbed wire fence surrounding the camp or were shot down by the SS guards. For every prisoner recaptured or shot while attempting to escape, the SS man responsible received three days' leave.

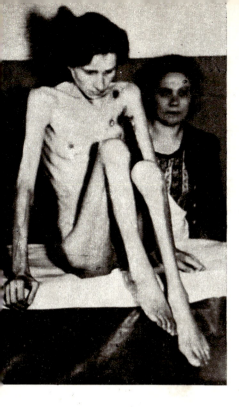

In *KL Auschwitz*, apart from direct annihilation, every conceivable method of indirect extermination was applied, from starvation to gruelling physical labour. Mortality among the prisoners was very high, in certain periods of the camp's existence reaching several hundred deaths a day.
Photo: A woman prisoner after the liberation of the camp.

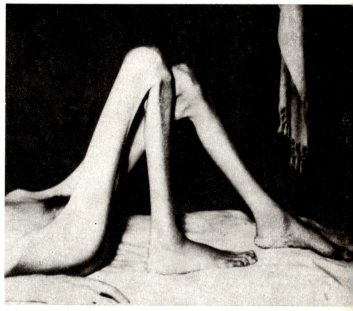

Epidemics of spotted typhus, typhoid fever, scabies, phlegmons and diarrhoea contributed to the constantly rising death rate among the prisoners.
Photo: Corpses of prisoners found in Block 11 after the liberation of the camp.

One way of exterminating the prisoners was by working them to death. Prisoners had to work from 10 to 12 hours daily.
Photo: Prisoners employed on the building of the IG Farben works.

Prisoners were employed in numerous factories situated in the vicinity of the camp. The work took place under the supervision of SS men who beat the prisoners for every transgression or wrote out punishment reports, which resulted in the *Lagerführer* imposing on the culprit one of the numerous camp punishments, of which one of the most frequently employed was relegation to the penal company, most of whose members ultimately perished.

Regardless of the time of year women prisoners had to perform heavy outdoor work.
Photo: A group of women working at Brzezinka.

The SS inflicted various punishments on the prisoners. One of the most frequently employed was flogging. The official maximum was 25 strokes, but cases of 50 and even 80 strokes being applied were not infrequent.
Photo: The flogging bench and the stick with which prisoners were beaten.

One very severe punishment was confinement in one of the standing cells in the cellars of Block 11. In each of these cells, measuring 90 by 90 cm., four prisoners had to spend the night. In the morning they had to go with the others to work.
Photo: Entrance to the cells.

In the courtyard of Block 11 was the Execution Wall, where a total of about 20,000 prisoners or persons sentenced by summary police courts, were shot.
Photo: Post-war reconstruction of the Execution Wall.

Block 11, known as the "Death Block".

On 19 July twelve Polish prisoners were hanged during roll call on a specially built gallows, having been suspected of maintaining contacts with the Polish civilian population living in the vicinity of the camp. The hanged men were: Stanisław Stawiński (No. 6569), Czesław Marcisz (No. 26891), Janusz Skrzetuski-Pogonowski (No. 253), Edmund Sikorski (No. 25419), Jerzy Woźniak (No. 35650), Józef Wojtyga (No. 24740), Zbigniew Foltański (No. 41664), Józef Gancarz (No. 24538), Mieczysław Kulikowski (No. 25404), Bogusław Ohrt (No. 367), Leon Rajzer (No. 399) and Tadeusz Rapacz (No. 36043).

Photo: The collective gallows by the camp kitchen.

The mobile gallows on which during evening roll calls prisoners who had tried to escape or who were suspected of participating in the resistance movement were hanged.

The photograph was taken in 1945 in the courtyard of Block 11 after the liberation of the camp.

Cell No. 18 in the cellars of Block 11 in which together with other prisoners condemned to death by starvation the Franciscan missionary Father Maximilian (Rajmund Kolbe) was confined, having volunteered to accept certain death in place of a fellow prisoner, whose life he thereby saved.

Photocopy of Kolbe's death certificate signed by Maximilian Grabner of the camp Gestapo.

Like Father Maximilian Kolbe, during one of the "weedings out" of victims for death by starvation the schoolteacher Marian Batko stepped forward as a volunteer. He also perished in the cellars of Block 11.
Photo: Photocopy of the page from the register of Block 11 on which Batko's death is entered under the date 27.4.41.

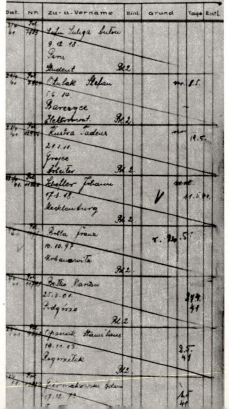

A tin of Cyclon B, the gas with which the SS murdered millions of people in the gas chambers. Cyclon B was produced by the firm of DEGESCH (Deutsche Gesellschaft zur Schädlingsbekämpfung), and delivered to the camp by the firm of TESTA (Tesch und Stabenow).

In order to implement their plans of mass extermination, the SS proceeded in 1943 to build gas chambers and crematoria at Brzezinka.
Photo: Part of crematorium III built by prisoner labour. The underground part, not visible here, contained the gas chamber, in which in the course of about 15 minutes 2,000-3,000 persons could be gassed with Cyclon B.

Each of the crematoria could dispose of the some 2,400 corpses of those gassed in the gas chambers in the space of 24 hours.
Photo: The ovens of crematorium II or III, in which bodies were cremated.

After the construction of the crematoria and gas chambers at Brzezinka, a special railway siding was built at the camp. The ramp adjoined crematoria II and III, which are visible to the left and right of the picture (the two high chimneys in the background).

In 1944 there arrived daily at the railway siding at Brzezinka several trains consisting of about fifteen waggons, each of which held about 100 persons. The waggons were emptied, the men being separated from the women and children. The new arrivals were told that they were to be taken to a bathhouse for a shower.

SS doctors and nurses, and often also other SS officers and NCOs, conducted selections, separating those whom they considered fit for work from the sick, the old, cripples and children. Mothers fit for work had their children forcibly removed. One of the doctors, Dr. Johann Paul Kremer, wrote in his diary that compared to the selections Dante's inferno seemed like a comedy and quoted the opinion of his colleague, Dr. Heinz Thilo, that the ramp at Brzezinka was the *anus mundi*.

The unfit for work (old people, pregnant women and mothers with children) were sent to their deaths immediately.
Photos: Groups of people headed for the gas chambers.

Some children were kept alive for the **purpose of conducting** pseudomedical experiments on them.
The photograph taken after the liberation of the camp shows a group of children showing the camp numbers tattooed on their arms.

People awaiting their turn for the gas chamber, situated in the wood at Brzezinka.

1

3

A prisoner belonging to the camp resistance movement took three illegal photographs which were later smuggled out of the camp. Their poor technical quality is attributable to the conditions in which they were taken. Anticlockwise from top left: women being herded to the gas chamber, preparations being made for burning the corpses on pyres (a method used because there were too many for the crematoria to cope with); the bodies being arranged on the pyre by members of the *Sonderkommando*, who were chosen from among new arrivals to the camp and after a certain period of time, as "persons in the know" (*Geheimnisträger*) about the scale of the crimes committed by the SS, were also sent to the gas chambers.

After the liberation of the camp on 27 January 1945 the corpses of hundreds of prisoners were found, which the SS had not managed to dispose of in the crematoria.

Photocopy of two pages of the manuscript of the memoirs of the former commandant of KL Auschwitz, Rudolf Höss, in which he writes of the "unmedical activities of the SS doctors at KL Auschwitz".

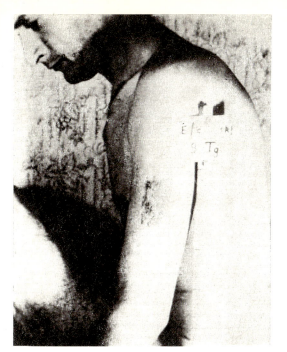 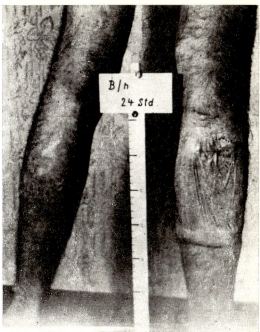

Healthy prisoners were subjected by SS doctors to the most varied pseudomedical experiments, as a result of which most of them perished, while those who survived were maimed for life.

In principle children who arrived at the camp were immediately sent to the gas chambers. Some, however, were kept alive — for example twins — so that SS Dr. Josef Mengele could carry out various experiments on them.

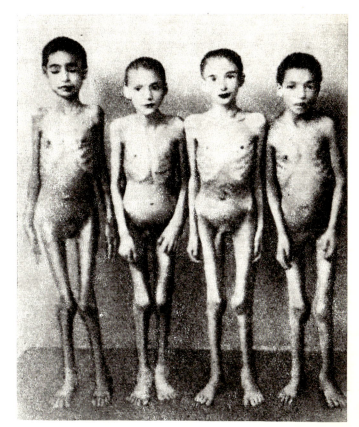

Block 10, in which the SS doctors carried out their criminal pseudomedical experiments.

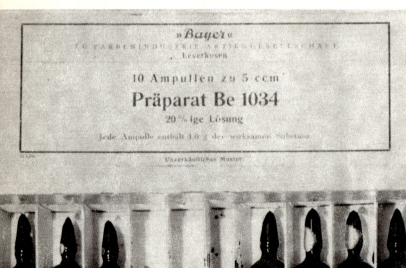

Pseudomedical experiments on prisoners were also conducted at the behest of famous pharmaceutical firms.
Photo: Ampules of the substance B 1034 produced by the firm of Bayer. This preparation was tried out on prisoners who had previously been injected with spotted typhus.

After the liberation of the camp hundreds of thousands of personal effects left behind by their murdered owners were found (shoes, clothing, articles of everyday use, artifical limbs). Also found were several tons of women's hair ready to be sent off to the Reich for use in the manufacture of such things as haircloth.

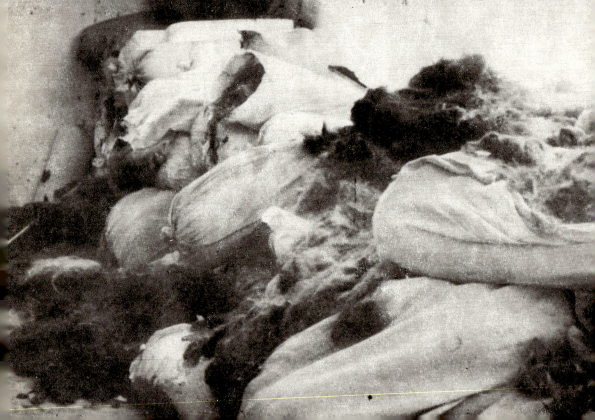

From the moment *KL Auschwitz* was founded the Poles were never passive. Despite enormous difficulties and great danger, a resistance movement emerged and was organized both in the camp and in the surrounding area.

Photo: Photocopy of a letter dated 22 July 1940 from the Higher SS and Police Leader in Wrocław, Erich von dem Bach-Zelewski, concerning the necessity of increasing security at *KL Auschwitz*.

Help in organizing illegal contacts with the camp at Oświęcim, preparing escapes and smuggling food, medicines, etc. to the prisoners, was furnished by the local Polish population.

The photograph, taken before 1939, shows a group of persons most of whom became members of the resistance movement in the area surrounding the camp. In the centre, seated, is Wojciech Jekiełek, later to become one of the most active resistance members in this area.

Photocopy of a letter dated 22 July 1940 from *SS-Gruppenführer* Erich von dem Bach-Zelewski in which he orders the shooting of five Poles for assisting in the escape of the prisoner Tadeusz Wiejowski. Further correspondence reveals that the sentence of shooting was commuted to flogging and confinement to the camp where they all, with the exception of Bolesław Bicz, eventually died.

Janina Kajtoch, one of those who organized assistance for the prisoners, standing before the house at Babice near Oświęcim from which she contacted prisoners from the surveying team.
Photograph taken before 1939.

Anna Zdrowakowa by the house in which she concealed escapers from the camp at Oświęcim. In 1944 a group of partisans, surrounded in this house, fought an SS detachment.
Photograph taken after the war.

A transfer point in the smuggling of medicines to the prisoners was the chemist's shop at Brzeszcze, through which considerable amounts of medicines passed on their way to the camp.
Photograph taken after the war

Maria Bobrzecka (died after the war), the proprietress of the chemist's shop at Brzeszcze.

The house of the Nikiel family at Skidzin near Oświęcim, where escapers from the camp used to hide. Photograph taken after the war.

The boarding house belonging to Julian Dusik (first from left) at Łęki-Zasole. In this house prisoners who escaped from the camp were concealed.

Konstanty Jagiełło, who together with Tomasz Sobański escaped from the camp. Jagiełło later fought as a partisan in the vicinity of the camp (Brzeszcze-Łęki) and was killed in a skirmish with the SS (when his unit was being joined by another group of escapers).

Escaped prisoners joined the ranks of the partisans operating in the vicinity of the camp.
Photo: Part of detachment led by Adam Rysiewicz ("Teodor") at the hostel on Babia Góra (Zawoja). In the centre, wearing a light coat, is the former prisoner Tadeusz Uszyński ("Cygan").

A group of prisoners (from left): Bolesław Janiszewski, Józef Baraś-Komski (standing), Otto Küsel and Bolesław Kuczbara whose escape from the camp was assisted by the family of Andrzej Hart (second from right) of Libiąż, near Oświęcim.

A great deal of assistance was rendered prisoners by members of the mining community at Brzeszcze and the partisan unit operating in the region.
Photos from left: Edward Hałoń ("Boruta"), the partisan commander; Władysław Pytlik ("Birkut"); and Marian Gach.

An important role in maintaining contacts with the camp resistance movement was played by women. Helena Szpak-Datoń (right) acted as messenger between the camp and the partisan detachment at Brzeszcze.

The camp resistance assisted in the escape of Alfred Klahr (Lokmani), a member of the Central Committee of the Austrian Communist Party, who subsequently perished in Warsaw. Photo taken before 1939.

Many members of the camp resistance movement died at the hands of the SS. Photos (taken before 1939): Janusz Skrzetuski-Pogonowski, hanged together with eleven of his comrades on a mass gallows for maintaining contacts with the civilian population (below left); Róża Robota, hanged together with three other women prisoners for helping to smuggle explosives to the members of the *Sonderkommando* who rebelled at Brzezinka in 1944 (below right).

1 2 3

In order to expand its contacts with partisan movement outside the camp, the camp resistance organized the escape of a group of five prisoners. They were: Bernard Świerczyna (above left), Piotr Piąty (above centre), Czesław Duzel (above right), Zbigniew Raynoch and the Austrian Ernst Burger (last two not shown). As a result of betrayal the escapers were caught by the SS. Duzel and Raynoch were killed on the spot. The remaining three, together with other Austrians Rudolf Frieml (below left) and Ludwig Vesely (below right) were hanged in the camp on 30 December 1944. Photographs taken before 1939.

4 5

Der SS-Standortälteste Auschwitz, den 29. April 1944.
Auschwitz.

Tgb.Nr. 150/44 geh.   G e h e i m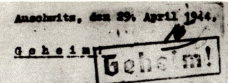

S t a n d o r t s o n d e r b e f e h l.

Betrifft: Verstärkter Terror und Sabotagetätigkeit der illegalen kommunistischen polnischen Widerstandsbewegung in der Zeit vom 27.4. bis 5.5.1944.

Das illegale Zentralkomitee der polnischen kommunistischen Arbeiterpartei "P.P.R." hat Funktionäre zu einer verstärkten Maiaktion für die Zeit vom 27.4. bis 5.5.1944 aufgefordert. Dabei soll der 1. Mai 1944 unter der Losung einer Arbeiterfront der Arbeiterklasse im Kampf um ein freies demokratisches Polen, der 3. Mai 1944 als 153. Nationalfeiertag geführt werden.
Von zuverlässiger Seite wurde dazu weiter in Erfahrung gebracht, dass die Terror- und Sabotagetätigkeit gegen deutsche Behörden und Wehrmachtsdienststellen in folgender Weise verstärkt werden soll:
a) Anschläge auf Eisenbahnzüge, Posten und Wachen der Gendarmerie, Kraftfahrzeugtransporte,
b) Überfälle auf Gefängnisse und Befreiung von Gefangenen, sowie bei Munitions- und Waffenarsenale.,
c) Attentate auf Beamte der Sicherheitspolizei,
d) Ermordung von Agenten,
e) Sabotage in grösseren Werken.
Für den gesamten Standort Auschwitz wird ab sofort bis zum 5. Mai 1944 einschliesslich **U r l a u b s s p e r r e** verhängt einschliesslich Standorturlaub und Stadturlaub.
Die einzelnen Dienststellen haben für ausreichende Bewachung Sorge zu tragen. Kontrolle der polnischen Zivilarbeiter ist besonders intensiv durchzuführen. Die jeweiligen Wachkompanien Auschwitz I und II haben für Sicherung des Lagers und der Wachgebäude Sorge zu tragen. Die übrigen Kompanien haben erhöhte Alarmbereitschaft anzuordnen. Dieses gilt besonders bei Einbruch der Dunkelheit. Die Truppenunterkünfte sind durch Innendienstler und Funktionsunterführer zu bewachen.
Die Kompanien Auschwitz I stellen gleichzeitig in Verbindung mit der Kommandantur II Streifen für das Interessengebiet K.L. Auschwitz einschliesslich der SS-Siedlung. Die Streifen sind so einzuteilen, dass keinerlei Ausfälle in der Gefangenenbegleitung eintreten.
SS-Hauptsturmführer **S t o p p e l** übernimmt die Einteilung des gesamten Streifendienstes, insbesondere für kriegswichtige Objekte.
Die Schutzhaftlagerführer treffen entsprechende Vorkehrungen zur Durchführung der Sicherheit ihres Lagers.
Kommandantur K.L. Auschwitz III regelt nach den örtlichen Verhältnissen die Sicherung der einzelnen Lager.
Jeder einzelne SS-Angehörige hat die Pflicht, in der Zeit bis zum 5. Mai 1944 mit besonderer Aufmerksamkeit seinen Dienst zu versehen und dort einzugreifen, wo gegebenenfalls Erscheinungen auftreten, die die Sicherheit des Lagers gefährden könnten.

F.d.R.   I.V.
SS-Hauptsturmführer   gez. Hartjenstein
und Adjutant.   SS-Sturmbannführer.

Photocopy of a special garrison order of the command of *KL Auschwitz* issued on 29 April 1944 in connection with the intensified sabotage operations being conducted by the Polish Workers' Party.

Photocopy of a smuggled letter of 18 October 1944 written in code by the prisoners Stanisław Kłodziński ("Stakło") and Józef Cyrankiewicz ("Tor"), mentioning *inter alia* the arrest of Stanisław Jasieński ("Urban") and Antoni Szlachcic ("Huzar").

The Nazi war criminals before the International Military Tribunal at Nuremberg.

Oswald Pohl, head of the SS economic administration (WVHA), sentenced to death by an American Military Tribunal for crimes committed in the concentration camps.

Immediately after the liberation of *KL Auschwitz* the USSR Supreme State Commission for the Investigation of German Crimes began work under the chairmanship of General Dr. Dmitri Kudryavtsev. The Commission examined and preserved the traces of the crimes committed by the Nazis in the camp, took evidence from former prisoners and organized medical aid for the sick.
Photo: Members of the Commission in session in the former office of the camp commandant.

The Polish Commission for the Investigation of Nazi Crimes made inspections of the places where the Nazis had carried out their programme of the mass extermination of millions of people.
Photo: Members of the Commission inspecting the remains of a combined gas chamber and crematorium (crematorium V) at Brzezinka, destroyed by the SS in order to remove the evidence of their crimes.

The crimes committed by the Nazis at *KL Auschwitz* shook public opinion throughout the world. Various delegations came to Oświęcim to see the traces of these crimes.
Photo: A British delegation consisting of the Dean of Canterbury, Dr. Hewlett Johnson, and Professor J. D. Eye of Oxford at Brzezinka in May 1945.

The first commandant of *KL Auschwitz*, Rudolf Höss, who was discovered hiding under the name of Franz Lang in the British zone of occupation in Germany, being extradited to Poland.

Rudolf Höss was tried before the Supreme National Tribunal in Poland. The trial was held in Warsaw and ended in Höss being sentenced to death. After a request for pardon had been rejected, he was hanged in 1947 at Oświęcim. Photo: Rudolf Höss in the dock.

In 1947 40 former members of the SS staff of *KL Auschwitz* were tried before the Supreme National Tribunal in Cracow.
Photos: Top left: the courtroom. Centre left: the accused (front row, from left) Arthur Liebehenschel, who succeeded Höss as commandant of the camp, Marie Mandel, head of the women's camp; and Hans Aumeier, *Lagerführer* of the main camp. Bottom left: front row of the dock with the wardresses (from left): **Therese Brandl, Alice Orlowski, Luise Danz, Hildegard Marthe Luise Lächert. Top right**: the accused (from left) Heinrich Josten, Wilhelm Gerhard Gehring, Kurt Hugo Müller, Ludwig Plagge, Richard Albert Schröder, Otto Lätsch and Fritz Wilhelm Buntrock. Bottom right: the accused stand as sentence is passed (front row, from left): Arthur Liebehenschel, Marie Mandel, Hans Aumeier, Karl Ernst Möckel and Maximilian Grabner; (second row, from left): Johann Paul Kremer and Erich Muhsfeld.

4

5

In the trial before the *Landsgericht* at Frankfurt am Main (Federal Republic of Germany), the chief accused was the last commandant of *KL Auschwitz*, Richard Baer. He died in custody before the trial began.

Part of the dock in the trial of Robert Mulka and others in Frankfurt am Main. Foreground (wearing glasses) the SS pharmacist Victor Capesius, behind him (with handkerchief in pocket) the former *Rapportführer* (camp marshal) Oswald Kaduk.

In the German Democratic Republic in 1966 the trial was held in Berlin of the former SS doctor Horst Fischer, who was sentenced to death.
Photo: Part of the courtroom with the accused giving evidence before the microphone.

In connection with trials being held in the Federal Republic of Germany of former members of the staff of *KL Auschwitz*, the government of the Polish People's Republic agreed to allow a Frankfurt court to visit Oświęcim.

Photo: The president of the *Landsgericht* in Frankfurt am Main, Judge Walter Hotz (wearing hat).

A second visit by the *Landsgericht* in Frankfurt am Main to the site of the former *KL Auschwitz*.

The site of the former *Konzentrationslager Auschwitz* where now stands the State Museum of Oświęcim — a Monument to the Martyrdom of the Polish and Other Nations, dedicated to the memory of the millions of victims murdered there by the Nazis in the years 1941—45.
Photo: The main entrance gate with the inscription *Arbeit macht frei*.

"We heard a grenade explode near the camp gate. We immediately looked out from the barracks and saw several Soviet scouts, their guns ready to shoot, advancing from the gate toward us. We right away put out white sheets with red stripes forming a cross sewn onto them. Upon seeing us, the scouts lowered their guns. A spontaneous greeting followed. As I could speak Russian, I addressed the scouts with these words: 'Zdrastvuitie pobieditieli i osvoboditieli!' In response, we heard: 'Uzhe vy svobodniy'." [2]

Altogether, 231 Soviet soldiers were killed in the fighting for the liberation of the Auschwitz subcamp of Monowitz, the Auschwitz main camp, the Birkenau camp, the town of Oświęcim, and the adjacent region. Sixty to seventy of them, including Sub. Lt. Ghildmudin Badriyevich, perished during the operation in the camp zone.

About 7,000 prisoners had survived until the liberation in the Auschwitz main camp, the camps in Brzezinka and Oświęcim-Monowice. A number of prisoners difficult to determine (most likely over 400) were liberated by Soviet soldiers on 27 January and shortly thereafter in the subcamps of *KL Auschwitz: Blechhammer* in Blachownia Śląska, *Eintrachthütte* in Świętochłowice, *Fürstengrube* in Wesoła, *Janinagrube* in Libiąż, and *Neu Dachs* in Jaworzno.

Among the prisoners freed in *KL Auschwitz*, there were some eminent persons, renowned and valued in Poland and abroad: the Polish sculptor and painter, Xawery Dunikowski; Bruno Fischer, a pediatrics professor at Prague University and head of the Children's Clinic there; Dr. Alfred Fiderkiewicz, a physician and author, activist of the Polish working class and peasant movement; Professor Stanisław Kętrzyński, a Polish mediaeval historian and diplomat; an activist of the Polish working class movement, Adam Kuryłowicz; Ferrand Henri Limousin, a professor of pathological anatomy at the University of Clermont; Geza Mansfeld, member of the Hungarian Academy of Sciences, a professor of pharmacology and experimental pathology in Pécs; Dr. Roman Łaba, a merited physician from Przemyśl.

On the site of the Auschwitz and Birkenau camps, the Soviet soldiers found the bodies of about 600 prisoners who had been shot by SS men during the withdrawal from Oświęcim or had died of emaciation at that time. These, however, were not the only traces of crimes which they encountered.

Part of the liberated Auschwitz prisoners who were in a relatively good physical shape immediately left for home.

---

[2] Account of Anna Chomicz. APMO. Zespół "Oświadczenia", t. 75, k. 13.

2. AID TO THE LIBERATED PRISONERS

Already in the first days after Oświęcim had been liberated, aid was extended to the prisoners by the Soviet military medical service and by the Polish authorities and society. Especially active in this respect were the workers of the Polish Red Cross (PCK) in Oświęcim, Brzeszcze near Oświęcim, and Cracow. The largest group of volunteers arrived from Cracow, among them Warsaw inhabitants, participants in the Warsaw Uprising, evacuated to Cracow by the Nazi authorities. In effect, next to the Soviet field hospitals, which changed as military units were redeployed and were headed, initially, by doctors (with the rank of major) Veitkov, Khitarov, and Mielai, and later by Zhilinska and Grobovoi, a PCK Camp Hospital was established on the site of the former camp, headed by Dr. Józef Bellert of Warsaw. Over 4,500 sick prisoners, citizens of twenty odd states, were placed in these hospitals. Among the 960 or so Polish citizens, there were 160 to 170 Polish women deported from Warsaw to *KL Auschwitz* during the Warsaw Uprising. Almost all of them were over 46 years of age, half of them over 60, and close to 30 over 70 years old. Among the prisoners, there were also more than 200 babies and children ranging in age from several days up to 15 years, many of them twins. Most of the former prisoners suffered from *Durchfall,* or hunger-induced diarrhoea, a symptom of the so-called hunger disease (*distrophia alimentaris*). In most cases, the disease was complicated by other diseases, chiefly T.B.

The staff of the PCK Camp Hospital included, next to Dr. Bellert, the physicians Jan Jodłowski, Jadwiga Magnuszewska, and Bolesław Urbański of Cracow, and Jan Szczęśniak of Oświęcim. As regards the staff of the Soviet field hospitals, next to the aforementioned commanders, those known by name include Mj. Dr. Polakov, the head physician under Mj. Mielai and Mj. Zhilinska, and the surgeon, Mj. Dr. Yeltanski.

Some of the volunteers, residents of Oświęcim, Brzeszcze, and the environs, took up work in the Soviet field hospitals before the arrival from Cracow of the PCK team, i.e. prior to 5-6 February 1945. Among them were inhabitants of Brzeszcze (e.g. Tadeusz Mleko, Roman Pęcikiewicz, and Wilhelm Wazdrąg), who came to Brzezinka out of their own accord and were the first Poles, beside the Soviet medical service, to take care of the sick. Other Brzeszcze inhabitants (e.g. Zdzisław Bosek and several others) and many residents of Oświęcim (Józef Mroziński and several others as well as Seraphite nuns) volunteered to cooperate with the Soviet medical service in the former main camp. Residents of Poręba Wielka and Włosienica worked together with the Soviet physicians and medical attendants in caring for the former prisoners of the subcamp in Monowice, whom they also supplied with food.

The changing Soviet field hospitals and the PCK Camp Hospital closely cooperated with each other. PCK nurses were added to the staff caring for a number of barracks under the exclusive Soviet administration. In time, mutual consultations between Soviet and Polish physicians became very frequent, as did joint rounds of the sick wards. Eventually, the Soviet and Polish staff were mixed together, and the forms of supervision of the treatment were regulated.

The work under the specific camp conditions posed many difficulties to the Soviet military medical service and the PCK volunteers. The biggest obstacles were encountered in Brzezinka. In order to maintain an appropriate temperature in the barracks, fire had to be kept day and night. Layers of excrement left by those suffering from diarrhoea were scraped off the clay floors, which were subsequently washed. The water necessary for washing the sick and cooking the meals was supplied from distant fire fighting reservoirs and wells, and in some instances lumps of snow were melted to obtain water. Since the number of medical attendants and other auxiliary staff was insufficient, it was impossible to remove immediately all the corpses lying in front of the barracks since the liberation to say nothing of removing excrement and all kind or refuse littering the whole site of the former camp.

, Initially in Brzezinka, there were about 2,200 sick former prisoners, who were looked after, aside from several physicians and few orderlies, by 12 PCK nurses, so each of them had the charge of about 200 patients. In order to cope with their duties, the members of the PCK staff worked ten odd hours a day, and at times two or three days running.

As the conditions existing in Brzezinka, and also in Monowice, did not ensure appropriate results in the treatment of the sick, all of them were gradually transferred, within the space of several weeks, to the brick barracks in the main camp. Members of the staff of the Soviet field hospitals and PCK volunteers invested a great deal of effort in adapting the barrack in the former main camp for hospital purposes. Hundreds of bedridden former prisoners were removed from the soiled bunks and taken to the freshly cleaned rooms. Gradually, difficulties of all kinds were overcome, e.g. shortage of medicines, of some food products, of bed linen, and of water. In time, specialist wards were created in the PCK Hospital: for T.B., internal diseases, surgery, and a ward for women suffering from grave nervous and mental disorders.

The specificity of the work of PCK volunteers on the site of the former main camp is illustrated by an account by a woman volunteer of her first turn of duty in a room accommodating 80 patients:

"Already during my first night shift, eleven women died in the room. I had to remove the bodies from the bunks and take them into the corridor all by myself. Early in the morning, the corpses were taken from the barracks by attendants. All night I heard cries coming from various corners of the room: 'Schwester! Schieber!' [Sister! Bed-pan!]. The sick were suffering from *Durchfall,* or diarrhoea caused by hunger. So all the time I was bringing them bed-pans. There was no one to help me." [3]

The patients were being gradually accustomed to eating by taking meals almost like doses of medicines; for example, they were fed soup of mashed potatoes: first a spoonful thre times daily, and later several spoonfuls at a time. For many weeks after the liberation, nurses would find bread under pallets and mattresses, hidden by some patients for the next day, since they did not believe they would receive new rations soon. The constant fear and the reflexes acquired in the camp by some patients were stronger than the sense of reality. For this reason, also, many patients directed to the bath would run away upon hearing the word "bath", and it would take a long time to explain to them that in the bath to which they were going they would not be in danger. They kept associating the bath with the camp "Saunas", in which — as was known — selection of prisoners was carried out those unift for work being put to death in the gas chambers. Nurses met with similar reactions as the case of baths while making intramuscular and intravenous injections. Some patients shunned or were averse to injections for fear of "phenol", i.e. for fear of being killed by a phenol injection, as many of their fellow inmates had been in *KL Auschwitz*.

Under the solicitous care of physicians, nurses, and hospital attendants, the patients would gradually rid themselves of the reflexes acquired in *KL Auschwitz*. However, the impact of the camp experiences upon their psyche was irreversible. For two to three months, nurses and male attendants looked after the sick working two shifts: day and night. These duties, however, exceeded their physical abilities. Under the circumstances, the care extended to the sick was in some cases incomplete and fragmentary. A radical improvement took place in April and May, i.e. after the forms of work of the Soviet field hospitals and the PCK Camp Hospital had been stabilized, and eight-hour shifts for nurses had been introduced.

One should stress the active participation of several scores of former men and women prisoners in the treatment of their colleagues in the Soviet field hospitals and the PCK Camp Hospital. Despite the unsatisfactory state of their own health, they performed the functions of physicians, nurses, attendants, and orderlies, thereby continuing the action of prisoners' self-aid commenced before the liberation. They included, amongst others: Dr. Irena Konieczna of Poland, Dr. Tibor Villányi of Hungary,

---

[3] Account of a former woman volunteer, participant in the PCK action in Oświęcim in 1945, nurse Maria Rożog. APMO. Zespół "Oświadczenia", t. 74, k. 175—176.

Dr. Otto Wolken of Austria, Terezie Jírová of Czechoslovakia, and Aldo Ragazzi of Italy.

Next to medical aid and nursing, other forms of assistance to former prisoners had developed. Noteworthy was the PCK's mediation in establishing correspondence between former prisoners and their families, and the information and inquiry activity conducted by the administration of the PCK Camp Hospital, an activity later taken over by the PCK information offices in Cracow and Warsaw and carried on, from 1945 onwards, also by an information section at the State Museum in Oświęcim.

Of considerable importance for many a patient was the aid extended by the Catholic clergy, among them the parish priest in Oświęcim, Father Jan Skarbek, and Father Stanisław Rokita (the director of the Salesian establishment in Oświęcim and the first chaplain on the site of the former camp after the liberation). This assistance was of both moral and material nature.

Most of the former prisoners left the Soviet field hospitals and the PCK Camp Hospital within three to four months from the liberation. Some of them set out for their home towns and home countries on their own, while others joined the transports organized by the Soviet military authorities. In spite of the shortage of vehicles, several scores of transports were formed dispatched from mid-February till July. Hundreds of former prisoners from countries other than Poland were taken to the repatriation points in Katowice, Bielsko, and Cracow. Many of them, just like the former inmates who had left the camp immediately after the liberation, received medical aid and meals and were accommodated in shelter homes established by Polish social institutions and organizations, among other places in Cracow.

The inhabitants of Oświęcim, Brzeszcze, and the environs not only cooperated in rendering aid to the sick on the site of the former camp, but also admitted over a hundred sick former inmates of the camp to the small hospitals they had set up in the town of Oświęcim and in Brzeszcze.

The PCK branch established in Oświęcim on 5 February 1945, and numbering, a'most from its inception, about 70 members, maintained close contacts with the PCK Camp Hospital and the Soviet military authorities in the field of assistance to former prisoners. The various problems were argeed upon with the management of the PCK Camp Hospital and the Soviet military authorities by the chairman of the board of the PCK branch in Oświęcim, Alojzy Ethens, and a member of the board, Antoni Leśniak. Under an agreement with the mentioned authorities, the branch sent groups of volunteers, called sanitary teams, to do the hardest and dirtiest work on the site of the liberated camp. The branch also admitted at least several scores of sick persons to the hospital it had established. The sick were cared for, voluntarily, by local physicians, among them Tadeusz Müller and Bogumił Pietrzyk.

Many sick ex-prisoners were admitted to the establishment of the Seraphite nuns in Oświęcim.

In the field of aid to former prisoners of *KL Auschwitz*, the PCK circle in Brzeszcze, re-established upon the liberation, played a role similar to that of the PCK branch in Oświęcim. In the hospital organized by the Brzeszcze circle, medical care was provided for, amongst others, 23 former women prisoners with 24 children, some of them babies, and a group of former prisoners suffering from T.B. The hospital was headed by Drs. Józef Sierankiewicz, Jan Drzewiecki, and Ernest Friebe. One of the nurses, Anna Krotosz, herself fell ill with tuberculosis and soon died. The hospital received medicines free of charge from the owner of the local pharmacy, Maria Bobrzecka, who until not long before had been very active in the clandestine movement for aid to Auschwitz prisoners. The PCK circle in Brzeszcze also extended care to 66 former prisoners freed on the site of the Auschwitz subcamp of *Jawischowitz* in Jawiszowice and provided medical aid for seven or eight former women prisoners from Brzezinka, looked after by the inhabitants of the nearby village of Wola. Moreover, in consultation with the circle, several local families took to their homes and cared for a number of former prisoners.

Just like Brzeszcze inhabitants, also residents of Oświęcim and other localities in the region (e.g. Poręba Wielka) and of Cracow admitted to their homes and cared for many former prisoners, frequently over a period of several weeks and even several months. Collections were organized, both officially and spontaneously, of food products for ex-prisoners.

Especially noteworthy is the fact that inhabitants of Oświęcim and Brzeszcze took care of a number of children from the camp in Brzezinka. In many instances, these children were after some time adopted by their foster parents. Some of them, after many years of searches, managed to find their closest relatives.

The sacrifice with which the PCK volunteers worked in the hospitals for the freed Auschwitz prisoners was greatly appreciated not only by the former prisoners, but also by the Soviet physicians. What determined the effects of the work of the PCK volunteers was doubtless the fact that most of them had been active, prior to the liberation, in the anti-Nazi resistance movement. They worked on the site of the liberated camp and in the hospitals in the town of Oświęcim and in Brzeszcze with the same zeal with which they had overcome extreme difficulties while in the underground movement. In conditions of the freshly regained freedom, the staff of the PCK Camp Hospital, the PCK branch in Oświęcim, and the PCK circle in Brzeszcze thus crowned their five years' activity in the clandestine centres for aid to Auschwitz prisoners situated in the vicinity of the camp, in Oświęcim, Cracow, and Upper Silesia.

The hospitalization in January and February 1945 of several thousand freed prisoners of *KL Auschwitz* was not the first case of this kind in the history of concentration camps. Previously, for example, many prisoners liberated from the Majdanek camp had found themselves in hospitals. Many other hospitals for the liberated prisoners of concentration camps (e.g. *KL Bergen-Belsen, KL Buchenwald, KL Mauthausen*) were organized by the military Allied authorities and the Red Cross organizations at a later time, during the last few weeks of the war. In all those hospitals, a unique confrontation occurred between medical science and a previously unknown category of patients, namely, former prisoners starved and emaciated both physically and mentally. The treatment of these patients was almost everywhere a pioneering effort. Nonetheless, the complex of Soviet and Polish hospitals on the site of the former *KL Auschwitz* and in its vicinity was unique in certain respects. This uniqueness was accounted for, above all, by the difficult frontline conditions in which several thousand former prisoners had to be given medical treatment. The scale of the difficulties which the Soviet physicians and PCK volunteers had to overcome in Oświęcim, Brzezinka, and Brzeszcze in January, February and March 1945 was certainly much bigger than in the hospitals organized for former prisoners during the last few weeks of the war. It is in this light that one should evaluate the effort and sacrifice of the 200 to 250 members of the staff of the hospitals in Oświęcim, Brzezinka, and Brzeszcze and of many other persons thanks to whom several thousand gravely ill ex-prisoners of *KL Auschwitz*, after a relatively short period of treatment, could return to their home towns and countries.

Noteworthy are the resolutions which the former Auschwitz prisoners staying in Oświęcim during the first months after the liberation addressed to the world public opinion, condemning Nazi crimes, warning against their repetition, and urging the world to counteract this menace. Three such resolutions are known. One was sent by a group of about a hundred Yugoslavs to the Yugoslav legation in Moscow, another was addressed by French communists to the Central Committee of the French Communist Party. The third resolution was handed to representatives of the Soviet authorities in Oświęcim in March 1945. It was signed by 27 persons: professors, physicians, engineers, lawyers, students, and other representatives of the intelligentsia from various countries. The resolution read:

"We the undersigned, liberated by the Red Army from the bloody Nazi rule, accuse before the international community the German government headed by Adolf Hitler of perpetrating the greatest mass murders and atrocities in the history of mankind...

"We request the international community to find out about the fate of millions of missing people of various nationalities and to save the prisoners who are still being held captive in Nazi Germany...

"In the name of humanism, we ask that everything possible be done in order to prevent a repetition in the future of the crimes committed by the Nazis and to ensure that the blood of innocent victims has not been shed in vain.

"We, about 100,000 prisoners of various nationalities, ask that the Nazi crimes should not go unpunished.

"As liberated prisoners, we owe our life to the heroic Red Army and we ask the international community and all governments to take cognizance of this and express gratitude on our behalf.

Prisoners of *KL Auschwitz*
(signatures of 27 former prisoners of *KL Auschwitz*)[4]

The liberation of Oświęcim by Soviet Army units on 27 January 1945 put an end to *KL Auschwitz*, which had been the largest Nazi camp and extermination centre, brought freedom to about 7,000 sick prisoners left in the Auschwitz camp, and presaged the regaining of independence by Auschwitz prisoners earlier evacuated inside the Third Reich.

However, 27 January 1945 was not the last day in the history of the Auschwitz camp. The camp has left a tremendous legacy which till this day manifests itself in various forms, in both the material and political-ideological spheres. To the world, Oświęcim-Auschwitz has become a symbol of Nazism. A social movement which could be termed the "Auschwitz movement" has developed in the Oświęcim region and wherever former Auschwitz prisoners and people concerned about the wartime history of Oświęcim are living. The movement was initiated, *inter alia*, by the events that occurred on the site of the former *KL Auschwitz* in the first months after the liberation of the camp.

The action of aid to the freed prisoners of *KL Auschwitz* taken up in late January and early February 1945 by the Soviet military medical service, the Polish authorities, and PCK workers preceded various actions of medical aid to ex-prisoners which have been organized till this day. The state of health of former Auschwitz prisoners, just as the state of health of ex-prisoners of other concentration camps, has become the object

---

[4] Resolution of a group of former prisoners of 4 March, 1945. APMO, Zespół "Materiały", t. 3, sygn. Mat. (29—30; t. 23, sygn. Mat. (459) copies in French, German, and Hungarian).

of study by many teams of physicians in various European countries. In effect of these studies, a new disease called "concentration camp syndrome" (*KL-syndrome*) has been included in the international classification of diseases. At the same time, the question of revindication of indemnities to former prisoners for the loss of health and material losses has assumed great significance.

Beginning from 1945, when PCK members proceeded to securing the camp documents and the remnants of the camp, various forms of commemoration of the Auschwitz camp have developed. The most significant event was the foundation on the site of the former camp in 1947 of a State Museum in Oświęcim as a site commemorating "the martyrdom of the Polish Nation and Other Nations". The martyrdom of Auschwitz prisoners is frequently referred to by participants in peace demonstrations held in various regions of the world. The history of the camp has been very widely reflected in publicist writings and scientific and popular literature all over the world. Moreover, the history of *KL Auschwitz* and its relics have provided many artist with the inspiration to create unique works of art, musical compositions, and films.

A considerable role in the "Auschwitz movement" in Poland is played by unions of former Auschwitz prisoners (so-called Auschwitz Clubs) which function at the local branches of the Union of Fighters for Freedom and Democracy, and on a global scale by the International Auschwitz Committee.

The history of the "Auschwitz movement" constitutes an integral complement of the history of *KL Auschwitz,* testifies to the concern which the existence of the camp evoked in the world and to the immensity of the tragedy of which the camp was the cause. Thus, the history of the camp fully deserves the attention of future researchers. Many of them will doubtless choose as the object of their research the significance of the "Auschwitz movement" in the international peace movement.

Kazimierz Smoleń

The Prosecution of the Auschwitz Criminals

1. LEGAL FOUNDATIONS OF THE PROSECUTION AND PUNISHMENT OF WAR CRIMINALS

No doubt the reader will be wondering if and to what extent the crimes committed in *Konzentrationslager Auschwitz* were punished, and if so, whether that punishment bore the character of revenge, or whether it was administered with the full majesty of the law.

Before an attempt is made to answer these questions, it would appear to be in order to draw attention to a number of problems, namely: were there earlier attempts at punishing war criminals and what were the results; how far in the light of existing international laws and usages is the punishment of such criminals possible; did the experience of the aftermath of the First World War influence the United Nations in the Second; and by what means did the latter solve this problem on the international plane? It would also appear to be desirable to show the influence of various acts of international law on the internal penal law of individual states, with special reference to the example of Poland. In this respect one should also give prominence to the role of Poland in consistently extending international legal assistance.

Each of the above problems is reflected in the abundant specialist literature which has appeared in many countries and in various language versions. From the extensive and complex material we shall discuss the most essential matters concerning directly or indirectly the punishment of the criminals of Oświęcim.

★

The problem of international punishment of war criminals appeared for the first time in the provisions of the Treaty of Versailles concluded in 1919 after the First World War. In Part vii of this treaty, entitled "Penalties", Article 227 accused the Emperor William II of "a supreme offence against international morality and the sanctity of treaties", and Article 228 directed the initiation of proceedings against persons accused of committing crimes "in violation of the laws and customs of war", as defined in the Fourth Hague Convention of 1907. After the Paris peace conference of 1919 a special commission on war criminals, also known as the "Commission of Fifteen", began work on determining precisely the rules of this Convention, fixing a definition of war crimes and establishing penal sanctions for their commission.[1] In accordance with these provisions an inter-allied "high tribunal" was to be appointed.

In practice these rules were not implemented, as Germany, being interested in hushing up the war crimes that had been committed, created its own legal machinery before the international allied tribunal had been constituted. The Supreme Reich Tribunal in Leipzig, which came into being in December 1919, refused to surrender the 900 or so criminals demanded (including the military commanders Paul von Hindenburg, Erich Ludendorff, August von Mackensen and Alfred von Tirpitz), reducing their number to 45, all of whom were lower ranking officers or NCOs.

Of the 45 accused only nine were sentenced, although in no instance was the death sentence applied. Some of the criminals were never apprehended at all, and the Emperor William II, who was to have stood trial before a special international tribunal of five judges (representing France, Italy, Japan, the UK and the USA respectively) evaded this fate by accepting the asylum offered him by Holland, where he lived after the war in the little town of Doorn. In a note of 16 January 1920, signed by the French premier Clemenceau, the Allied powers demanded that Holland surrender William, but the Dutch government refused.

The commission of Allied lawyers which studied the results of the activities of the Leipzig Tribunal found that most of the accused had been acquitted or that proceedings against them had been waived. The Tribunal's activity was referred to as the "farce of Leipzig". The accused left the courtroom as national heroes with experience which was to be of use to them in future.

The immensity of the war crimes committed by the Third Reich during the Second World War intensified the necessity of working out new acts

---

[1] Alfons Klafkowski, *Ściganie zbrodniarzy wojennych w Niemieckiej Republice Federalnej w świetle prawa międzynarodowego* (herafter *Ściganie zbrodniarzy...*). Poznań 1968, p. 49, Note 20.

of international law which, being based on the existing foundation of the Fourth Hague Convention of 1907 (ratified by all the belligerent states, including the Axis powers), would make possible the just punishment of war criminals. The scale and nature of the crimes committed was such that "when the international community and the international law which governs it were threatened with ruin, the powers guiding the United Nations proceeded to organize an effort aimed at restoring respect for international law"[2] and in particular to supplement the legal norms contained in the above-mentioned Convention.

Information concerning the crimes committed by the Nazis had been passed on to the Polish government-in-emigration while the war was still on by the Polish resistance movement, which thus contributed to many international initiatives and intensified diplomatic activity concerning the prosecution and punishment of war criminals. Appeals, diplomatic notes, government statements, declarations, treaties and research findings became the basis for an intensive development of international law regarding the prosecution of war criminals, the development of procedural principles and ways of meting out appropriate punishment to the guilty.

As early as April 1940 an appeal had appeared addressed "To the Conscience of the World", signed by the governments of Britain, France and Poland, in which it was stated that "the three undersigned governments are profoundly shocked by news of the crimes being committed in Poland by the German occupation authorities and forces". In this document, which arose on Poland's initiative, the responsibility of Germany for these crimes was again affirmed and decisions were taken to right the wrongs visited on the Polish people.

The involvement of the United Nations in the business of conducting the war prevented any more major statements being made in this matter for almost another eighteen months. Not until 25 October 1941 was anything more heard on the subject, when two statements were issued almost simultaneously, one by Roosevelt and the other by Churchill. The President of the United States declared that terror would never bring peace to Europe, that it only sowed hatred which would some day produce a terrible punishment. The British premier stated that the atrocities perpetrated in the occupied countries, especially in the territories of the Soviet Union which were engulfed by hostilities, exceeded everything which had been seen since the darkest and most bestial ages of mankind.

These matters were formulated even more clearly in two notes from the Soviet Union (25 November 1941 and 6 January 1942) addressed "To all governments with whom the USSR maintains diplomatic relations". In them attention was drawn to the crimes committed against Soviet

---
[2] *Ibid*, p. 49.

POWs: "Prisoners are tortured with red hot irons, their eyes are gouged out, their feet, hands, ears and noses are cut off and their bellies are ripped open, they are tied to tanks and crushed under them." The Soviet government placed responsibility for these inhuman deeds on the German military and civil authorities of the criminal Nazi government of the Third Reich.

One of the earliest legal groups which arose to deal with the problem of punishing war criminals was the International Commission for the Reconstruction and Development of Penal Law, formed in 1940 in Cambridge. Its members included distinguished lawyers. The Commission's main task was to consider the possibility of establishing principles of retribution for war crimes, to work out definitions of these crimes and ways in which penalties might be imposed by future courts. Among many other principles the Commission laid down that the war criminal should be tried both in accordance with international law and the penal law applying in the territory where the crimes were committed. Important work in this field was also done by another group called the London International Assembly. Neither group, however, had an official character. Their conclusions, which were even framed in part in the form of draft laws, were passed on to the United Nations War Crimes Commission, whose first session took place on 20 November 1943. This Commission assembled evidence of war crimes, drew up lists of criminals and principles ensuring their effective prosecution. It began its work in January 1944, and so-called national offices were formed in association with it. One of the first of these was the Polish office.[3]

The first document of the United Nations concerning culpability for war crimes was the Declaration of Allied Countries Occupied by Germany of 13 January 1942, which was released after a conference in London convened on the initiative of Poland and Czechoslovakia and chaired by the Polish premier, General Władysław Sikorski. The Declaration contained a demand for the punishment of those guilty of violating the principles of international law. It contained a statement to the effect that one of the basic aims of the war was "the punishment by means of an organized system of justice of those who are guilty of crimes and responsible for them — regardless of whether these crimes were committed on their instruction, by them personally or with their participation in any form". It also announced the creation of mechanisms for the extradition of war criminals.

The Declaration had not only great diplomatic, but also legal significance, as a unified standpoint had been agreed among the occupied coun-

---

[3] Tadeusz Cyprian and Jerzy Sawicki, "Komisja Zjednoczonych Narodów do Spraw Zbrodni Wojennych", in: *Wojskowy Przegląd Prawniczy*, 1947, no. 4, p. 404—413.

tries (Poland, Czechoslovakia, Belgium, France, Greece, Luxemburg, the Netherlands, Norway and Yugoslavia) and the representatives of the Great Powers who had been invited to London: the UK, USSR, USA and China. From this moment on one may note on the part of these states a number of collective acts aimed at elaborating principles of the prosecution and sentencing of war criminals, and of seeing to it that sentences would be carried out. A large number of notes were exchanged in which the criminal activities of the authorities of the German Reich in the occupied countries were described. On 7 October 1942 President Roosevelt issued another statement affirming that the United States would prosecute the Nazi leaders.

A legal act of great significance was the Moscow Declaration on war crimes issued jointly on 30 October 1943 by the USSR, UK and USA in the name of the thirty-two states belonging to the United Nations. It stated that "At the time of the granting of any armistice to any Government which may be set up in Germany, those German officers and men and members of the National Socialist Party who have been responsible for or have taken a consenting part in the above atrocities, massacres, and executions will be sent back to the countries in which their abominable deeds were done in order that they may be judged and punished according to the laws of these liberated countries and of the free Governments which will be erected therein." Lists of criminals will be drawn up in all these countries with all possible exactitude.

It was also stated in the Declaration that all war criminals would in principle be surrendered to those countries in whose territories they had committed crimes, and only the so-called major war criminals, whose activities were not limited to a precise geographically defined territory (i.e. who had been active in several countries or who had given orders concerning several or all of the occupied countries), would be punished on the basis of a joint decision of the United Nations. The Declaration warned further that with the greatest certainty the three Allied powers would pursue these criminals even to the furthest corners of the earth and deliver them to their accusers so that justice might be done.

The contents of the Declaration exercised an enormous influence on the decree of 22 January 1946 on the creation of a Supreme National Tribunal in Poland and the resolution of the Polish Supreme Court concerning the application of the decree of 31 August 1944 on the punishment of Fascist and Nazi war criminals and traitors to the Polish nation.

In the Declaration concerning Germany adopted by the Great Powers after the Yalta Conference (also known as the Crimean Conference) on 11 February 1945, it was recalled that the United Nations had decided to bring all war criminals to justice and swift punishment and exact reparation in kind for the destruction wrought by Germans. Moreover the Declaration contained decisions concerning the necessity of completely uprooting national socialism and German nationalism in order to ensure that Germany would never again be able to disturb the peace and security of the whole world.

The question of punishment for war criminals was also dealt with by the Potsdam Agreement of 2 August, a whole chapter (Chapter VII: War Criminals) being devoted to it, while Art. 5 of Chapter III contains the following statements: "War criminals and those who have participated in planning or carrying out national socialist undertakings involving or resulting in atrocities or war crimes shall be arrested and brought to judgement. National socialist leaders, influential Nazi sympathizers and high officials of Nazi organizations and institutions and any other persons dangerous to the occupation and its objectives shall be arrested and interned."

2. THE INTERNATIONAL MILITARY TRIBUNAL

On 8 August 1945, a few days after the Potsdam Agreement, an Agreement concerning the prosecution and punishment of the major war criminals of the European Axis countries was signed in London by the four Great Powers, and later by a further 19 of the states belonging to the United Nations. To the Agreement was attached the Charter of the International Military Tribunal.

The London Agreement referred to the principles laid down in the Moscow Declaration and contained seven basic articles. Article I dealt with the creation of an International Military Tribunal to try war criminals whose criminal deeds could not be linked with any specific locality, regardless of whether they were accused individually or as members of organizations or groups, or in both capacities. Article III stated that each of the signatories would take the steps necessary to put at the disposal of the International Military Tribunal for the examination of charges against and the trial of those of the major war criminals whom it was holding in custody and who were to appear before the Tribunal. The signatories would also do everything in their power to place at the disposal of the Tribunal for examination of charges and trial by the Tribunal those of the major criminals who were not on the territory of any of the signatories. Article IV stated that the Agreement did not impair the decisions contained in the Moscow Declaration concerning the surrender of war criminals to these countries in whose territories they had committed their crimes.

The Charter of the International Military Tribunal is an integral part of the Agreement and is composed of thirty articles contained in seven chapters. It defines *inter alia* the constitution, competence and powers of the Tribunal. In Chapter II, Article 6, three kinds of crimes are mentioned which come under the jurisdiction of the Tribunal and entail personal accountability:

(a) Crimes against peace, i.e. the planning, preparation, initiation or waging of a war of aggression or war which is a violation of international treaties, agreements, or participation in planning or conspiring to commit one of the above-mentioned acts;

(b) War crimes, i.e. violation of the laws and customs of war. Such violations will include but not be limited to murder, ill treatment or deportation for forced labour or any other purpose of the civilian population in occupied areas or from these areas, murder or ill treatment of prisoners of war or persons at sea; the killing of hostages; the looting of public or private property; the wanton destruction of settlements, towns or villages, or devastation not justified by the exigencies of war;

(c) Crimes against humanity, i.e. murder, extermination, enslavement, deportation and other inhuman acts perpetrated against any civilian population before or during the war, or persecution for political, racial or religious reasons in the commission of any crime coming within the competence of the Tribunal or in connection with such a crime, regardless of whether this was in accordance with or contrary to the law of the country in which the crime was committed.

In the conclusion to this article it is clearly indicated that: "Leaders, organizers, instigators and accomplices who took part in the making or execution of a joint plan or conspiracy to commit one of the above-mentioned crimes will answer for all deeds perpetrated by anyone in connection with the implementation of such a plan."

On the basis of Article IX of the Charter the International Military Tribunal could also in the course of a trial recognize as criminal a group or organization a member of which had been charged individually. Article X contains the further formulation: "In cases where some group or organization will be recognized by the Tribunal as criminal, the proper authorities of each signatory will have the right to deliver individuals to a national or occupation court for membership in this group or organization. In such cases the criminal character of such a group or organization will be considered as proved and will be called in doubt."

The place chosen for the trial before the Tribunal, which had hitherto been based in Berlin, was Nuremberg, it being added that successive trials would be held in places to be determined by the Tribunal. But the International Military Tribunal only sat once, in what has become known as the Nuremberg Trial of 1945—46.

Proceedings before the International Military Tribunal lasted from 20 November 1945 to 31 August 1946, after which the Tribunal retired to consider its verdict which was announced, together with supporting judgement, on 30 September and 1 October 1946.

With reference to its stautory provisions the IMT recognized in its verdict the following Nazi organizations as criminal: the political leadership of the *Nationalsozialistische Deutsche Arbeiterpartei* (National Socialist German Workers' Party, or NSDAP), the *Geheime Staatspolizei* (Gestapo) and *Sicherheitsdients* (SD), the *Schutz-Staffeln* (SS) and with certain reservations the *Sturmabteilungen* (SA).

The matter of the crimes committed in the concentration camps cropped up frequently in the course of the proceedings at Nuremberg, especially in connection with the recognition of the SS as a criminal organization. In its findings the Nuremberg Judgement had this to say: "The evidence adduced indicates beyond all doubt that the constant brutal treatment of the inmates of the concentration camps was a result of the general policy of the SS, in accordance with which the people confined in concentration camps were to be treated as belonging to an inferior race and regarded with contempt..."

The Nuremberg Judgement considered the concentration camps as one "...of the most shameful means of terror in relation to the population of the occupied territories" and called them "death factories" in which hunger and starvation rations, sadism, lack of clothing, lack of medical care, diseases, beating, hanging, freezing, forced suicide and shootings played the main role in achieving the aim. The Judgement also contains the finding that "a certain number of concentration camps were equipped with gas chambers for mass killing of prisoners and with ovens for burning the bodies" and the statement that "it is simply impossible to point to even a single section of the SS which did not participate in this criminal activity".

The legal norms laid down in the London Agreement of 8 August 1945 between the four powers and in the attached Charter of the International Military Tribunal, and later repeated and justified in the judgement of the IMT in the trial of the major war criminals, were confirmed by the General Assembly of the United Nations and under the official name of the Nuremberg Principles have become part of international law.

3. THE NUREMBERG TRIALS OF 1947—49

In the various occupation zones of Germany special Military Tribunals operated, called into being in execution of Statute No. 10 of the Allied Control Commission for Germany of 20 December 1945 concerning punishment for war crimes, crimes against peace and crimes against humanity. In the American occupation zone, in the building of the IMT in Nuremberg, twelve major trials were held in the years 1947-49. The guiding principles of these trials were those of the Nuremberg Trial of 1945-46. Of those trials those in particular should be mentioned in which the question of crimes in concentration camps was raised. These were:

(i) Case I — against doctors of the Wehrmacht and SS guilty of carrying out criminal, pseudomedical experiments on concentration camp inmates and POWs;

(ii) Case IV — against the leadership of WVHA. The main accused was the chief of this office, Oswald Pohl. In the trial it was proved that the accused had been guilty of war crimes and crimes against humanity, the extermination of POWs, the reduction of the population of the occupied countries and crimes in the concentration camps;

(iii) Case V — which embraced matters concerning the organization and system of deportation of civilians to forced labour and of slave labour in the concentration camps;

(iv) Case VI — against the board of directors of IG Farben which made use of the slave labour of civilians and concentration camp inmates, thus contributing to mass murder. The trial also established the responsibility of this concern for pseudomedical experiments conducted on the inmates of concentration camps, including *KL Auschwitz*;

(v) Case VIII — against the Race and Resettlement Head Office (RuSHA) as organizers of extermination actions directed at foreign peoples (Slavs, Jews, Gypsies) and the extermination of the latter in concentration camps. The proceedings of this trial *inter alia* registered and verified the documentation concerning the mass deportation of Poles from the Zamość region and their relegation to concentration camps, especially to Oświęcim, and documentation concerning the abduction of 200,000 Polish children to Germany for Germanization;

(vi) Case X — against the firm of Krupp. This trial revealed crimes connected with the exploitation of the labour of concentration camp inmates and POWs. It was also proved that prisoners of the concentration camp at Oświęcim had been forced to work for Krupp;

(vii) Case XII — in which the main defendants were the higher officers of the High Command of the Armed Forces (OKW). Among many proven crimes the extermination of over 13,000 Soviet POWs in the concentration camp of Oświęcim was also examined.

It follows from the albeit fragmentary material here adduced that war crimes and crimes against humanity committed in the concentration camps occupied, besides crimes against peace, a large part of the evidence presented before both the International Tribunal and the Military Tribunals operating in the various occupation zones of Germany. The crimes revealed during the trials shook world opinion once again and threw into relief the inhuman face of Hitlerite fascism. In all judgements it was stated that the responsibility for the crimes committed was borne by the entire political, party, economic and military apparatus of the Third Reich.

4. THE LEGAL BASES OF THE PUNISHMENT OF WAR CRIMINALS IN POLAND

Poland belonged to the countries which suffered most under German occupation during the Second World War. The basic official Poli h document "Report Concerning Poland's War Losses and Damage in the Years 1939-45" prepared by the War Reparations Bureau of the Presidium of the Council of Ministers in January 1947 and consisting of three parts (descriptive, general statistical tables and detailed statistical tables), mentions in Table 1 — "Biological Losses of the Polish People during the Second World War" — the figure of 6,028,000. Of this number 644,000 persons, or about 10.7 per cent, were killed as a result of hostilities, while the remainder, i.e. 5,384,000, or 89.3 per cent, lost their lives as a result of the terrorist rule of the occupation authorities.

A second important official document was the indictment submitted at the end of 1945 by the Polish delegation to the International Military Tribunal in Nuremberg, in which as many as 32 pages were devoted to crimes committed in concentration camps. This material for the prosecution was extended by the addition of a report by the Polish-Soviet Supreme State Commission appointed to investigate the crimes committed by the Nazi invaders at Oświęcim, which was presented by the Soviet delegate Colonel L. N. Smirnov. The Nuremberg Judgement, in the part dealing with the sentence passed on one of the main Nazi criminals, the former governor general of Poland Hans Frank, states that at the root of "the occupation policy lay the destruction of Poland as a national entity and the ruthless exploitation of its human and material resources for the war being waged by the Germans... In the GG * a system of concentration camps was introduced with the setting up of the universally known camps as Treblinka and Majdanek. As early as 6 February 1940 Frank gave a picture of the means by which the terror would be implemented in his cynical comment on a press report about von Neurath's poster announcing the shooting of Czech students. Frank said on that occasion: "If I were to order posters to be displayed announcing the shooting of every seven Poles, all the forests in Poland would not suffice to provide paper for these posters'."

The scale and nature of the crimes committed caused the Polish autho-

---

* General Government

rities to issue on 31 August 1944, a few days after the creation of the Polish Committee of National Liberation, a decree concerning punishment of Nazi criminals guilty of killing and ill treating civilians and POWs and punishment of traitors to the Polish nation who had cooperated with the Nazis. To the crimes encompassed by this decree all the general provisions of the then existing Penal Code were to have application, and special penal courts were set up by a decree of 12 September 1944 to try these cases. While the war was still on, namely between 27 November and 2 December 1944, six SS men who were former members of the camp staff of the concentration camp at Majdanek and who had been captured at the scene of their crimes, were tried by a Special Court in Lublin.

The decree of 31 August 1944 was updated several times, for example on the occasion of Poland's accession to the London Agreement. It introduced the Nuremberg Principles into Polish law, proof of which is to be found in the judgement of the Supreme Court of 23 February 1948, in which it was stated that "close jurisdictional liaison between Polish and international sentencing practice in this field allows the Polish courts to draw upon the judgement of the Nuremberg Tribunal in interpretation of the Polish statute based on this judgement".[4]

5. THE AUSCHWITZ CRIMINALS BEFORE THE SUPREME NATIONAL TRIBUNAL

With the cessation of hostilities and the surrender to Poland in acordance with the London Agreement of several hundred war criminals (including the high-ranking Nazis Artur Greiser, Ludwig Fischer, Albert Forster, Josef Bühler and Rudolf Höss), the necessity arose of summoning a special tribunal which, in view of the gravity of the problem, would be a national equivalent of the International Military Tribunal at Nuremberg. Thus there arose on the basis of a decree of 22 January 1946, for the purpose of trying these major war criminals, the Supreme National Tribunal. All matters pertaining to the investigation were conducted by the Procurator's Office of the Supreme National Tribunal and a special organ of the Ministry of Justice — the Chief Commission for the Investigation of Nazi Crimes in Poland, called into being by a decree of 10 November 1945.

The Chief Commission for the Investigation of Nazi Crimes operated through regional commissions. The chairman of the Commission was the minister of justice, who appointed the chairmen and members of the re-

---

[4] E.S. Rappaport, "Z zagadnień prawa międzynarodowego w orzecznictwie sądów polskich", in: *Rocznik Prawa Międzynarodowego*, 1949, p. 233.

gional commissions. The task of the Chief Commission was to investigate and gather evidence concerning German crimes committed during the years 1939-45 either in Poland or beyond her frontiers in relation to Polish citizens or persons of Polish nationality, or else in relation to foreigners who were in Poland at the time the crimes were committed. The decree also envisaged the publication from time to time by the Chief Commission of materials and the results of its investigations and also that they be made accessible or referred to the organs of justice, in Poland and abroad.

The Supreme National Tribunal had a lay character, insofar as in addition to three professionally qualified judges it consisted of four assessors who had to be members of the Home National Council.* The decree clearly established that the Tribunal was hierarchically equal to the Supreme Court.

The accused had the right to defence counsel either chosen by themselves or appointed by the Tribunal. The latter were chosen from among barristers resident in Poland.

The Tribunal's judgements were final and those convicted had the right to appeal for pardon to the President of the Home National Council.

In the years 1946-48 seven trials were held before the Supreme National Tribunal, two of which were connected with the concentration camp at Oświęcim.

The first of these lasted from 11 to 29 March 1947 and ended with the announcement of the verdict and sentence on 2 April. The accused was the first commandant (a post he had held for three years) of *KL Auschwitz*, Rudolf Franz Ferdinand Höss, who had been handed over to Poland by the British occupation authorities in Germany in May 1946. The trial of Rudolf Höss had enormous international significance, since, being the trial of the commandant of the largest of the camps, it constituted both an exemplification of how the whole system of Nazi concentration and extermination camps functioned, and an indictment of the ideology which had made them into instruments for implementing the criminal national and racist policies of the Third Reich.

The process of investigation began almost immediately after the liberation of the camp at Oświęcim by Soviet soldiers on 27 January 1945. i.e. when the war was still on. Despite the fact that the camp command had attempted from August 1944 onwards to obliterate all traces of their criminal activity (after the liberation of the concentration camp at Majdanek), many proofs were found, which were secured thanks to the speed with which the Supreme State Extraordinary Commission of the Soviet Union began its work under the chairmanship of General Professor

---

* The first post-war Polish parliament.

Dmitri Kudryavtsev. The Commission made an inspection of the entire site and the buildings to be found on it, particularly those serving the aims of mass extermination — the gas chambers and crematoria. Testimony was taken from many prisoners who as unfit for evacuation had been marked down for liquidation but who were liberated as a result of the rapid shift of the front. Parallel with the activity of the Soviet State Commission, investigations were conducted on behalf of the Polish authorities by the Cracow Regional Commission for the Investigation of Nazi Crimes presided over by Judge Jan Sehn, a member of the Main Commission for the Investigation of Nazi Crimes in Poland. The material gathered comprised 21 volumes containing the depositions of witnesses, the statements of the accused Höss, the testimony of experts and the most important documents from the period of the camp's existence.

The main questions examined during the trial of Höss were: the tasks and aims set by the Nazis for the concentration camps, the function of the latter in the policy of persecuting opponents, the way in which the personnel who staffed the camps had been trained and the scale on which the crimes were committed, especially the dimensions of the extermination policy conducted in the camp at Oświęcim against Slavs, Jews and Gypsies with the help of the gas Cyclon B used in specially constructed gas chambers. The Tribunal also dealt with the matter of the experiments which had been conducted in the camp either for pseudoscientific aims or for the purpose of finding methods of exterminating whole nations, chiefly Slavs.

The trial was held in Warsaw and the proceedings were simultaneously translated into English, Russian, French and German. It was attended by many foreign observers and correspondents. The eight-man American delegation included the assistants of General Telford Taylor, Chief Prosecutor of the US Military Tribunal in Nuremberg.

Opening the session, the president of the Supreme National Tribunal, Judge Alfred Eimer, recalled that in the camp at Oświęcim millions of people had been done to death for no other reason than that they either represented different political, social or religious views than the rulers of the Third Reich, or that they belonged to a different race. He appealed to the judges of the Tribunal to weigh precisely every word spoken by the witnesses and the defence, so that the Court might uncover the real and undissimulated truth. The president of the Tribunal closed his address with the following words:

"Citizen Judges! Mindful of our great responsibility towards the dead and the living, let us not lose sight of what the fight of the freedom-loving nations was for.

"Respect for the dignity of man constituted that great aim, so let it also be the share of the accused, for it is first and foremost a man who stands before the Court.

"This also authorizes me to call upon those present to remain serious in this courtroom. To do so will not only be an obeisance before the laws of the Republic, under whose protection the accused finds himself, but also before the dignity of human suffering."[5]

Even while the investigation was going on, the accused Höss had realized that in the light of the material assembled, to which new depositions, expert testimony and documents were constantly being added, there was no sense in concealing the truth. He was also aware of the punishment awaiting him for the crimes he had committed and awaited the ultimate penalty with the utmost calm. The best proof of this is constituted by his memoirs (*My Soul, Education, Life and Experiences*)[6] written in a prisons cell while awaiting trial. The shattering descriptions they contain of such things as the mass killing of people in gas chambers read like the factual accounts of a completely disinterested observer. While giving evidence Höss answered briefly and to the point, without hesitation. It is worth quoting here two extracts from the trial record.

After the deposition of the witness Walter Gnojny of Katowice that on one occasion Höss, pointing to the returning penal company whose members were with difficulty dragging along those of their comrades who were no longer able to walk, said: "I don't want to see this trash tomorrow (*Diesen Mist will ich morgen nicht sehen*) and that these prisoners had been killed the same evening, the following exchange took place:

President of the Tribunal: Does the defence have any questions?

Defence Counsel Ostaszewski: I should like the accused to say something about this perhaps.

President of the Tribunal: If he wants to say something, let him do so by all means. Does the accused wish to say anything in this matter?

The accused Höss: No.[7]

Höss reacted similarly to the testimony of the witness Jan Korczyński, who described how at one period of the camp's existence every prisoner

---

[5] Quoted in: *Zbrodniarze hitlerowscy przed Najwyższym Trybunałem Narodowym* (hereafter *Zbrodniarze hitlerowscy...*) by Janusz Gumkowski and Tadeusz Kułakowski. Warsaw 1961, p. 85.

[6] The manuscript of these recollection is in the Archives of the State Museum in Oświęcim, sygn. Wsp. (Höss) 96, nr inw. 49757. They were published in book form in Poland and a number of other countries (including the FRG) in various language versions.

[7] Quoted in: *Zbrodniarze hitlerowscy...* by Janusz Gumkowski and Tadeusz Kułakowski, p. 137.

returning to camp after an exhausting day's work had to carry with him five bricks (a load of about 20 kilograms). Höss had stood by the gate observing the scene to see that each prisoner proceeded independently. In this connection the prosecutor Tadeusz Cyprian put a question to Höss:

Prosecutor: I have a question for the accused. Did the accused see this carrying of bricks into the camp?
Accused: I did.
Prosecutor: Did the accused not consider that this work was too arduous for these people?
Accused: No.[8]

Höss only became roused to a certain extent when describing the mass extermination of millions of human beings, which he spoke of like a kind of mass production process and "occasionally produced the impression of the manager of a factory who tries to explain certain shortcomings in the work of his plant with reference to difficulties of an objective nature: excessively large transports, the fact that the capacity of the crematoria was too low, hold-ups caused by mechanical faults. It was as if he wanted to explain to the Tribunal that he had done everything in his power to conduct the 'special action' [as the Nazis described mass extermination — K.S.] as efficiently as possible, and if he had not succeeded in producing such results as Himmler and Eichmann thought possible, it was not his fault... The calm with which he spoke of the extermination seemed all the more uncanny. Listening to him one had the impression that in carrying out his task he had tried to eliminate completely from his consciousness the factor of human life, which was after all the central issue. At times his voice contained almost a slight note of pride when he spoke of the difficulties he had succeeded in overcoming, and at others a note of guilt or shame that he had been unable to discharge his obligations and been unworthy of the trust placed in him by his superiors..."[9]

The Supreme National Tribunal found the accused Höss guilty on the following counts:

(i) belonging to a criminal organization called the SS and to the National Socialist German Workers' Party (NSDAP);

(ii) as a joint creator of the Nazi system of concentration camps, which were intended to torment and exterminate people, he had directed the implementation of this task;

(iii) deliberately taking part in the killing of about 300,000 people entered in the camp register, and of a further number impossible to establish precisely but amounting to at least 2,500,000 persons not included in the camp register, and of at least 12,000 Soviet prisoners of war who

---

[8] *Ibid*, p. 133.
[9] *Ibid*, pp. 141—142.

had been placed in the concentration camp in violation of international law;*

(iv) acting to the detriment of civilians, military personnel and prisoners of war, keeping them in a state of slavery combined with the most varied physical and moral torments (starvation, forcing them to work beyond their strength, torture, the infliction of inhuman punishments, disregard of human dignity) and taking part in the mass plunder of property taken from persons brought to the camp and sent straight to their death in the gas chambers or taken from the already dead, which was linked with profanation of the bodies (removal of artificial limbs, gold teeth and women's hair).

In its judgement the Tribunal stated that it "considers the figure of 2,500,000 victims as indubitable, and also minimal, for when the depositions of the witnesses, the expert testimony of Professor Roman Dawidowski and the findings of the Soviet Extraordinary Commission are taken into account, a figure of three to four millions bears all the features of probability".[10]

The Supreme National Tribunal sentenced Rudolf Höss to death by hanging. The sentence was carried out on 16 April 1947 at Oświęcim beside the building of the former commandant's office from which he had governed the camp in former years.

In the second trial held before the Supreme National Tribunal there were forty accused, including: Arthur Liebehenschel, who succeeded Höss as commandant; Maximilian Grabner, former head of the camp Gestapo; Hans Aumeier, former *Lagerführer;* Karl Ernst Möckel, head of the supply department; Marie Mandel, formerly in charge of the women's camp at Brzezinka; Franz Xaver Kraus, assistant to the *Lagerführer;* Dr. Johann Paul Kremer, camp doctor; Heinrich Josten, deputy *Lagerführer;* Dr. Hans Münch of the SS hygiene institute at Auschwitz; Erich Muhsfeld, head of the crematorium; Hermann Kirschner, overseer; Karl Seufert, overseer; Hans Koch, overseer; Wilhelm Gerhard Gehring, overseer; Ludwig Plagge, *Rapportführer;* Otto Lätsch, *Rapportführer;* Fritz Wilhelm Buntrock, *Rapportführer;* August Reimond Bogusch, *Blockführer:* Kurt Hugo Müller, *Blockführer;* Paul Goetze, *Blockführer;* Paul Szczurek, *Blockführer;* Richard Albert Schröder, *Blockführer;* Herbert Paul Ludwig, *Blockführer;* Eduard Lorenz, *Blockführer;* Therese Brandl, wardress in the women's camp; Alice Orlowski, wardress in the women's camp; Luise Danz, wardress in the women's camp; Hildegard Marthe Lui-

---

* The number of victims accepted by the Supreme National Tribunal was based on data arising from the then state of studies of the history of the former KL Auschwitz.

[10] For the full text of the verdict see *Siedem wyroków Najwyższego Trybunału Narodowego.* Poznań 1962, p. 95.

se Lächert, wardress in the women's camp; Hans Hoffmann, member of the political department; Arthur Johann Breitwieser, member of the works department; Hans Schumacher, member of the works department; Adolf Medefind, member of the works department; Franz Romeikat, member of the works department; Anton Lechner, overseer; Josef Kollmer, overseer; Detleff Nebbe, overseer; Alexander Bülow, overseer; Erich Dinges, driver; Johannes Weber, overseer; and Karl Jeschke, overseer.

Among the accused were people of various social backgrounds and different levels of education. They included for example a doctor of philosophy and medicine and *Privatdozent* of Münster University (Johann Paul Kremer); a master of laws (Arthur Breitwieser) as well as a former baker's assistant (Erich Muhsfeld) and former waitress (Therese Brandl).

The Cracow trial lasted from 25 November to 16 December 1947. The trial proceedings were based on the same material as in the case of Höss, only supplemented by additional depositions of witnesses. The tactics pursued by the accused, however, differed from those of Höss. At the beginning of the trial they pleaded not guilty, and only a few admitted beating prisoners. The accused attempted to throw responsibility for the deeds committed on absent superiors, particularly Höss, sheltering behind a plea of orders received. They frequently gave false testimony in an insolent manner. They obstinately denied proven facts, strove to discredit the depositions of witnesses, while at the same time fawning before the Tribunal in the hope of receiving a lenient sentence.

Many of the accused — especially one of the most deeply implicated, Maximilian Grabner, the former head of the camp Gestapo — assured the court that they had had no power in the camp. The former *Lagerführer*, Aumeier, declared that if he died he would be a "penitential offering for Germany". The accused Josef Kollmer asked with bitterness and resentment where Hitler and Himmler were. The accused Liebehenschel tried to prove to the Tribunal that from the moment he took over as commandant the living conditions of the prisoners had improved.

In the course of the three-week trial the Tribunal analyzed the criminal activity of the concentration camps and the people who had run them and acquainted itself with the life of the prisoners, the plunder of property, forced labour and the whole mechanism of mass extermination.

The sentences were announced on 22 December 1947. Twenty-three of the accused were sentenced to death, six to life imprisonment, seven to fifteen years imprisonment each, and two to ten and a half and three years imprisonment respectively. One of the accused (Hans Münch) was found not guilty.

At the beginning of Chapter IV of its judgement in the trial of the forty former members of the staff of the camp at Oświęcim, the Supreme National Tribunal stated that the indictment did not only charge the accused for committing individual deeds or belonging to either the NSDAP or the SS — which the Nuremberg Judgement and the Polish decree on the punishment of Nazi criminals had recognized as criminal organizations — but also for belonging to another criminal organization, namely the command, administration and staff of the concentration camp at Oświęcim. In dealing with this question the Tribunal explained that "the Nuremberg Judgement is undoubtedly the first step forward in the direction of codifying international penal law, but it is not a penal code in the sense that acts not covered by it could not be recognized as crimes by the proper courts. Thus from the point of view of international law there are no obstacles to the supplementing of the legal principles contained in the Nuremberg Judgement by new principles which do not contradict the content of the judgement. ...The Nuremberg legislation has also found its reflection in Polish legislation. The above-mentioned decree on the punishment of Nazi criminals in Article 4, Paragraph 2, recognized as criminal organizations those organizations which have as their aim crimes against peace, war crimes or crimes against humanity, and also organizations which have other aims, but strive to achieve them by means of the above-mentioned crimes..."

Next the Tribunal analyzed the provisions of Polish law in the light of the Nuremberg Judgement, stating in Point 14: "...The organization of the German concentration camps was therefore an organization having as its aim crimes against humanity, which were at the same time crimes according to the penal codes of all civilized nations, and also war crimes, insofar as the Soviet prisoners of war were concerned." In conclusion the Supreme National Tribunal recognized the members of the commands, administration and staffs of the German concentration camps in Poland, especially the one at Oświęcim, regardless of the name of these camps, as a "criminal group" (the Tribunal used the term "group" and not "organization" in view of the fact that Article 4 of the Polish decree used both these terms; the word "group" in this case is more appropriate in view of the etymology of the word "organization").

The records of the trials of Höss and the forty former members of the staff of the camp at Oświęcim together run to about 12,000 pages.

Besides the war criminals tried by the Supreme National Tribunal, many, including a high proportion who had held high office in the Nazi hierarchy, appeared before the Polish regular courts. About 700 Oświęcim criminals who had been extradited to Poland also appeared before these courts.

Among the trials held before these courts one should mention the Cracow trial (in 1951) of the former chief of Office DII of WVHA, *SS-Standartenführer* Gerhard Maurer. The sphere of competence of this office had embraced all matters concerning the exploitation of concentration camp inmates as slave labour. The 25 volumes of evidence assembled in the Maurer case prove that the programme of exploiting the prisoners' labour had been initiated by the big German concerns. When the programme was at its height there were over 500,000 prisoners employed in the German economy. They worked in nearly every industrial establishment. Leading industrialists constantly demanded increases in the number of prisoners available for work. This trial showed against a broad background the links of Hitlerism ever since its inception with industrial and banking capital. The accused Maurer was sentenced to death.

6. THE AUSCHWITZ CRIMINALS BEFORE THE COURTS OF OTHER COUNTRIES

More or less during this same period (1945-48) a number of Oświęcim criminals appeared before the Military Tribunals in the American, British, French and Soviet occupation zones of Germany. These were cases of individuals who had left Oświęcim in order to ply their bloody trade in other camps and were being tried for crimes committed there, and also of criminals from the concentration camps of Buchenwald, Bergen-Belsen, Dachau, Ravensbrück, Natzweiler, Sachsenhausen, Mauthausen and others. Such trials were held in Lüneberg, Dachau, Landsberg, Hamburg and elsewhere. Criminal collaboration with the Oświęcim concentration camp was the subject of trials held in Paris (Helmuth Knochen), Prague (Hanel), Budapest (László Baky and others), Vienna (Anton Alois Brunner), Bratislava (Dieter Wisliceny), and other cities. The above-mentioned individuals had been emissaries of RSHA and had on the orders of Adolf Eichmann (who was later tried in Jerusalem) prepared and organized in particular countries the death transports of Jews bound for Oświęcim.

One should also mention the trial of the supplier of Cyclon B to Oświęcim — Gerhard Peters, director of the firm of Degesch, a subsidiary of IG Farben. In the years 1949—55 Peters appeared eight times before the court in Frankfurt am Main. His defence was that he had produced Cyclon B in the sincerest conviction that in so doing he was bringing relief to people condemned to death anyway. He was finally found not guilty "for lack of evidence", the court taking the view that "today it cannot be proved beyond doubt that people really were killed with the help of Cyclon B at Oświęcim". A middleman in the supply of this poison to Oświęcim had been the firm of Tesch und Stabenow (Testa) of Dessau. The partners Bruno Tesch and Karl Weinbacker were condemned to death in Hamburg in 1946.

Between 10 and 25 March 1966 one of the camp doctors of Oświęcim, Horst Fischer, was tried by the Supreme Court of the German Democratic Republic in Berlin. This trial was extensively documented, *inter alia* by materials supplied from Poland. Depositions were made by dozens of witnesses from various countries. The trial revealed in particular the criminal role of the SS doctors, their share in sending people brought to the camp to the gas chambers, the making of selections among the sick and the killing of the latter with phenol injections or in the gas chambers, the appalling sanitary conditions, the absence of medical care, participation in executions and the falsification of death certificates. The accused Fischer confessed to the charges. The court sentenced him to death having proved his share in the killing of about 80,000 people. The trial also revealed the criminal links between the camp authorities and German concerns, in particular IG Farben.

The behaviour of the courts in the Federal Republic of Germany regarding the prosecution and punishment of war criminals has been neither consistent, systematic nor coordinated. They have taken no initiatives on their own and have tried only those who were handed over to them with incontrovertible proof of the crimes they had committed. Links with other criminals were not investigated, nor were the latter prosecuted.

For example, the trial of Professor Carl Clauberg, charged in Kiel with having conducted experiments on prisoners in the Oświęcim camp with the aim of finding a swift and effective method of exterminating the Slavs by mass sterilization, was never held, as Clauberg died in 1957 during the lengthy preliminary investigation. Former *SS-Obersturmführer* Wilhelm Reischenbeck was sentenced in Munich in 1958 to five years imprisonment for the murder of thirty people during the evacuation of Oświęcim. Johann Paul Kremer, whose death sentence from the Supreme National Tribunal in Cracow was commuted to life imprisonment as an act of clemency, after an early release found himself before a Federal German court in Münster in 1960. He was deprived of his title of professor, his doctor's degree was withdrawn and he was sentenced to ten years' imprisonment, which he was considered to have served while in Poland. At the trial of Otto Hunsch, one of Eichmann's associates, in Frankfurt in 1962, the name of Rudolf Höss was mentioned, whereupon the president of the court, in order to confront the testimony of the accused with the facts concerning the Oświęcim camp, proposed that Höss be summoned as a witness!

Lethargy and the absence of good will meant that a good many war criminals could (and can) remain at liberty in the Federal Republic of Germany. For example it was not until December 1960 that the last commandant of *KL Auschwitz*, Richard Baer, and one of the camp's worst sadists, Wilhelm Boger, a former functionary of the camp Gestapo, were arrested, by which time most of the crimes they had committed had become subject to the German statute of limitations.

At present prosecutions may still be brought in the Federal Republic for crimes of murder, complicity or assistance in murder, incitement to murder, or attempted murder.

After the creation in Ludwigsburg in 1958 of the *Zentralstelle der Landesjustizverwaltungen zur Aufklärung von NS-Gewaltverbrechen* (Central Office of Land Justice Institutions for the Clearing Up of Nazi Crimes) files were opened on about 1,000 persons suspected of committing crimes at the Oświęcim camp. This figure constitutes about a third of the SS camp complement in 1944, making no allowance for rotation over the years 1940–45.

A large proportion of the recorded criminals have so far not been caught. Some of them, such as Dr. Josef Mengele, are in hiding or residing abroad. Under the pressure of public opinion and the representations of the International Auschwitz Committee, the Federal Republic of Germany applied to the government of Ghana for the extradition of Dr. Horst Schumann, which took place in 1966. His trial began in Frankfurt am Main in September 1970 and was interrupted in April 1971 as a result of the illness of the accused. The main charge against Schumann was his part in the "euthanasia" (*Aktion T-4*) programme carried out on mentally ill citizens of the Third Reich. Horst Schumann had, however, been at Oświęcim where he had made a selection as a result of which 575 sick prisoners had been sent to Sonnenstein (near Dresden) and killed. Generally dressed in the uniform of a Luftwaffe officer, Schumann also carried out criminal experiments (castration) at Oświęcim and Brzezinka, following which prisoners died.

One of the most important trials of Oświęcim criminals to be held in the Federal Republic of Germany was that of "Robert Mulka and others", which was held between 20 December 1963 and 20 August 1965 before the *Schwurgericht* in Frankfurt am Main. The preliminary investigation had lasted for years and embraced 24 suspects, including the last commandant at Oświęcim, Richard Bear. Because the chief accused died before the trial began, and another (Hans Nierzwicki) was excluded from the trial on account of illness, 22 accused finally appeared in the dock: Robert Mulka, Karl Hoecker, Wilhelm Boger, Hans Stark, Klaus Dylewski, Perry Broad, Jochmann Schoberth, Bruno Schlage, Franz Hofmann, Oswald Kaduk, Stefan Baretzki, Heinrich Bischoff, Arthur Breitwieser, Franz Lucas, Willi Frank, Willi Ludwig Schatz, Victor Capesius, Josef Klehr, Herbert Scherpe, Emil Hantl, Gerhard Neubert and Emil Bednarek.

The indictment entered on 16 April 1963 charged that the accused had on the site of *Konzentrationslager Auschwitz* in the years 1940–45, out of a desire to murder or other base motives, personally or in association with others, deliberately killed people. The accused Richard Baer (who was not before the court) was furthermore charged with committing similar crimes in the concentration camps of Neuengamme and Mittelbau-Dora.

As the proceedings dragged on for months the number of the accused shrank to twenty. On 13 March 1964 Bischoff was excluded from the trial on grounds of ill health, and Neubert on 13 July for the same reason.

At the beginning of the trial as many as thirteen of the accused answered the charges while remaining free in their own custody, but by the final phase this figure had shrunk to three (Schoberth, Breitwieser and Schatz). In the course of the preliminary investigation the prosecutors took testimony from about 1,300 witnesses from various countries, the resulting material being assembled in 88 volumes (a total of about 15,000 pages). In this way the indictment presented the truth about Oświęcim. The accused constituted a mixed group, ranging from majors to lance corporals, from a woodchopper (Baer) and stoker (*Lagerführer* Hofmann) to a butcher (sanitary orderly Scherpe). They represented the entire camp hierarchy. This made it possible (as in the trial before the Supreme National Tribunal in Cracow of the forty members of the Oświęcim camp staff) to achieve a rounded view of the activity of all accused and to recognize them as a consciously and purposefully organized criminal group; at the same time this made it possible to define the role of every member of the group in the organization and mechanism of its functioning. These possibilities, however, were unfortunately not exploited by the *Schwurgericht* in Frankfurt am Main.

The trial abounded in instances of offensive behaviour by the defence counsel towards former camp inmates. One who particularly distinguished himself in this respect was Dr. Hans Laternser, who had specialized for years in the defence of former SS men, almost identifying himself with them in the course of the defence. His arrogant remarks frequently met with the disapproval of the president of the court, Dr. Hans Hofmeyer, and with determined reaction from the prosecution.

Equally arrogant was the behaviour of the accused themselves, who denied the crimes with which they were charged. They all continued to be a criminal group operating in total collusion, giving evasive or mendacious testimony or refusing to give any testimony at all. The behaviour of the accused may be explained chiefly by the fact that they knew they would not be sentenced to death, as the death sentence had been abolished in the Federal Republic in 1949. From the practice of German courts they also knew that sentences tended to be light and remissions frequent. The most frequently heard response of the accused was: "That is unknown to me" or "That is not true".

On 8 June 1964, the 53rd day of the trial, the civil prosecutor Dr. Henry Ormond proposed a visit to Oświęcim, informing the court that the government of the Polish People's Republic was ready to express its agreement. Ormond justified his suggestion by saying that even the most precise depositions of witnesses, sketches and photographs were no substitute for seeing with one's own eyes. President Hofmeyer pointed out that this proposal aroused certain reservations in the light of international law, as the judiciary acts of a German judge on the territory of another state could be construed as a violation of the sovereignty of that state. Dr. Hofmeyer's opinion was immediately supported by the defence counsel, Dr. Laternser, who added that in his opinion the government of the Federal Republic would not agree to any kind of judical proceedings on foreign territory. A different attitude was adopted by defence counsel Hans Schallock, who supported the proposal to go to the site of the former concentration camp at Oświęcim, stating that it aroused no reservations on his part. Similar statements were made by the prosecution and some of the other counsel for the defence. The second civil prosecutor, Professor Friedrich Kaul (of the German Democratic Republic) associated himself with Ormond's proposal, adding that the GDR would undoubtedly be prepared to guarantee transit facilities. The court returned to this matter several times.

Characteristic was the attitude of Laternser, who stated that in the event of the proposal being accepted all the defence counsel would have to go, and he personally did not like the idea of a journey behind the "iron curtain". Therefore every defence counsel who for these reasons did not visit Oświęcim would in future have the right to lodge an effective argument for revision. Moreover he added that the question of guarding those of the accused who were at liberty required clarification. He supposed that a German policeman would only be able to enter Poland unarmed and in civilian clothes. Thus the accused would find themselves in the custody of a foreign state, in contradiction to the general principle of German law that no German citizen could be surrendered to a foreign authority. This doubt was dispelled by Dr. Ormond who explained that the Polish authorities had agreed to let German police exercise supervision over the accused on Polish territory. Using camp jargon, he explained that the German police would constitute the "little sentry cordon" (kleine Postenkette), while the Polish militia would form the "big sentry cordon" (grosse Postenkette), and the latter would isolate and secure the camp site during the court's inspection.

Not until 15 October (i.e. after a lapse of five months) did the court appeal to the opinion of the examining magistrate, Dr. Hans Düx, who before the trial had been at Oświęcim. That same month the president of the court announuced that it had been decided to conduct — if it should be possible — an inspection of the site of the former camp at Oświęcim, describing this action of the court in visiting the scene as an *Ortsbesichtigung*, and that this would be conducted by a member of the panel of judges.

On 14 December 1964 there arrived at the site of the former concentration camp at Oświęcim a group of twenty-three persons comprising *Gerichtsrat* Walter Hotz of the panel of judges, all the prosecutors, eight of the defence counsel and one accused (Franz Lucas). In the administrative building of the State Museum at Oświęcim a room was made available in which sessions could be held. Present at the session on behalf of Poland were Professor Jan Sehn, plenipotentiary of the Minister of Justice; the Director of the Museum, Kazimierz Smoleń, as an expert witness; the co-plaintiff (*Nebenkläger*) Mieczysław Kieta and his counsel Henry Ormond.

Before the court went into session, Professor Jan Sehn made a statement which included the following passage:

"The forensic activities which the *Schwurgericht* in Frankfurt am Main has decided to conduct on this site are intended to establish the material truth about the events which took place here in the past and which are at present the subject of proceedings before this Court... The government of the Polish People's Republic — being guided by this same aim — has expressed its agreement to the conduct of these activities. As requested it has guaranteed all participants in these activities of the court personal safety by the granting of safe conduct and necessary assistance by the proper organs of our people's power."

Judge Hotz, opening the session, expressed thanks to the Polish authorities for making possible this visit to Oświęcim and ensuring proper conditions for the Court to conduct its business.

The purpose of the visit was to find answers to 32 questions concerning the depositions of individual witnesses and accused. After the first day the prosecutor, Dr. Hans Grossmann, stated that everything he and his colleagues had seen had shaken them, and that although the prosecutor's office had for a number of years been dealing with this problem in detail, it had never realized its immensity so clearly as now. The visit came to an end on 16 December 1964 with the signing of a protocol,[11] which was read out during the trial in Frankfurt. Some of the accused (Klehr, Bednarek) and counsel for the defence entered reservations concerning certain explanations put forward by the Polish expert. Dr. H. Stolting II for the defence objected that during the visit the Museum director, Kazimierz Smoleń, had been heard as an expert witness when

---

[11] A copy of the protocol with all photographs is in the Archives of the State Museum in Oświęcim, sygn. Dpr-Zo (Frankfurt) 4, nr inw. 149011.

his statements were open to doubt, as the accused Bednarek had also been a prisoner and did not consider Smoleń's opinion to be correct. Stolting moved for another visit to the scene. This request was supported by defence counsel Benno Erhard and Hans Laternser. In view of these reservations the Museum director was summoned once again to Frankfurt am Main. In the course of his cross examination, however, it turned out that all the explanations previously furnished by him and entered in the court record were correct. Thus the motion for a second visit to the scene fell through. It should be added that during the cross-examination of Kazimierz Smoleń before the *Schwurgeircht* Laternser and Stolting were both absent from the courtroom, a fact that President Hofmeyer ordered with particular emphasis to be entered in the record.

Thus the objections raised by some of the accused and their counsel were intended solely to prolong the trial, a practice known in press circles as "dilution". Such tactics had been used by the defence right from the start of the trial. Finally, on 19 August 1965, sentences were passed. They fell far short of the severe penalties the prosecution had asked for. Six of the accused were senteced to life imprisionment, one to fourteen years, one to ten, five to five to nine years and four to three to four years imprisonment. Altogether seventeen of the accused were found guilty and sentenced, and three were found innocent (Schatz, Schoberth and Breitwieser).

The attitude of the Polish side in the matter of agreeing to permit the court to visit Oświęcim was commented on in 1968 by Professor Alfons Klafkowski, a Polish expert on international law, as follows:

"...the Polish government expressed consent to an utterly unconventional agreement with the court of a country with which our country not only does not have any treaty on legal cooperation, but does not even have diplomatic relations. On 31 March the plenipotentiary of the Polish minister of justice, Professor Jan Sehn, signed with the president of the Frankfurt Tribunal, Dr. Hofmeyer, an agreement on the strength of which our courts heard witnesses summoned by plaintiffs and defence on Polish territory in the presence of prosecutors and defence counsel and also civil prosecutors.

"What is more, our government gave its consent to safe conduct for these defence lawyers regarding whose past, especially that part connected with activities on Polish territory, we may have serious reservations." [12]

This visit described above, which was the first, was followed by several others, including three to the Oświęcim site. All were connected with trials held in Frankfurt.

The next trial of Oświęcim criminals, known as Trial II, was also held

---

[12] Alfons Klafkowski, *Ściganie zbrodniarzy...*, p. 242.

before the Frankfurt *Schwurgericht* and lasted from 14 December 1965 to 16 September 1966. The accused were Gerhard Neubert, Wilhelm Burger and Josef Erber, also known as Josef Hustek. All three were found guilty, Erber being sentenced to life imprisonment, Burger to eight years and Neubert to three-and-a-half years imprisonment.

According to the prosecutor's office, to the so-called Trial III was to embrace the following accused: Bruno Hugo Albrecht, Karl Reinhard Broch, Eugen Doerr, Reinhard Edele, Alois Frey, Karl Friedrich Gaar, Erich Alfred Grönke, Adam Kradil, Kurt Hans Jurasek, Johann Josef Mirbeth, Elisabeth Ruppert, Willi Rudolf Sawatzki, Anton Wilhelm Siebald, Robert Sierek, Georg Swierczynski, Otto Vollrath and Josef Windeck. At the same time it was also announced that the prosecutor's office was gathering material for a new trial in which charges would be brought against the following individuals, who were mentioned by name: Friedrich Ontl, Karl Egersdörfer, Jakob Fries, Richard Böck, Hubert August Christoph, Helmut Pomereinke, Johann Sabo, Franz Tomaszewski, Arthur Willi Wildermuth, Anton Glaser, Richard Gunter Hinze, Ludwik Holze, Josef Kaufmann, Josef Hofer and Bernhard Heinrich Bonitz.

This announcement was implemented only to a minimal degree, since of the thirty-two persons mentioned above only two, the former Kapos Bonitz and Windeck, were finally brought to trial. This was to so-called Trial III, held in Frankfurt between 30 August 1967 and 14 June 1968, which ended in the two accused being sentenced to life imprisonment.

In Trial IV, held between 18 December 1973 and 3 February 1976, the accused were former *SS-Oberscharführer* Willi Sawatzki and former *SS-Unterscharführer* Alois Frey. The accused were charged *inter alia* with taking part in the liquidation of the Gypsy camp and the murder of prisoners during the evacuation of the camp of January 1945. On 25 November 1974 Alois Frey was released for lack of evidence, and on 3 February 1976 the prosecutor dropped the charges against Sawatzki. Thus the trial ended with neither of the two accused being sentenced.

In Austria, which also has Oświęcim criminals on its territory, two of the builders of the gas chambers and crematoria at Brzezinka were tried between January and March 1972. These were the former SS officers Walter Dejaco and Fritz Ertl. The *Schwurgericht* in Vienna found them not guilty. A similar verdict was reached in a second trial (April 1972), also held in Vienna, in which the accused were Frantz Wunsch and Otto Graf, former SS men who had taken part in the selections on the ramp at Oświęcim.

As has already been mentioned, the United Nations took up the matter of the punishment of war criminals while hostilities were still going on.

Both the concept of war crimes and the procedural matters connected with prosecution, punishment, extradition, etc. were precisely defined. The International Military Tribunal at Nuremberg punished the major war criminals regardless of the position they occupied and in so doing helped to restore respect for the law regulating the way nations live together. In all the liberated countries the practitioners of genocide were brought to trial. These trials were conducted in accordance with the law, and were not acts of vengeance but acts of justice.

On the basis of international treaties and agreements Poland not only prosecutes and punishes war criminals, but also helps other countries to do so, by passing on evidence and furnishing witnesses. Particular services in this regard have been performed by the Main Commission for the Investigation of Nazi Crimes in Poland.

On Poland's initiative, the General Assembly of the United Nations passed on 26 November 1968 a Convention on the non-application of Statutory Limitations to war crimes and crimes against humanity (this Convention, although open to non-members of the UN, was not acceded to by the Federal Republic of Germany). Poland also lobbies in the Human Rights Commission for the further protection of mankind against war crimes by urging the following measures: introduction of an international obligation to render legal assistance in the prosecution of war criminals; definition of the duty to extradite; introduction of an unambiguous ban on the granting of asylum to war criminals; and the setting up of a Permanent International Tribunal to try them.

During five years of occupation the name *Konzentrationslager Auschwitz* awakened dread among the peoples of all the countries conquered by the Third Reich, for it was one of the largest centres of mass extermination in which the Nazis implemented their cruel purpose of wiping out their opponents regardless of their nationality, citizenship, political convictions, social origin or religious creed.

The Nazis were aware of the enormity of their crimes and for this reason attempted, as their military defeats at the hands of the Allies multiplied, to remove at all costs the traces of their deeds. In this they were only partially successful.

When on 27 January 1945 troops of the Red Army liberated Oświęcim, the Extraordinary Soviet State Commission immediately set about conserving these parts of the camp which had not been destroyed. Many fundamental facts were established on the spot and a wealth of documentary material was assembled testifying to the immensity of the crimes committed.

The idea of the necessity of preserving the site of the camp as a Monument of Struggle and Martyrdom, the idea of honouring the memories of fathers and mothers, brothers and sisters — of all those who perished — was no doubt born among the prisoners in the dark days of Nazi domination, when the sky over Oświęcim was obscured by the smoke from the flaming pyres containing thousands of human bodies.

On 31 December 1945 at a plenary session of the Home National Council Dr. Alfred Fiderkiewicz, a former prisoner of the concentration camp at Oświęcim, submitted in the name of a group of deputies a proposal for the commemoration of places of Polish and international martyrdom. The submission of such a proposal was demanded by the whole Polish nation, which had lost one in every five of its citizens at the hands of the Nazi invader. On 2 July 1947 the government of People's Poland issued a decree on the conservation of the site of the former concentration camp at Oświęcim-Brzezinka together with all structures and installations built thereon as a Monument to the Martyrdom of the Polish and Other Nations and on the establishment there of a State Museum.

The State Museum of Oświęcim-Brzezinka does not limit itself to the administrative work of conserving this cemetery of about four million people. It also conducts wide-ranging research, collects documents, publishes papers on the history of Nazi crimes, organizes symposia, lectures, exhibitions — making its contribution to the fulfilment of the appeal of the liberated prisoners: "Never again".

SS Ranks and their Wehrmacht Equivalents

SS rank	Wehrmacht equivalent	Rough English translation
SS-Mann	Grenadier	private
SS-Sturmmann	Gefreiter	lance-corporal
SS-Rottenführer	Obergefreiter	senior lance-corporal
SS-Unterscharführer	Unteroffizier	corporal
SS-Scharführer	Unterfeldwebel	junior sergeant
SS-Oberscharführer	Feldwebel	sergeant
SS-Hauptscharführer	Oberfeldwebel	sergeant-major
SS-Stabsscharführer	Stabsfeldwebel	staff sergeant-major
SS-Untersturmführer	Leutnant	second-lieutenant
SS-Obersturmführer	Oberleutnant	lieutenant
SS-Hauptsturmführer	Hauptmann	captain
SS-Sturmbannführer	Major	major
SS-Obersturmbannführer	Oberstleutnant	lieutenant-colonel
SS-Standartenführer	Oberst	colonel
SS-Oberführer	Brigadekommandeur	brigadier-general
SS-Brigadenführer	Generalmajor	major-general
SS-Gruppenführer	Generalleutnant	lieutenant-general
SS-Obergruppenführer	General	general
SS-Oberstgruppenführer	Generaloberst	colonel-general
Reichsführer SS — Himmler's personal title as head of the SS	no equivalent	

BIBLIOGRAPHY

Bartoszewski, Władysław, *Prawda o von dem Bachu* (The Truth About v. dem Bach), Warsaw—Poznań 1961

Baum, Bruno, *Wiederstand in Auschwitz* (Resistance in Auschwitz), Berlin 1957

Borowski, Tadeusz, *Pożegnanie z Marią. Kamienny świat* (Farewell to Maria. Stone World), Warsaw 1972

Ciesielski, Edward, *Wspomnienia oświęcimskie* (Recollections of Oświęcim), Cracow 1968

Cyprian, Tadeusz and Sawicki, Jerzy, "Komisja Zjednoczonych Narodów do Spraw Zbrodni Wojennych" (United Nations War Crimes Commission) in *Wojskowy Przegląd Prawniczy*, 1947, No. 4

Cyprian, Tadeusz and Sawicki, Jerzy, *Sprawy polskie w procesie norymberskim* (Matters of Polish Concern in the Nuremberg Trial), Poznań 1956

Cyprian, Tadeusz and Sawicki, Jerzy, *Siedem wyroków Najwyższego Trybunału Narodowego* (Seven Verdicts of the Supreme National Tribunal), Poznań 1962

Dokumenty i materiały z czasów okupacji niemieckiej w Polsce (Documents and Materials from the Period of the German Occupation of Poland), Vol. 1: *Obozy* (Camps), Oświęcim, Łódź 1946

Döring, Hans Joachim, *Die Ziegeuner im NS-Staat* (The Gypsies in the Nazi State), Hamburg 1964

Fiderkiewicz, Alfred, *Brzezinka*, Warsaw 1965

Friedman, Filip and Hołuj, Tadeusz, *Oświęcim*, Bydgoszcz 1946

Gumkowski, Janusz and Kułakowski, Tadeusz, *Zbrodniarze hitlerowscy przed Najwyższym Trybunałem Narodowym* (Nazi Criminals Before the Supreme National Tribunal), Warsaw 1961

Henkys, Reinhard, *Die nationalsozialistischen Gewaltverbrechen* (The National Socilist Crimes of Violence), Stuttgart—Berlin 1964

Hołuj, Tadeusz, "W odpowiedzi na artykuł K. Moczarskiego: Czy można było uwolnić więźniów Oświęcimia?" (Reply to K. Moczarski's Article "Could the Oświęcim Prisoners Have Been Set Free?") in *Tygodnik Demokratyczny* 1957, No. 48.

Hołuj, Tadeusz, "Nie byliśmy biernymi ofiarami" (We Were Not Passive Victims), in *Za wolność i lud*, 1963, No. 2

I. G. Farben, Auschwitz, Experimente, Berlin 1965

Kamiński, Andrzej Józef, *Hitlerowskie obozy koncentracyjne i ośrodki masowej zagłady w polityce imperializmu niemieckiego* (The Nazi Concentration Camps and Mass Extermination Centres in the Policy of German Imperialism), Poznań 1964

Kaul, Friedrich Karl, *Ärzte in Auschwitz* (Doctors in Auschwitz), Berlin 1968

Kielar, Wiesław, *Anus mundi. Wspomnienia oświęcimskie* (Anus Mundi. Recollections of Oświęcim), Cracow 1972

Klafkowski, Alfons, *Podstawowe problemy prawne likwidacji skutków wojny 1939—1945 a dwa państwa niemieckie* (Basic Legal Problems of the Liquidation of the Results of the 1939—45 War and the Two German States), Poznań 1966

Klafkowski, Alfons, *Obozy koncentracyjne jako zagadnienie prawa międzynarodowego* (The Concentration Camps as a Problem of International Law), Warsaw 1968

Klafkowski, Alfons, *Ściganie zbrodniarzy wojennych w Niemieckiej Republice Federalnej w świetle prawa międzynarodowego* (The Prosecution of War Criminals in the German Federal Republic in the Light of International Law), Poznań 1968

Kluz, Władysław, *Czterdzieści siedem lat życia* (47 Years of Life), Cracow 1973

Kowzan, Tadeusz, "Francuzi w oświęcimskim ruchu oporu" (French Participants in the Oświęcim Resistance Movement, in *Za wolność i lud* 1956, No. 4.

Kraus, Ota and Kulka, Erich, "Továrna na smrt" (Death Factory), in *Naše Vojsko*, Prague 1959

Langbein, Hermann, *Die Stärkeren, Ein Bericht* (The Stronger. A Report), Vienna 1949

Lesch, Franz-Xaver, *P. Maximilian Kolbe* (Father Maximilian Kolbe), Würzburg 1964

Moczarski, Kazimierz, "Czy można było uwolnić więźniów Oświęcimia"? (Could the Oświęcim Prisoners Have Been Set Free?), in *Tygodnik Demokratyczny*, 1957, No. 43

Nyiszli, Miklós, *Pracownia doktora Mengele. Wspomnienia lekarza z Oświęcimia* (Dr. Mengele's Laboratory. Recollections of a Doctor from Oświęcim), Warsaw 1966

Oświęcim w oczach SS. Höss, Broad, Kremer (Oświęcim Through the Eyes of the SS), Oświęcim 1972

Przegląd Lekarski — Oświęcim. Periodical published by the Cracow Branch of the Polish Medical Society, Cracow 1961—75

"Obóz koncentracyjny Oświęcim w świetle akt Delegatury RP na Kraj" (The Oświęcim Concentration Camp in the Light of Documents of the Polish Republic's Delegation to the Homeland), in *Zeszyty Oświęcimskie*, special issue I, Oświęcim 1968

Rajewski, Ludwik, *Oświęcim w systemie RSHA* (Oświęcim in the RSHA System), Warsaw 1946

Rajewski, Ludwik, *Ruch oporu w polskiej literaturze obozowej* (The Resistance Movement in the Polish Camp Literature), Warsaw 1971

Rappaport, E. S., "Z zagadnień prawa międzynarodowego w orzecznictwie sądów polskich" (Problems of International Law in the Judgements of Polish Courts), in *Rocznik Prawa Międzynarodowego* 1949

Ryszka, Franciszek, *Noc i mgła* (Night and Fog), Wrocław 1962

Ryszka, Franciszek, *Państwo stanu wyjątkowego* (The State-of-Emergency State), Wrocław—Warsaw—Cracow 1964

Schnabel, Reimund, *Mach ohne Moral. Eine Dokumentation über die SS* (Power Without Morality. A Documentation on the SS), Frankfurt a. Main 1957

Schuldig im Sinne des Rechts und des Völkerrechts (Guilty Under the Law and Under International Law), Berlin 1966

Sehn, Jan, *Obóz koncentracyjny Oświęcim-Brzezinka (Auschwitz-Birkenau)* (The Concentration Camp of Oświęcim-Brzezinka; Auschwitz-Birkenau), Warsaw 1964

Sehn, Jan, Introduction in *Wspomnienia Rudolfa Hössa, komendanta obozu oświęcimskiego*, Warsaw 1965

Smoleń, Kazimierz, *Oświęcim 1940—1945. Przewodnik po Muzeum* (Museum Guide), Oświęcim 1974

Stryj, Franciszek, *W cieniu krematoriów* (In the Shadow of the Crematoria), Katowice 1960

Strzelecki, Andrzej, "Wyzwolenie KL Auschwitz" (The Liberation of KL Auschwitz), in *Zeszyty Oświęcimskie*, special issue III, Oświęcim 1974

Szmaglewska, Seweryna, *Dymy nad Birkenau* (Smoke Over Birkenau), Warsaw 1946

Witek, Teofil, "Norbert Barlicki" in *Za wolność i lud*, 1956, No. 8

Witek, Teofil, "Dwa spotkania z Julianem Wieczorkiem" (Two Encounters with Julian Wieczorek), in *Za wolność i lud*, 1955, No. 6

Wspomnienia Rudolfa Hössa, komendanta obozu oświęcimskiego (Memoirs of Rudolf Höss, Commandant of the Camp at Oświęcim), Warsaw 1965

"Wśród koszmarnej zbrodni. Rękopisy więźniów Sonderkommando odnalezione w Oświęcimiu" (Amidst a Nightmare of Crime. Notes of Prisoners of Sonderkommando, found in Oświęcim), in *Zeszyty Oświęcimskie*, special issue II, Oświęcim 1971

Zabochen, Milkhail, "Antifasistkoye podpolye Osventsima" (The Antifascist Underground of Oświęcim), in *Nova i noveyshaya istoriya*, Moscow 1965

Zeszyty Oświęcimskie, Publication of the State Museum in Oświęcim, Oświęcim 1957—75, No. 1—17

Witek, Teofil, "Wspomnienia o Stanisławie Dubois" (Recollections Stanisław Dubois in *Za wolność i lud*, 1955, No. 7

Żywulska, Krystyna, *Przeżyłam Oświęcim* (I have survived Oświęcim), Warsaw 1960

Historical consultant:
PROFESSOR JÓZEF BUSZKO

Translated by
IAIN W. M. TAYLOR and LECH PETROWICZ (pp. 159—171)

Cover and design by
JERZY KĘPKIEWICZ

Production editor:
WIESŁAWA ZIELIŃSKA

Sketches and plans by
TADEUSZ KINOWSKI

Illustrations:
Archives of the State Museum in Oświęcim
Photographs by Lidia Foryciarz, Zofia Łoboda and Andrzej Piotrowski

This book is also available in Polish, French, German and Russian

*This is the two thousand and sixty-ninth book
from Interpress Publishers*

© INTERPRESS 1978, 1985

PRINTED IN POLAND

ISBN 83-223-2069-8

PRASOWE ZAKŁADY GRAFICZNE RSW „PRASA-KSIĄŻKA-RUCH" — ŁÓDŹ